Transgender

Recent Titles in the
CONTEMPORARY WORLD ISSUES
Series

Books in the **Contemporary World Issues** series address vital issues in today's society such as genetic engineering, pollution, and biodiversity. Written by professional writers, scholars, and nonacademic experts, these books are authoritative, clearly written, up-to-date, and objective. They provide a good starting point for research by high school and college students, scholars, and general readers as well as by legislators, businesspeople, activists, and others.

Each book, carefully organized and easy to use, contains an overview of the subject, a detailed chronology, biographical sketches, facts and data and/or documents and other primary source material, a forum of authoritative perspective essays, annotated lists of print and nonprint resources, and an index.

Readers of books in the Contemporary World Issues series will find the information they need in order to have a better understanding of the social, political, environmental, and economic issues facing the world today.

Transgender

A REFERENCE HANDBOOK

Aaron Devor and Ardel Haefele-Thomas

ABC-CLIO ™

An Imprint of ABC-CLIO, LLC
Santa Barbara, California • Denver, Colorado

Library of Congress Cataloging-in-Publication Data

Names: Devor, Aaron H., 1951- author. | Haefele-Thomas, Ardel, author.
Title: Transgender : a reference handbook / Aaron Devor and Ardel Haefele-Thomas.
Description: Santa Barbara : ABC-CLIO, [2019] | Series: Contemporary world issues | Includes bibliographical references and index.
Identifiers: LCCN 2018048697 (print) | LCCN 2018049771 (ebook) | ISBN 9781440856914 (ebook) | ISBN 9781440856907 (cloth)
Subjects: LCSH: Transgender people. | Transgender people--Identity.
Classification: LCC HQ77.9 (ebook) | LCC HQ77.9 .D4948 2019 (print) | DDC 306.76/8--dc23
LC record available at https://lccn.loc.gov/2018048697

ISBN: 978-1-4408-5690-7 (print)
978-1-4408-5691-4 (ebook)

23 22 21 20 19   1 2 3 4 5

This book is also available as an eBook.

ABC-CLIO
An Imprint of ABC-CLIO, LLC

ABC-CLIO, LLC
147 Castilian Drive
Santa Barbara, California 93117
www.abc-clio.com

This book is printed on acid-free paper ∞

Manufactured in the United States of America

With all of the current media attention on gender-diverse people, it would be easy to be fooled into thinking that trans, non-binary, and Two-Spirit people just came on the scene in the past few years. After all, it is almost impossible to look at any kind of media today and not see stories about trans and non-binary lives. Ex-Olympian Caitlyn Jenner was interviewed in, and appeared on, the front cover of *Vanity Fair* magazine in 2015; trans actress Laverne Cox was featured on the cover of *Time* magazine in 2014 and on the cover of many other major magazines since then; trans celebrity Chaz Bono appeared on *Dancing with the Stars* in 2011. The news has also been full of stories about people like Texas trans high school wrestler Mack Beggs, who went all the way through high school asking to be able to wrestle on the boys' wrestling team rather than being forced to wrestle on the girls' team.

Twenty-first-century news has also been full of stories about controversies over bathrooms. Canada and Sweden both have been on the cutting edge of providing "bathrooms for all genders." In the United States, however, bathroom laws vary radically from state to state, and range from a 2017 California law that requires all single-use bathrooms in public buildings to be both fully accessible and gender inclusive, to a Texas bathroom bill that would deny trans people access to bathrooms aligning with their gender identity and would force them to use facilities according to their sex assigned at birth.

Trans, non-binary, and Two-Spirit people are not new to the twenty-first, or even the twentieth century. In Chapter 1,

"Background and History," we briefly discuss some of what we know about gender-diverse people in the centuries before we had the words *trans, non-binary,* and *Two-Spirit,* and the social categories that they define. We include a discussion of how, in many Indigenous cultures, some dating back thousands of years, there were special names and social positions for people who were neither male nor female and who were often revered as shamans and healers. In the rest of the chapter, we look at some pivotal moments in the development of trans as a diagnosis, as an identity, and as a social movement.

Chapter 2, "Problems, Controversies, and Solutions," looks at various issues concerning trans people and their rights. We start with a discussion of terminology and consider some of the debates about who should be included under the trans umbrella. We then look at research about the causes of trans, non-binary, and Two-Spirit identity as well as treatment issues for those who seek this sort of intervention. We also provide information about what is happening for trans, non-binary, and Two-Spirit youth in schools; for trans, non-binary, and Two-Spirit people of all ages in sports and in institutions; and we look at some legal issues concerning gender-diverse people. In all of this, we explore the ways that the trans, non-binary, and Two-Spirit people and communities have become empowered over time.

In Chapter 3, "Perspectives," you will find writings from people around the world who have contributed original works specifically for this reference text. They have made contributions to trans, non-binary, and Two-Spirit medicine, law, art, culture, and society. Their ages range from a teenager to trans elders, and they focus on topics from trans rights and history in the Netherlands to changing a Canadian Catholic high school's policies to be welcoming to people of all genders.

Chapter 4, "Profiles," reviews key people, events, and organizations that have changed the ways that gender-diverse people have been understood around the world. We start with a number of important historical figures, including short biographies of some of the first people known to have medically transitioned.

We then look at some of the medical clinics that focus on gender affirmation procedures. We follow that with profiles of some trans, non-binary, and Two-Spirit activists, politicians, attorneys and judges, celebrities, and artists. We round out the chapter with brief introductions to a number of history projects and advocacy organizations.

Chapter 5, "Data and Documents," offers graphs, charts, and excerpts from key documents that focus on various important trans issues around the world including the disparities that many trans, non-binary, and Two-Spirit people continue to face.

Chapter 6, "Resources," offers brief descriptions of books, periodicals, films, websites, and organizations for further research into trans, non-binary, and Two-Spirit topics.

The book concludes with a chronology and a glossary for further reference.

Acknowledgments

We would like to thank ABC-CLIO for making this text a priority. We give a special "hats off" to Robin Tutt, who has been an amazingly fast and patient editor. Most especially, we send huge thank-yous to all of the people who wrote for the Perspectives section of this book. We have appreciated your patience and the opportunity to engage with you about the field of trans studies.

We are each grateful to our families for their forbearance and generous support during all of the time that producing this book has taken. In addition, Ardel's work here is in memory of Daine Gray, a young gay trans man whose early death reminds us how very much we need books like this one. Both of us humbly acknowledge and thank all of those who have worked so very hard to bring us to where we are today, only a few of whom are mentioned in these pages. We stand on the shoulders of giants.

Transgender

Introduction

This first chapter covers some of the background and history of gender diversity around the globe from the ancient world to the present. We begin the chapter with important terminology and a look at the evolution of words and definitions for trans, non-binary, and Two-Spirit people. Then, we explore ancient Indigenous cultures and the respect that they had for gender diversity—often honoring third-, fourth-, and fifth-gender identities. From the ancient world, we move to an exploration of the science of sexology, which created many of the ideas and terms that are still prevalent today in terms of trans, non-binary, and Two-Spirit people. Finally, the chapter will look at examples of laws, popular culture, and policies from various decades leading up to the current moment in trans, non-binary, and Two-Spirit history. Of particular note, there is an in-depth focus on the decade between 1959 and 1969 when many political actions in the United States advanced social and political change for trans, non-binary, and Two-Spirit people. This chapter is not meant to be exhaustive, but rather to give readers a sense of the breadth of the history of trans, non-binary, and Two-Spirit people.

Pictured are three *hijras*, whose gender identity rests outside of the gender binary. Hindu goddess Bahuchara Mata is known as a special deity to the *hijras*, who have existed in Indian culture for well over 4,000 years. (Alain Lauga /Dreamstime.com)

Terminology

The words *transgender* or *trans*, and the concepts that they attempt to convey, are quite new in historical terms, really only becoming widely used in the 1990s. *Two-Spirit* was a term created by Indigenous people in the early 1990s ("The term is a translation of the Anishinaabemowin term *niizh manidoowag*, two spirits." Researching for LGBTQ2S+ Health, https://lgbtqhealth.ca/community/two-spirit.php). Two-Spirit is an umbrella term meant to convey an openness to gender diversity and sexual orientation outside of heterosexuality and serve as a contrast to earlier European terms that were not respectful. The term *non-binary* is even newer, coming into common usage in the early 2000s. Earlier in the twentieth century, the words *transvestite* and *transsexual* were more commonly used in Western societies to describe people who cross-dressed periodically, or who pursued complete hormonal and surgical transitions. Prior to the beginning of the twentieth century, there were no words in the English language specifically to describe those whom we now think of as trans or non-binary people. However, evidence of people who were gender diverse is as old as are our historical records, and many Indigenous peoples around the world have long had language to describe gender diversity as it has been understood in their cultures. Today, the term Two-Spirit is used in English among North American Indigenous people.

The contemporary language used to describe gender-diverse people is rapidly changing and a subject of much debate. Members of various gender-diverse communities have their own preferences for how they want, and do not want, to be understood. Scientific and medical communities often use terminology that is quite different from that used by gender-diverse people themselves. Journalists and social media authors may use still other language. Those cisgender people (not trans) who wish to be seen as allies will often use quite different language from those who are hostile to gender-diverse people.

Underlying all discussions of gender diversity are the concepts of sex and gender. For most everyday purposes, these two words are commonly used interchangeably. When considering gender-diverse people, these become important and distinct concepts.

Sex

Sex refers to one's biological status as male, female, or intersex. Sex has several components: assigned sex, legal sex, sex identity, and attributed sex.

Sex assignment is most commonly done by way of a visual inspection of the genitals at birth. Those newborns with penises are assigned as male. Those newborns with vulvas are assigned as female. When the genitals cannot be clearly labeled as penises or vulvas, a newborn is considered to have a difference of sex development (DSD), commonly called intersex, and further investigations are undertaken to attempt to make a clear sex determination. Other evidence that is most commonly used includes genetics (those with XY chromosomes are usually assigned male; those with XX chromosomes are usually assigned female; other chromosomal configurations, such as XXY, XYY, and Fragile X, are considered to be intersex), and internal reproductive organs (those with external or internal testes and associated structures are usually assigned male; those with ovaries, uterus, and associated structures are usually assigned female; others are assigned intersex). The vast majority of newborns can be easily assigned as male or female. Estimates of the number of newborns who may be assigned intersex on the basis of genitals, chromosomes, internal reproductive structures, and hormonal conditions that may not show up until later in life are as high as 1.7 percent (Sax 2002). Generally, every effort is made to determine whether to assign a newborn as male or female. It is very rare that anyone remains legally or socially assigned as intersex for very long, although their medical facts may remain unchanged.

Cisgender people, as the term is most commonly used, are those who identify with their assigned sex and feel that their corresponding legal sex, and the sex that other people attribute to them, are all correctly aligned. Individuals on the trans spectrum do not identify with the sex assigned to them at birth; they may work to change their legal sex and take other steps to ensure that people do not misattribute to them the sex that they were assigned at birth.

Although sex may appear to be a simple biological determination, it is important to bear in mind that the criteria that are considered to be valid are a result of social negotiations and can vary at different times and places. The socially decided nature of what counts as sex is easily seen in the fact that many gender-diverse people are able to acquire a legal sex designation that is not the same as their originally assigned sex, sometimes without undertaking any physiological changes. Furthermore, another indicator of the socially decided aspect of sex assignments is the fact that the criteria for determining when trans people have changed their sex are hotly debated, constantly changing, and differ from jurisdiction to jurisdiction.

Gender

Gender is generally assumed to follow from those biological elements that make up one's sex. Gender has several components: assigned gender, legal gender, gender identity, gender expression, and gender attributions. Genders are assigned to people at birth on the assumption that anyone assigned as a female should be known as a girl (and later a woman) and that anyone assigned as a male should be known as a boy (and later a man). Intersex newborns are usually assigned a sex soon after birth, and their assigned gender corresponds to that sex. In cases where a sex cannot be clearly assigned on the basis of medical information, the usual practice is to assign a gender on the basis of a best approximation.

Legal gender can be changed in many places around the world, although the requirements for doing so vary widely. In general, a legal gender change happens as part of a legal sex change.

Typically, legal gender starts out as the same as assigned gender. However, trans, non-binary, and many Two-Spirit people do not identify with the gender assigned to them at birth, or with their assigned legal gender. They may adopt a range of other gender identities, and they may find that different identities may work better for them at different times and under different circumstances. The number of gender identities that people may feel best fit them is constantly changing and expanding. The 2015 U.S. Transgender Survey of 27,715 people found that those who answered the survey used more than 500 different gender identities, with many people reporting more than one gender identity. The most commonly chosen identities were: transgender (65 percent); trans (56 percent); trans woman, MTF, male to female (32 percent); trans man, FTM, female to male (31 percent); non-binary (31 percent); genderqueer (29 percent); gender nonconforming, gender variant (27 percent); gender fluid, fluid (20 percent); androgynous (18 percent); transsexual (18 percent); and agender (14 percent) (James et al. 2016, 44).

Many people are not able to express their gender identities fully, or in ways that garner correct gender attributions from other people, often because of the dangers they face from widespread pernicious transphobia. Even among those who do express their gender identities in some way, not all gender expressions are recognized or respected by others.

In many parts of the world it is possible to change one's legal sex and thereby to legally change one's gender. In many other parts of the world, this remains forbidden. Nonetheless, many people effectively change their gender in their everyday lives by way of altering their gender expression such that they are able to conduct most of their lives in their correct gender. However, people who are unable to obtain legal validation of their binary (males/men or female/women) or non-binary (sometimes designated as X on official identity documents) gender identities are at all times vulnerable to a wide range of abuses and victimizations.

Other Terms

Transgender or **trans** are both umbrella terms used to describe a range of people who share the feature of not feeling that the sex and gender assignments made for them at birth were correct. **Transsexual** people identify as the binary sex and gender that they were not assigned at birth. Some wish to alter their bodies using hormones of the sex with which they identify and using surgeries to craft bodies that affirm their sex and gender identities. **Transvestite** is an older term that has been mostly replaced by the words **cross-dresser**, or transgender, trans, or non-binary. People who identify in this way were usually assigned male at birth and dress themselves part-time as women. Each of these terms is contested in ways that are discussed further in Chapter 2.

People who identify as **non-binary** reject the either/or nature of a binary. Where gender identity is concerned, non-binary people see the male or female gender binary as a restrictive social construct. Non-binary people use various pronouns to reflect this rejection of the male/female binary. Currently, in the English language, the most common pronouns that non-binary people use are gender neutral *they, them,* and *theirs.*

Two-Spirit is a term adopted in Winnipeg, Manitoba, at the 1990 Third Annual Inter-tribal Native American, First Nations, Gay and Lesbian American Conference. It was suggested by Albert McLeod because an English-language term was needed to replace a term then in use by anthropologists, which was felt to be both inaccurate and insulting. Two-Spirit is meant to be a general-purpose term that approximates many variously nuanced traditional terms extant in Indigenous languages. Traditionally, people who in English could be called Two-Spirit were different from women and men on the basis of their temperament, work roles, clothing, personal habits, spirituality, or sexuality. Today, Two-Spirit functions as an umbrella term including lesbian, gay, bisexual, trans, non-binary, intersex, queer, and questioning people. Some people identify more with one or more aspect of gender or sexuality under the Two-Spirit umbrella, and other people prefer to identify simply as Two-Spirit (Filice 2015).

While it is valuable to know the words that are commonly used today to talk about trans, non-binary, and Two-Spirit people, our contemporary understandings are neither universally agreed-upon, nor are the same now as they have been in the past. Every time and place has its own social rules and practices about gender. Every time and place has always had people whose behaviors vary from the norms of their societies. While we can learn about variations in gender presentations from a range of different kinds of reports and records, in most cases, that is all that we can know. We cannot know about how such people identified. Thus, when speaking about other times and places, sometimes it is better to frame discussions as being about **gender-diverse** people while making no assumptions about their gender identities.

From the Ancients to the 1700s—Recognition of Gender Diversity

The classical Greeks believed that there was only one sex with two variations. According to the great thinkers of their day, everyone was inherently male, and all sex organs were penises and testicles. However, some individuals were more highly developed due to having been exposed to greater "vital heat" during gestation. Those who were more highly developed had external penises and testicles. Those were less highly developed had internal versions of the same. There were no unique words for female reproductive organs because they were not seen as different in quality, only in location. These beliefs supported a social system in which females/women were seen as inherently underdeveloped compared to males/men and were therefore excluded from positions of power and authority. These ideas persisted in Western thought until at least the year 1600, in some ways as late as 1800. During these centuries, there were numerous stories in circulation about females who miraculously experienced postnatal bursts of vital heat sufficient to cause their penises and testicles to become external (Laqueur 1990).

Numerous ancient cultures around the world recognized and respected gender diversity; in many cases, these societies and cultures recognized and embraced three or more gender identities. People within these cultures who embodied a third-, fourth-, or fifth-gender identity were often seen as special within their community. They may have been healers or spiritual guides. For example, before Hawai'i was colonized by Western explorers and missionaries and a strict gender binary was put into place, the *māhū*, who were outside of the gender binary of male/female, were accepted and honored as a crucial part of the community. The Wizard Stones (ancient lava rocks) on public display in Waikiki tell the legend of four *māhū* who, around 400 CE, came from Tahiti to Hawai'i as healers (Anbe and Xian 2001). These healers were neither men nor women, but rather *māhū*—a gender identity and expression that simultaneously combined masculine and feminine in a third gender outside of this binary. This is an important story in the history of the land that we know today as the Hawaiian Islands.

Some other places around the world where gender diversity was known to exist and to be fully accepted were, among others, the continental Americas, Egypt, Indonesia, Italy, New Zealand, Siberia, and Uganda. In Maori culture in New Zealand, for example, *Wakawahine* are people assigned male at birth who pursue more traditional women's roles. Meanwhile, also in Maori culture, *Wakatane* are people assigned female at birth who pursue more traditional men's roles. In Indonesia, five genders have been recognized. Throughout the Americas, there are numerous Indigenous groups who recognized third, fourth, and fifth genders—and in all cases, there were precise names given to the people who embodied this gender diversity (PBS 2015).

Gender Diversity and the Imposition of Eurocentric Laws and Religion

Many of these cultures, however, experienced the violence of Western imperialism and subsequent colonization of their societies. Indigenous cultures suffered during first contact, which refers to the time when Indigenous communities first encountered Western men of European descent who were sailing around the world to "discover" different people, animals, and places. Sacred lands that had been theirs for centuries were stolen from Indigenous peoples; they were forced to relocate; traditional clothing and spiritual practices were criminalized; and languages were stripped away.

Back in Europe, there was a large market for tales of adventure. On numerous occasions, not only were plants and animals carted off to Europe to be put on display in the great halls of science and for popular amusement, but often Indigenous people were also caged against their will, put on ships, and then displayed in cities like Berlin, London, and Paris. Indigenous communities did not need to be discovered, since they already knew where they were, who they were, and what their own cultural practices were. As the Europeans went around the globe, they believed that their own ideas about religion, language, dress codes, culture, and gender were superior, and they set about imposing them on others. Hinaleimoana Wong-Kalu, a twenty-first-century *Māhū*, explains:

Before the coming of foreigners to our islands, we Hawaiians lived in Aloha, in harmony with the land and with one another. Every person had their role in society whether male, female, or *Māhū*. . . . *Māhū* were valued and respected as caretakers, healers, and teachers of ancient traditions. We passed on sacred knowledge from one generation to the next through hula, chant, and other forms of wisdom. When American missionaries arrived . . . they were shocked and infuriated by these practices and did everything they could to abolish them. Many chiefs and commoners adopted this religious mindset, seeing even hula and chant as immoral. . . . all kinds of traditions came to be viewed as ignorant or bad. (PBS Hawai'i 2015)

Part of the misunderstanding that many of the explorers had when they visited places like the Hawaiian Islands was that they mistook gender diversity to be homosexuality. In 1778, Captain Cook, a British explorer and cartographer in the Royal Navy, first came ashore on the beach in Hawai'i where he was met by people he identified as men, but who were wearing what he thought of as women's clothing. It is not clear if the first people Cook encountered were *Māhū* because Cook could have been confused by any clothing with which he was not familiar. He assumed that men wearing women's clothing were homosexual, which was both sinful and illegal according to European religions and laws.

The historian Kathleen Wilson writes the following about Cook's misrecognition:

Within the gender complementarity of eastern Polynesian culture, the *mahu* were seen possibly as a third gender, or as women; men having sexual relations with them did not think of themselves as "sodomites," nor did *mahu* have sex with each other. . . . The social acceptance of the *mahu* in eastern Polynesian societies may have actually expressed the associations of women's reproductive functions with the divine—and hence the identification of the feminine with positive, rather than negative, hierarchies and characteristics. (Wilson 2004)

One of the problems Cook and most of the other European explorers had was their inability to translate Indigenous terms like *māhū* (Hawai'i), *hijra* (India), *nádleeh* (Navajo), *muxe* (Zapotec), *winkte* (Sioux), *asegi udanto* (Cherokee), and *fa'a fafine* (Samoa) into European words (English in this case) that respectfully and accurately described the identities and the gender diversity in these numerous cultures. European words, and the binary concepts inherent in them, were imposed and, with them, the nuances and complexities of the words in Indigenous languages were nearly lost. Cultures with a richness of gender diversity that had existed for thousands of years were neither honored nor preserved.

Problems with Western Terminology: Case in Point, the *Hijras* of India

Queen Elizabeth I of England chartered the East India Company in 1600 so that the British could expand their wealth by colonizing India, which they did over the next 335 years until Indian independence in 1947. Numerous explorers and travel writers from Britain went to India to chronicle the people, animals, plants, cultural customs, and religions there. One travel writer in particular, James Forbes, was part of the East India Company when he traveled extensively throughout India in the 1700s. His large leather-bound books, still in existence in library archives today, are filled with journal entries and hand-painted drawings of all the life he encountered there. The following is an excerpt from his diary about an unusual encounter he had with a group of people:

Among the followers of an oriental [*sic*] camp, at least of the Mahratta camp to which we were attached, I must not omit the hermaphrodites; there were a great number of them in the different bazaars, and I believe all in the capacity of cooks. In mentioning these singular people, I am aware I tread on tender ground. . . . There were a considerable number of human beings called hermaphrodites in the camp, who were compelled, by way of distinguishing them from other castes, to wear the habit of a female, and the turban of a man. I was called into a private tent, to a meeting between the surgeon-major and several medical gentlemen of the army, to examine some of these people: my visit was short and the objects disgusting. (Forbes 1813)

In this entry, Forbes demonstrates that he is both fascinated and disgusted with the people he meets. It is interesting to note that he points out there are a "great number" of the people whom he has labeled "hermaphrodites." In other words, they were not unusual in Indian culture at that time.

The people whom Forbes refers to as "hermaphrodites" were, in fact, *hijras*. When the British arrived, the *hijras* had already been in existence for at least 3,500 years. *Hijras*, assigned male at birth, are traditionally categorized as neither male nor female. The term comes from Urdu, but "no English term is adequate to capture the complexity of *Hijra* identity, which cannot be understood solely in terms of sexuality or gender" (Boyce 2015). Often, though, *hijras* are explained within Western terminology as "hermaphrodites" (which is an antiquated term for people with differences of sex development) or as eunuchs (people whose testicles are removed). However, many *hijras* start their lives as people assigned male at birth, but once they feel called to become *hijras*, they go through a spiritual ritual that includes both castration and a penectomy (the removal of the penis); these procedures may be done in the temple of a goddess known as the *hijra* deity, Bahuchara Mata.

Forbes (and many others after him) imposed his own terminology on a group of people who already had a culturally appropriate traditional name. Before British colonization, *hijras* had a place in society, often at the bottom of the caste system, even though it was believed that they had special spiritual powers to provide blessings at a wedding or for a newborn baby. Even today, it is bad luck to turn a *hijra* away from such life-cycle events because they are believed to have the power to bless *or* to curse. Not only do *hijras* embrace a gender identity and expression outside a male-female binary, but they also often exist within Indian Hinduism, Islam, and Jainism or one of the other multitude of religions found in India. It is clear, though, that Western terminology cannot do justice to the complexity of the *hijras.*

De-Colonial Recovery Projects

In the twenty-first century, many Indigenous cultures have been carrying out de-colonial recovery projects to revitalize traditional languages and customs. Gender diversity is one of the areas of focus for numerous groups grappling with recovering from colonization. In Hawai'i, for example, several schools have brought back the Indigenous Hawaiian anthem that is sung at the beginning of the school day, ancient hula is in the course curriculum for grades K–12, and the history of the *māhū* is again being told with pride. In India, the term *hijra* never disappeared, even though the British misunderstood the *hijras'* cultural roles. One of the ways that India is showing increased respect for *hijras* is that there is now a third gender category available on government identification materials put into place specifically because of the *hijras.*

Gender Diversity in Spiritual and Religious Practices

In many ancient cultures, deities were also seen as gender diverse. An inherent part of the sacred power of these deities was their ability to encompass all genders. Throughout the history of ancient cultures, there are accounts of gender-diverse deities and ancient practices and rituals in which third-, fourth-, and fifth-gender people participated. In the ancient *māhū* tradition, for example, there are specific hula dances and rituals to honor gender-diverse gods. And in Navajo culture, there are special songs and chants that are sung by *nadleeh* people to invoke gender-fluid spirits. The following are a few examples of gender diversity in ancient cultures.

Ancient Egypt

Gender-fluid deities were very common in ancient Egypt. For example, the creation story of the Egyptian gods focuses first on Atum, a deity who is both male and female. This gives a clue to how important gender diversity was in ancient Egyptian spirituality. In the ancient Egyptian cities of Canopus (a religious center) and Thonis-Heracleion (a major trading hub), which both sank to the bottom of the Nile River over 1,200 years ago, the gigantic statue of Hapy (sometimes spelled Hapi), the god of the Nile, used to tower over the water's edge. A rediscovered statue of Hapy, which weighs six tons and is eighteen feet tall, depicts a deity that is both masculine and feminine with a male beard and female breasts. An embodiment of divine androgyny, Hapy was worshipped throughout Canopus and Thonis-Heracleion.

India and Nepal

In Indian culture, there are several deities that embody gender diversity, most notably the deity worshipped by the *hijras,* Bahuchara Mata. Bahuchara Mata is often depicted in colorful drawings riding a large rooster with her sisters dancing in a circle on the ground below her. According to legend, Bahuchara Mata and her sisters were traveling on a road when a male bandit tried to rob, rape, and kill them. To avoid being raped, Bahuchara Mata cut her own and her sisters' breasts off because, at that time in India, a woman without breasts was seen as neither male nor female. She also cursed the bandit with impotence. Similarly, *hijras* who perform a ritual penectomy (removal of the penis) become neither male nor female (Das n.d.). One of the most important Hindu gods, Shiva, the creator and destroyer, is often depicted in statues with one masculine earring and one feminine earring. Another gender-fluid Hindu deity from Nepal is Lakshminarayan, who "represents the male god Vishnu and his female consort Lakshmi . . . sometimes shown as a single figure whose body is half male and half female" (Parkinson 2013).

Ancient Judaism

Rabbi Elliot Kukla, who is the first out trans person to be ordained as a rabbi by the Hebrew Union College–Jewish Institute of

Religion in Los Angeles, and currently serves as the rabbi at the Bay Area Healing Center in San Francisco, has discussed six different terms for gender identities found in ancient Jewish texts: *zachar*, male; *nekevah*, female; *androgynos*, someone we would refer to today as having differences of sexual development (DSD) or intersex—a person who clearly embodies sex traits of both males and females; *tumtum*, someone whose sex is not determined; *ay'lonit*, a person who is assigned female at birth who begins to display male characteristics; and, finally, *saris*, someone assigned male at birth who begins to display female characteristics (Kukla 2006).

Nineteenth- and Twentieth-Century Sexology

The science of sexology rose out of eighteenth-century European Enlightenment ideas and philosophies about the need to create taxonomies for all living species. Sexology, which began to develop and become a popular field of study in the late 1800s, focused predominantly on Western European populations.

Generally speaking, sexologists fell into two categories in their approach to the burgeoning scientific field. The first approach took cisgender reproductive heterosexual orientation as the norm. In other words, a normal person was someone assigned either male or female at birth, and whose gender identity and gender expression aligned with this sex classification at birth. A normal person also did not engage in any homosexual activity. And, ultimately, a normal person, according to sexologists who used this model, did not engage in sex outside of marriage and outside of the realm of procreation. In other words, a normal person did not have sex for pleasure. Anyone deviating outside of these parameters of normal was seen to have a pathology or a disease. This included anyone exhibiting what were labeled homosexual tendencies, which ran the gamut from desire for people of the same sex to dressing in clothing of the opposite sex (cross-dressing). It also included heterosexuals who engaged in sex with more than one partner, engaged in masturbation, or who fetishized body parts, such as feet. In this first approach, sexologists attempted to diagnose, label, and then cure the pathology.

The second approach included sexologists who studied and labeled various modes of sexual orientation, gender identity, and/or gender expression as natural variations within the human species. Some sexologists, of course, fell somewhere between these two approaches, often mixing and matching them, and in some cases, coming up with new approaches. Many of the sexologists who were interested in natural variation wanted to make life better for the people who fell outside of these areas of "normal."

The majority of the sexological writings in the late nineteenth and early twentieth centuries were written predominantly in Latin and German. These writings were not accessible to a general reading public; they were reserved for only the most highly educated people. In that time period, education was reserved for men who were socioeconomically advantaged. Women of all socioeconomic backgrounds were barred from higher education, as were people who were in the working class or at poverty level.

There were, however, numerous educated men who were not scientists who found the writings of the sexologists to be of interest. The Royal Society of London was an intellectual hub for educated gentlemen in the nineteenth century, and it was there, during various scientific presentations, that these intellectuals first learned of Charles Darwin's theories about evolution, as well as the theories of some of the earliest sexologists. The evenings at the Royal Society were not restricted to men in a specific field of study, but rather open to all educated gentlemen who were members of the society. It was at lectures like these that people like John Addington Symonds and Edward Carpenter, both homosexual men who, for the time period, were very open about their sexual orientation, most likely first heard about the sexological theories of "urnings"—a word for homosexuality as well as what, today, we would understand to be transgender identity.

Symonds and Carpenter were both poets and philosophers, not scientists; however, they both felt compelled to write arguments against the sexologists who saw "urnings" as diseased and in need of a cure. They are examples showing that, very early in the field of sexology, there were people who were pathologized by the first type of sexological approach and who stood up for themselves and for their communities. In his lifetime, Edward Carpenter wrote several theories about same-sex desire between men, referring to homosexuality and gender-fluid people as a "third sex." John Addington Symonds wrote letters to the sexologists who only wanted to cure "urnings" to argue that, perhaps, "urnings" seemed sick because society (and specifically the sexologists) had pathologized them. Magnus Hirschfeld took note and helped open up another less judgmental avenue to sexological research.

As the field of sexology began to further develop in the twentieth century, more and more of those who would have fallen under the diseased label took matters into their own hands in order to broaden the field of sexology and to focus on the second type of sexological research: that of the nonjudgmental study of nature's diversity. Although, at least to our knowledge, none of these earlier sexologists would necessarily fit under the trans umbrella today, it is crucial to remember that the concepts of sexual orientation and gender identity had not yet been separated, and that in order to understand the history of gender diversity, one also has to look at the history of homosexuality.

The major institution for the study of sexology in the European world from 1919 to 1933 was Magnus Hirschfeld's Institut für Sexualwissenschaft (Institute for Sexual Science), located in Berlin, Germany. Not only was the institute highly regarded in scientific circles, but Hirschfeld also strove to make it a safe place for people of all gender identities and sexual orientations. Some of his pioneering work centered on differentiating gender identity from sexual orientation. Hirschfeld noted the difference between homosexual men who dressed in drag for entertainment and people assigned male at birth who wore women's clothes because they felt that they were women. In a radical move, Hirschfeld worked with the police authorities in Berlin to help get identification papers labeling people as *transvestites* so that they would not be arrested under Paragraph 175 of the German Penal Code, which criminalized male homosexuality. In 1910, Hirschfeld published the first book about transvestism. With the rise of the Third Reich in Germany in the 1930s, Magnus Hirschfeld came under particular scrutiny because he was Jewish and he was homosexual. In 1933, the Nazis raided and burned the contents of his institute and the forward motion of many of the world's leading sexologists at the time was halted. World War II, which started in Europe in the early 1930s and raged until 1945, not only put a stop to the advancement of sexological inquiry; rather, the war nearly erased it entirely. By the early 1940s, almost the entire globe was feeling the effects of war in Europe and in the Pacific. In the aftermath, much work was being put into the task of rebuilding countries, cities, and towns at all levels.

By the time the science of sexology became active once again, the intellectual center had moved from Europe to the United States where Alfred Kinsey, a scientist who originally started out researching gall wasps, founded one of the world's premiere institutions in sexology that is still going strong in the twenty-first century: the Kinsey Institute for Research in Sex, Gender, and Reproduction at the University of Indiana. When discussing the field of sexology, Kinsey said, "We are the recorders and reporters of facts—not the judges of the behaviors we describe" (Kinsey Institute n.d.). Harry Benjamin (who was originally from Germany) was preparing to write his groundbreaking 1966 book that would be accessible to all people who could read, *The Transsexual Phenomenon*. Kinsey, Benjamin, and many of the sexologists following in their footsteps, have embraced the sexological approach that sees nature as diverse.

The 1890s to the 1940s: Popular Culture

While the sexologists debated whether gender diversity was a disease or a natural variation, popular culture outside of the realm of the educated men of science seemingly not only tolerated, but often embraced various types of gender transgressions. From literature to underground performances and Hollywood films, the 1890s to the 1940s saw gender diversity in a range of venues.

The 1890s, also known as the "Gay Nineties," saw a rise in both male and female impersonation on the stage. In Boston in the 1890s, Julian Eltinge was a hugely popular female impersonator who staged several shows in Boston and New York. At the age of ten, when his family lived in Montana, Eltinge started wearing women's clothing and sneaking out to perform at local saloons. His father rejected him, but his mother apparently supported him and, worried for his safety at home, sent him to live with her sister in Boston where his career took off. Eltinge is credited with making drag a comedic form in popular culture because serious female impersonation would have marked him as perverted (Goodman 2018). In England, during this same time period, Matilda Alice Powles, aka Vesta Tilley, was a popular male impersonator in London's music halls. In shows like *Burlington Bertie,* Tilley performed and sang as a man (Loguidice 2014). In both cases, there is no way to know if Eltinge and Tilley felt more like the gender they performed or not; however, their immense popularity and the popularity of these shows with the general public certainly illuminates the ways that the general population was fascinated by, and also tolerated, their gender transgression.

Virginia Woolf was a famous British writer and member of the Bloomsbury group, which was a group of Modernist artists and writers, most of whom were gay, lesbian, bisexual, and/or transgender in today's terms. In 1928, she published her novel *Orlando: A Biography.* The novel was dedicated to her female lover, Vita Sackville-West. Both Woolf and Sackville-West were bisexual in a time when bisexuality not only denoted a sexual orientation but also a gender identity in that a bisexual person was seen as someone who had a mixture of male and female attributes. The novel, which is a fanciful look at English history from the Renaissance to the early twentieth century, focuses on Orlando, who, for the first 150 years of his life, is a man. After

150 years, on a trip to Turkey, Orlando (who does not age) falls into a dreamlike trance for several days and then wakes up as a woman. In a statement directed specifically at all of the sexological debates, Woolf writes the following:

> The change seemed to have been accomplished painlessly and completely and in such a way that Orlando herself showed no surprise at it. Many people, taking this into account, and holding that such a change of sex is against nature, have been at great pains to prove (1) that Orlando had always been a woman, (2) that Orlando is at this moment a man. Let biologists and psychologists determine. It is enough for us to state the simple fact: Orlando was a man until the age of thirty; when he became a woman and has remained so ever since. (Woolf 1928, 127–128)

Woolf's novel was very successful and she earned quite a bit of money from it, not just from the novel, but also the numerous stage adaptations that were based on it. Woolf's success also points to a general audience interested in gender diversity and gender transgressions. Woolf's novel can be easily read as a transgender text, and the Orlando story continues to be popular into the twenty-first century.

The year 1928 also saw Gladys Bentley become the "queen" of the Harlem Renaissance as she sang to sold-out crowds who came to the famous Clam House on 133rd Street in Harlem, New York City. Bentley always performed in her tuxedo and top hat, and carried a cane to go with her dapper masculine look. Bentley was famous as a cross-dressing blues singer whose fame lasted into the early 1930s. She even broke the racial barrier by marrying a white woman in a civil ceremony in New Jersey in 1931 (Harten 2017).

On the silver screen, audiences were captivated by the gender fluidity of both Marlene Dietrich and Greta Garbo. Dietrich had been born in Berlin, Germany, in 1901. During the 1920s and 1930s, on screen as well as on stage in cabarets, she often wore a tuxedo and top hat, which were seductive to men and women alike. With the rise of the Third Reich in Germany, she was asked to be a star dedicated to the Nazis, but she refused; in 1937 she became an American citizen and worked to help get Jews out of Nazi Germany through various underground resistance efforts. Throughout the 1930s, 1940s, and 1950s, Dietrich could be seen cross-dressed and performing in a cabaret. During World War II, in particular, she not only refused to help the Nazis, but she spent much of her time visiting U.S. and British military men and performing for them in her tux and top hat. Similarly, Greta Garbo became famous for her 1933 role in *Queen Christina,* a biographical drama about the life of Sweden's queen who cross-dressed and ruled as a man. Since the film was made in 1933, it predated Hollywood morality laws that forbade cross-dressing in a serious dramatic role.

Gay historian Allan Bérubé devotes an entire chapter of his groundbreaking book *Coming Out under Fire: The History of Gay Men and Women in World War II* (Bérubé 2010) to drag shows in the U.S. military. Although drag does not necessarily denote any sort of actual gender identity—specifically a transgender identity—in all of these cases from the late nineteenth century through the 1940s, drag does point to ways that gender transgressions were constantly happening and were constantly supported in public venues. It is also noteworthy that these gender transgressions happened across racial, socioeconomic, cultural, and national boundaries.

The 1950s: Underground Trans Culture

While there were numerous public examples of gender diversity and gender transgressions in art and culture from the 1890s through the 1940s and continuing into the hyper-heteronormative and hyper-cisnormative 1950s, there were also underground transgender cultural productions and underground transgender communities.

In 1953, Ed Wood Jr.'s first film, *Glen or Glenda?* (which was also released at various venues under the titles *I Changed My Sex* and *I Led Two Lives*), opened in small independent movie theaters around the United States and the United Kingdom. Of note, the film was released one year after Christine Jorgensen's famous coming out after her gender affirmation surgery in Copenhagen, Denmark. Although the film is difficult to follow and mixes together science fiction, gothic horror (Bela Lugosi has a feature role), and a sensationalist documentary style, the story at the heart of Wood's first film is one of a man who is a transvestite. He tries desperately to fit into 1950s society as a man, but he spends all of this time thinking about dressing like and being a woman. The film opens with the suicide of another trans person who cannot handle the pressures of normative culture, and then the film looks at the ways binary gender roles are thrust on people. To this day, the film does not get favorable reviews; however, given that it was made in 1953 and takes a sympathetic approach to a transgender person who is struggling with their transgender identity, it was a radical film for its time. And, in many ways, it was ahead of its time. The power of this film rests in the fact that many closeted trans people who saw it at the time were able to relate to the film and may have been bolstered by the empathy to trans issues displayed in the film. In the twenty-first century, this film is an important piece of historical transgender popular culture.

In the late 1950s, a very important safe space for trans women was created in the Catskill Mountains resort area in New York State. In Hunter, New York, a broken-down property was purchased by Marie Valenti, who owned a wig shop in Manhattan. She was the wife of a cross-dresser whose male name was Tito, but who preferred to use the name Susanna. Thus, Casa Susanna was born. According to the trans historian Dallas Denny, people arriving at Casa Susanna for a weekend away would drive up to the mountains in masculine business suits, but "they drove to the Catskills with the trunks of their cars filled with female attire." Upon arrival at the renovated weekend resort, they would "soon change into cocktail dresses and sweater sets to begin a weekend as the women most of them wished they were" (Denny 2014). Archival photographs from Casa Susanna still exist and researchers can see some of the various women who spent weekends at this early trans safe house. Some of the photos in the Casa Susanna series are "glam" shots and what today would be called "selfies." But the majority of the photos show a group of people who came together as chosen family to create a safe space to be, if only for a weekend, the women that, as Dallas Denny said, most of them wanted to be.

Developments from the 1950s to the 1970s

While the film *Glen or Glenda?* and Casa Susanna were more underground phenomena, Christine Jorgensen's very public coming out as a trans woman made international headlines. Jorgensen was a U.S. military veteran who, in 1950, went to Copenhagen, Denmark to begin her gender affirmation procedures, which, at that time, took several operations. In 1952, her gender affirmation became public knowledge and she became a household name. For most people, Jorgensen was their first introduction to trans issues. While many people ridiculed Jorgensen, many others were truly interested in her story. Throughout the 1950s, she made herself available for magazine interviews. For trans people who didn't know that anything could be done about how they felt, Jorgensen provided an example and gave them hope.

Two other trans pioneers who were not as well known to the general public at this time but whose work has positively influenced trans culture are Louise Lawrence and Virginia Prince. Louise Lawrence lived in San Francisco and worked with physicians to help educate them about trans issues. In one of her presentations at a University of California Medical School class, Lawrence met Virginia Prince, another trans woman. Together with Edith Ferguson and Joan Thornton, they created and published *Transvestia,* which would later, under the leadership of Virginia Prince, become one of the most important underground trans magazines in the United States.

The second half of the twentieth century saw many groups in the Western world increase their agitation for, and achievement of, greater recognition of their long-denied rights. The post–World War II era of the 1950s in the United States saw sharp socioeconomic and racial inequities. In the American South, Jim Crow laws (enacted in 1877) that enforced racial segregation were even more stringently enforced by white police officers and other white governmental officials than they had been before the war. African American soldiers returning home after fighting for the United States in World War II were greeted by increased racist violence as well as increased socioeconomic disparity because many companies prioritized hiring white veterans returning from the war. The post–World War II era also saw "white flight," which referred to middle-class and working-class white citizens moving out of the urban centers of the United States and into swiftly growing suburban areas. The people who remained in the urban centers were predominantly people of color living at or below the poverty line, and many people who, today, we would understand to be LGBTQ2+.

By the mid-1950s, African American communities in the South, in particular, began to organize to dismantle the Jim Crow laws. The civil rights movement continued to gain momentum into the 1960s, culminating in the spectacular 1963 March on Washington where Dr. Martin Luther King Jr. delivered his famous "I Have a Dream" speech. Many other marginalized communities took notes from the civil rights movement, and many people in these other marginalized communities were also a large part of the civil rights movement.

Between 1955 and 1975, the United Farm Workers movement fought for the rights of migrant farmworkers; the second wave of the feminist movement worked to pass the Equal Rights Amendment; the American Indian Movement reoccupied Alcatraz Island in San Francisco Bay and demanded that the U.S. government return and recognize stolen lands; the peace movement against the American war in Vietnam grew exponentially; and various riots and protests ushered in the modern LGBTQ2+ rights movement. As Sylvia Rivera, a trans woman who is often thought of as a grandmother of the LGBTQ2+ rights movement, said, "All of us were working for so many movements at that time. Everyone was involved with the peace movement, the women's movement, the Civil Rights movement. We were all radicals" (Rivera 1998).

Anti-Masquerading Laws and Police Violence

In the ten years encompassing 1959–1969, there were three riots and one protest in the United States that helped usher in the modern American LGBTQ2+ rights movement. All four incidents were a reaction to police harassment around anti-masquerading (anti-cross-dressing) laws. In the 1950s and 1960s, several states, including California, New York, and Pennsylvania, had anti-masquerading laws on the books, which made it illegal for someone to wear clothing not seen as appropriate to their sex assigned at birth. The laws varied from state to state, but the general rule was that a person had to be wearing at least three articles of "appropriate gender" clothing (according to the police) in order not to be arrested. These anti-masquerading laws gave police and other officials an immense amount of power; raids on diners, restaurants, and bars that were known to serve LGBTQ2+ people occurred frequently.

When the police raided an establishment, they would often force people into the bathroom and make them strip off all their clothes, ostensibly to check that they were wearing the requisite number of gender-specific items of clothing. Names of people arrested on these anti-masquerading charges would be printed in local newspapers, which often led to them losing their jobs, or losing their families. The following four incidents show some of the ways in which people who cross-dressed—people who today might very well identify as trans, non-binary, or Two-Spirit—stood up to police harassment and, ultimately, helped to pave the way for the American LGBTQ2+ rights movement.

May 1959: Cooper's Do-Nuts—Los Angeles

In the 1950s, the area of Los Angeles known as Skid Row exemplified the aftermath of "white flight" from urban centers. It was a poor neighborhood that was home to a predominantly Latinx and Indigenous population. Two gay bars, Harry's and the Waldorf, were also located in this neighborhood. Both bars had signs that said "no drags," which meant that the bars were not open to cross-dressers. This was because the Los Angeles Police Department often staked out these two bars, waiting to find people violating the anti-masquerading laws, which they would then use as a reason to raid the bars.

Located between these two bars was a twenty-four-hour doughnut shop named Cooper's. Although the two bars did not allow people who were cross-dressed to come in, from all contemporaneous accounts, the doughnut shop never refused to serve anyone. The customers at the shop included police officers, sex workers, hustlers, and drag queens, and they were very ethnically and socioeconomically diverse. One evening in May 1959, the police entered Cooper's and began arresting people who looked gender nonconforming. As the handcuffed patrons were being marched out to the patrol cars, they began to resist arrest. The customers still left in Cooper's, many of whom were LGBTQ2+ people of color and wearing the "wrong clothing," stormed out of Cooper's and began throwing cups of coffee, doughnuts, and garbage at the police. Upon hearing the noise, gay men who were at Harry's and the Waldorf also ran out to fight against the arrests.

The riot at Cooper's Do-Nuts did not make the national news; however, it does mark one of the first known instances of LGBTQ2+ resistance in the United States, and it was led by people who, today, might very well identify as trans:

Cooper's Donuts symbolized a sanctuary for not just the gay population of Los Angeles, but also for the overlooked transgender population. Their presence brought irrational prejudice, violence, and judgement, but Cooper's allowed them a space to take part in conversations and be who they were without the fear of scrutiny. The gathering and joint effort of LGBTQ+ people on the night of the riot is representative of the family that Cooper's created. (Cooper's Donuts n.d.)

April 1965: Dewey's Famous—Philadelphia

Dewey's Famous, near 13th, Camac, and Chancellor Streets in Philadelphia, was a twenty-four-hour diner that was locally famous for being "noisily packed late into the night with a whole spectrum of drag queens, hustlers, dykes, leather men and Philly cops looking for a cup of coffee, a cross section of life on 13th Street" (Skiba 2013). From all accounts, this particular Dewey's location was very welcoming to everyone; however, when some of these same customers started appearing at another Dewey's location on 17th Street near Rittenhouse Square, the management did two things: (1) they called the police to come enforce the anti-masquerading laws, and (2) they told the servers to refuse service to anyone who either looked homosexual or who was wearing the "wrong gender" clothing.

Word spread quickly through the LGBTQ2+ community in Philadelphia, which resulted in the Janus society, an early LGBTQ2+ rights group there, organizing a lunch counter sit-in modeled on the lunch counter sit-ins that had gone on all over the United States to protest Jim Crow laws. The sit-in was a success in that over 150 people showed up wearing "wrong gender" clothing. Once the police arrived, almost everyone left peacefully (there were three arrests, but the people were released). This protest was a success because the Dewey's diner chain began requiring their employees to serve everyone at all locations regardless of gender expression. It was also a success because an entire community comprised of LGBTQ2+ people came together to support the cross-dressers who had been initially denied service.

Monica Roberts, an African American trans activist, scholar, and blogger, wrote the following about the importance of the peaceful lunch counter protest at Dewey's in 1965:

> As a person who has been involved for a decade in the struggle for transgender rights, it is deeply gratifying to know that African American transgender activism isn't a new phenomenon. I'm estatic [*sic*] to discover another nugget of my African American transgender history. I'm gratified to know that I'm a link in a chain that will eventually expand the "We The People" in the constitution to include transgender ones as well. (Roberts 2007)

August 1966: Compton's Cafeteria—San Francisco

In August 1966, sixteen months after the peaceful sit-in at Dewey's Famous in Philadelphia, another uprising against police harassment of trans people occurred in the Tenderloin district of San Francisco. Like Cooper's and Dewey's, Gene Compton's twenty-four-hour cafeteria was a safe place for drag queens, trans women, sex workers, and hustlers, most of whom were people of color. Felicia Flame, a navy combat Vietnam veteran, AIDS activist and survivor, and trans resident in the Tenderloin in 1966, says that the night the riot broke out was like any other:

> It was just one of those ordinary nights when all of the girls would come to Compton's to drink coffee or just hang around to see what the night would bring. Every night at around two or three, we ["the girls," that is, trans women] would gather around to make sure we had made it through the night. (Stryker and Silverman 2005)

When the police came in to carry out one of their usual raids at Compton's, the customers fought back by throwing shoes, purses, saucers, food, and anything else they could hurl at the police. As the fighting broke through the front plate-glass windows and out onto the streets of the Tenderloin, the radical

LGBTQ2+ youth group Vanguard joined in. By the end of the night, a police car had been turned over and set on fire. Many of the trans women interviewed in Susan Stryker and Victor Silverman's 2005 documentary film, *Screaming Queens: The Riot at Compton's,* noted that there were two major changes during that summer of 1966. One was the riot and the aftermath when the San Francisco Police Department eased up on their raids in the wake of the events. The second was that, for many of the trans women present at Compton's that night, the release of Dr. Harry Benjamin's *The Transsexual Phenomenon* would suddenly give them hope for a way to finally fully become the women they wanted to be. Harry Benjamin's groundbreaking book was the first book-length discussion of transsexualism, and the first book to argue that transsexual people should be treated with hormones and surgeries. Unlike the texts of earlier sexologists written specifically for medical practitioners, Benjamin's work was fully accessible for anyone who could go to a bookstore or a public library and read it.

June 1969: Stonewall Inn—New York
On Sunday, June 28, 1969, the Stonewall Inn, a bar in Greenwich Village, was crowded with a combination of drag queens, gay men, trans women, butch dykes, hustlers, and sex workers, many of whom were people of color. The police raided the bar, even though they had just raided it a few days earlier. They came in and demanded that everyone dressed in the "wrong gender" clothing start stripping, and began arresting people. However, on this particular night, many of the bar's clientele began fighting back by throwing drinks and shoes at the police. The tension rose so quickly that veterans from the riot, Sylvia Rivera and Miss Major Griffin-Gracy, noted that the police were frightened and locked themselves in the bar with some of the protesters. The fighting quickly erupted out into the streets.

What sets the Stonewall Riots apart from the other previous riots and protests is that the fighting lasted, on and off, for over a week, and news of the rioting made it into national and international newspapers. Most LGBTQ2+ communities around the world view the Stonewall Riots as the moment when the modern LGBTQ2+ rights movement began. What very often gets lost to history, though, is that the main group of people who stood up to police violence that night were trans people of color.

In the decades since Stonewall, a lot of the true history of that night has been pushed aside for more whitewashed versions of the story that have the riots being led by cisgender white gay men and lesbians. The arguments over the history of who was at Stonewall and which group of people truly started the rioting are one of the causes of a split that has developed within the gay, lesbian, bisexual, and transgender community. At this point in time, though, it is clear that some of the most marginalized people in our society—trans people of color, many of whom were also sex workers and living on the streets—were at the forefront of the people who ushered in the modern American LGBTQ2+ rights movement.

The 1970s

Transphobia in the LGBTQ2+ Community

Shortly after their actions during the Stonewall Riots, Sylvia Rivera, a Venezuelan and Puerto Rican trans woman and her soulmate, the African American trans radical Marsha P. Johnson, were purposefully excluded from the newly forming gay political groups. By 1973, when New York City's Pride March included speeches from people in the community, Rivera was nearly forced off the stage by cisgender gay men and cisgender lesbians heckling her. The irony was painful: one of the women whose actions on the night of the Stonewall Riots had made the 1973 Pride March possible was nearly dragged off the stage. In response to the heckling, Rivera commented: "I am not even in the back of the bus. My community is being pulled by a rope around our neck by the bumper of the damn bus. . . . Gay liberation but transgender nothing!" (Rivera 2007, 120).

In response to the transphobia they encountered from cisgender gay and lesbian groups, Rivera and Johnson founded the Street Transvestite Action Revolutionaries (STAR). STAR was a radical social justice group comprised predominantly of trans people of color. One of the first issues that they addressed was homelessness among LGBTQ2+ youth (the group may have been focused on "transvestites" but they did not discriminate against anyone who needed their help). The first STAR House was in a trailer truck, which was towed away one day with over twenty street youth inside. After this incident, Rivera and Johnson, as the housemothers, knew they had to find an actual building. In 1972, with the help of several community members, STAR was able to open the second STAR House in a building, a safe place for LGBTQ2+ street people to go to have a roof over their heads. Both Rivera and Johnson spent their adult lives working to help homeless LGBTQ2+ youths in New York City to have a safe place to stay, even though Sylvia and Marsha were often homeless themselves.

In 1992, while she was struggling to get clean and sober, Sylvia woke up to the news that Marsha P. Johnson had been found dead, floating in the Hudson River. The New York City police (NYPD) ruled Johnson's death a suicide; however, the trans community, led by Rivera, rose up to demand justice because they all knew that Johnson had not been suicidal. The NYPD had made it clear that Johnson's death was not high on their list of investigations. As of 2018, the truth behind Marsha P. Johnson's death has still not been learned, and members of the trans community are still advocating for the police to reopen the case, and for justice to be done.

In 2002, Sylvia Rivera died from complications of liver cancer. She struggled with alcoholism and drug addiction her entire life. She was also homeless for the majority of her adult life. Even on her deathbed, Rivera was advocating for New York City to adopt a fully inclusive non-discrimination policy that would cover sexual orientation and gender identity. In 2015, the National Portrait Gallery in Washington, D.C. displayed a photograph of Rivera, making it the first time the gallery had displayed a portrait of a trans person.

Trans in Popular Culture

The moment the Stonewall Rebellion in New York City happened, it was as if the floodgates of activism had opened. Even though a split between the gay, lesbian, bisexual, and transgender communities happened soon after Stonewall, popular culture exploded with various trans representations. The year 1970 was a watershed year for many transgender milestones. It was the year that Sylvia Rivera and Marsha P. Johnson first formed the Street Transvestite Action Revolutionaries (STAR) in response to transphobia, racism, and classism within the gay, lesbian, and bisexual movement. It was also the year that Andy Warhol's protégé, trans woman Holly Woodlawn, debuted in the film *Trash*. This was also the year that the now iconic gay director from Baltimore, John Waters, released his first low-budget film that he wrote, directed, and recorded on a hand-held camera, *Multiple Maniacs*. The black-and-white satire about heterosexual, cisgender, and middle-class American norms only played at the midnight movies at small urban theaters because the content was often seen as disgusting. This film, however, marked the birth of one of the most iconic cross-dressed actors in film— Divine. Harris Glenn Milstead, who was a quiet man, first donned his makeup and feminine clothing to play Divine, and as John Waters notes in the documentary *The Cockettes*, there was no going back for Milstead. Although Divine was not transgender per se, she was often portrayed as a trans woman who had to deal with hate crimes starting, specifically, in the final scene of *Multiple Maniacs*. Divine represents a moment when drag representation and trans representation came together.

Another culturally important work was the 1973 London stage show *The Rocky Horror Show*, written by Richard O'Brien, who in 2017 came out as non-binary. The science fiction comedy features Frankenfurter, a mad scientist who, like Dr. Frankenstein, tries to create a man. Frankenfurter embraces his trans identity and sings the song "Sweet Transvestite." While the stage play was popular, it was not until 1975 that the play was turned into the cult classic film *The Rocky Horror Picture Show*, which still shows at midnight in theaters around the world. For over forty years, the screening of this film has given a safe space to gender "freaks," wherever they live. As a major popular culture phenomenon, the power of *Rocky Horror* is that it continually, for two generations, has brought together all types of people, and it creates a safe space for everyone who wants to transgress the gender binary. For many trans, non-binary, and Two-Spirit people, this film (although its language may be a bit outdated in the twenty-first century) serves as a refuge since it is an audience-participation film that asks everyone in the theater to be gender fluid.

Research and Community-Building in the 1970s and 1980s

The 1970s was a time when trans people, researchers, and service providers all started to build communities. One of the most notable was the Erickson Educational Foundation (EEF), started and funded by wealthy trans man Reed Erickson. Incorporated in 1964 and functioning into the early 1980s, the EEF did most of its trans work in the 1970s. That work included publishing a newsletter chronicling news about advances in trans rights and research; publishing informational pamphlets on a variety of subjects; compiling and providing a referral list to sympathetic service providers; running a speakers bureau for educational institutions and the media; funding research projects, including the first gender clinic in the United States; and organizing the first conferences for researchers.

The conferences organized by the EEF became the inspiration for the 1979 founding of the Harry Benjamin International Gender Dysphoria Association (HBIGDA), which later was renamed the World Professional Association for Transgender Health (WPATH). The same year that HBIGDA was founded also saw that group create the first version of the standards of care meant to ensure that trans people who wished to undergo medical transitions were provided with state-of-the-art care.

The year 1975 saw the start of Fantasia Fair in Provincetown, Massachusetts, now the longest-running trans gathering in the Western world. It was started by Ariadne Kane, Betty Ann Lind, and several others from "The Cherrystones," a trans support group from Boston. Fantasia Fair's founding mission was to provide trans people with an opportunity to learn about themselves in an open, socially tolerant environment.

Around the same time, in 1976 and 1977, ophthalmologist and trans woman Renée Richards was thrust into the national news when she successfully sued the United States Tennis Association for the right to compete in women's tennis. Richards has served as an inspiration for trans athletes ever since. After she retired from tennis, Richards went on to coach Martina Navratilova to win twice at Wimbledon.

Meanwhile, Lou Sullivan started the first organization for trans men in the United States, and Rupert Raj was working in a number of Canadian cities to build community by starting a series of organizations and publishing newsletters advocating for trans rights. Raj began with the Foundation for the Advancement of Transsexuals (FACT) and followed that with the Metamorphosis Medical Research Foundation, among others. Raj was also part of a wave of trans people in the 1980s who, for the good of others, allowed themselves to be interviewed by television and radio talk show hosts. By and large, such talk shows portrayed trans people in a derogatory and sensationalist manner for cisgender audiences to laugh at and gawk at. However, despite the apparent intent of the producers of these shows to make horrifying or humorous spectacles of trans people, such shows were life-saving for many trans viewers because it was the first time they became aware that there were other people like them, and that it was actually possible to change their gender.

The 1980s: AIDS and the Trans Community

In 1980 Ronald Reagan was elected president of the United States. Under his administration, which was largely tied to a growing and more politicized religious right, many of the laws and positive forward motion that the LGBTQ2+ community saw over the course of the 1970s were suddenly at risk. It is important to remember that there were trans people who were also gay, lesbian, or bisexual and that transgender communities also had some different struggles at that time from those of the gay, lesbian, and bisexual communities. For example, in 1973, the American Psychiatric Association finally removed "homosexuality" as a mental disorder from the *Diagnostic and Statistical Manual of Mental Disorders* (DSM). However, gender dysphoria (being trans) was first included in the DSM in 1980 and remains in the DSM to this day.

In the summer of 1981, reports emerged from New York, Los Angeles, and San Francisco that young gay men were dying of a rare cancer. At first, there were only a few cases; however, within a year, the disease that would come to be known as Acquired Immune Deficiency Syndrome (AIDS) had started to ravage the LGBTQ2+ community in the United States. President Reagan and his entire administration looked at the unfolding pandemic as a sign that "homosexuality" was evil, and some people said that everyone suffering from AIDS deserved it. It took President Reagan until 1986 to publicly say the word "AIDS." Meanwhile, thousands of people died because there was no governmental money going into research and prevention.

At the time, and continuing into the twenty-first century, AIDS is often thought of as a gay man's disease, even though it is clear that anyone can contract HIV and/or get AIDS. During this pandemic that began in the 1980s, trans, black, and Indigenous Two-Spirit communities, in particular, were (and continue to be) hit hard. However, scientists and doctors are only now beginning to take note that a disproportionately large percentage of trans people have been affected since the beginning.

In the mid-1980s, several studies showed that Indigenous people, who were already marginalized where health care was concerned, were proportionately at greater risk of contracting HIV. And within that population, Two-Spirit individuals were at even higher risk.

Thousands of trans women, many of whom were trans women of color in urban centers, died from AIDS-related complications. However, since many trans women were unable to afford gender affirmation procedures at that time, they were not recorded as transgender, but rather placed under the umbrella category of "men who have sex with men." In 1986, in the midst of the AIDS pandemic in San Francisco, gay trans man Lou Sullivan founded FTM International, the first international outreach and information group for trans men in the world. Lou contracted AIDS and died in 1991.

The numbers of trans people who were misrecorded as gay during the early years of the pandemic leaves a gaping hole in trans, non-binary, and Two-Spirit history and limits our understanding of the ways that AIDS also devastated trans, non-binary, and Two-Spirit communities. To this day, trans, non-binary, and Two-Spirit people, particularly poor trans women of color, are often at higher risk of contracting HIV than other marginalized people. In San Francisco, there are groups like El/La Para TransLatinas that are attempting to rectify this situation and give support and health care regarding safe sex practices and harm reduction for trans, non-binary, and Two-Spirit communities.

The 1990s: The Power of Internet Access

In the 1980s, the AIDS crisis galvanized lesbian and gay communities to mass activism. It wasn't until the 1990s that gender-diverse people's activism significantly increased.

Trans, non-binary, and Two-Spirit people, at about 0.5 percent of the general population (Meerwijk and Sevelius 2017), are a priori a small proportion of the population. As well, many trans, non-binary, and Two-Spirit people have had good reasons to not wish to be publicly known for being gender diverse: due to rampant transphobia, in many places it is simply not safe to be out; while many people just want to get on with their lives in their correct gender and be known for their personalities and accomplishments, not for being gender diverse. Until access to the Internet started to become widespread in the 1990s, these factors combined to leave almost all trans, non-binary, and Two-Spirit people feeling extremely isolated. It also meant that it was very difficult to organize for rights when it was almost impossible to make contact with others who were trans, non-binary, or Two-Spirit.

When trans, non-binary, and Two-Spirit people came online in the 1990s, it didn't matter so much that they didn't know anyone else like them who lived nearby. They were able to start to find much needed support online and to build online communities that had strength in the numbers necessary to make change in laws, policies, attitudes, and the ways that things got done. Trans, non-binary, and Two-Spirit people were also quick to take advantage of the rise of social media in the early 2000s. The interactivity of Web 2.0 applications allowed trans, non-binary, and Two-Spirit people to engage more actively with mainstream media when the media got things wrong; to have their own voices heard in ways that have profoundly altered public understandings of what it means to be trans, non-binary, or Two-Spirit; and to organize and deploy resources more effectively.

While the Internet is crucial to connecting people who might otherwise feel isolated, in San Francisco in 1997, founders of the first transgender film festival in North America wanted to create an open and safe venue for trans-themed films, filmmakers, and audience members. San Francisco was already host to one of the largest LGBT film festivals in the world; however, founders of the Transgender Film Festival wanted to give up-and-coming gender-diverse filmmakers a venue. In the face of many LGBT film festivals being more focused on big-budget,

Hollywood-style films, the Transgender Film Festival focuses, instead, on less established talent and the diverse stories of trans, non-binary, and Two-Spirit lives. Many of the films also are made available on the Internet for free after the festival's conclusion, so that there can be access for anyone who has the ability to go online.

The Twenty-First Century: Global Changes

The twenty-first century, generally speaking, has been a fast-paced time of change where transgender rights are concerned, and most of the changes have been for the better. During the first two decades of the twenty-first century, several countries have begun to recognize third-gender possibilities on government documents, which helps not only people with differences of sex development, but also people who identify as non-binary, agender, genderqueer, or any other term that falls outside of the gender binary. In the twenty-first century, several countries have lifted bans on trans people serving in the military, and there have been numerous trans people elected to public office around the world. At the same time, with the rise of visibility, there has also been a rise in hate crimes against trans, non-binary, and Two-Spirit people around the world. From Sasha, an agender youth being set on fire on a public bus in Oakland, California, in 2013 to an all-time high murder rate of transgender women in Brazil in 2017, there are still many laws, policies, and cultural attitudes that need to be changed around the world.

2000 to 2010

At the beginning of the twenty-first century, Monica Helms created the transgender flag, which was first put on display at a march in Phoenix, Arizona. Although the rainbow flag, which stands for LGBTQ2+ Pride, is meant to be all-embracing, this special trans flag has now become iconic around the world and is often flown next to the rainbow flag.

In 2002, in Newark, California, a town in the San Francisco Bay Area, Gwen Araujo, a young trans woman of color, was murdered by young men she knew from high school. In the case of Gwen Araujo, her family honored her name and her gender identity when they spoke about her to the press, and when they buried her. This issue of families often not respecting their loved one's gender identity and chosen name sadly happens far too often even in the twenty-first century when there is more understanding than ever about trans, non-binary, and Two-Spirit issues. Gwen's murderers attempted to use the "trans panic" defense—saying that they had become terrified when they found out that she was trans. Gwen's family's rage about her death, and a huge activist response to the murderers' transphobic tactics, resulted in a 2006 law called the Justice for Gwen Araujo Act, which set a precedent that courts were not allowed to entertain a "trans panic" defense argument to lessen the sentencing of murderers in hate crimes.

In 2007, the Supreme Court of Nepal issued a decision on third-gender identity that is, globally, the most comprehensive law enabling people to legally identify outside of the gender binary. Nepal was not the first country to legalize a third-gender identity, but this decision set a legal precedent for the rest of the world. The law went into effect in 2011.

2011 to 2018

On May 24, 2012, Argentina's president, Cristina Fèrnandez de Kirchner, signed the Gender Identity Bill into law, making Argentina the first nation in the world where people can legally change their gender identity without a judge's or doctor's signature. The law also obligates their health care plans to cover gender affirmation treatments and obligates clinics to prescribe hormones and provide gender affirmation procedures on demand.

In the United States, in 2016, President Barack Obama and his administration supported two trans-positive moves at the national level. His administration lifted the military ban that excluded transgender people from serving in the U.S. military, following the lead of numerous other countries that had already done so (starting with the Netherlands in 1974). In November 2016, President Obama worked with the Department of Education to sign a new portion of Title IX into law stating that Title IX, which forbids sex discrimination in schools that receive government funding, needed to include trans, non-binary, and Two-Spirit people (the actual legislation uses only the term "transgender"). However, in 2017, President Donald Trump and his head of the Department of Education, Betsy DeVos, overturned the Obama administration's amendment to Title IX so that trans, non-binary, and Two-Spirit people are no longer covered. In 2018, President Trump also began making moves to ban transgender people, once again, from the U.S. military.

In 2017, a newborn, Searyl Atli Doty, in British Columbia, Canada, became the first known baby in the world to be issued a "U" gender-neutral sex marker on a health card. The baby's parent, Kori Doty, who is non-binary trans, fought a legal battle to make sure that a binary gender marker was not placed on the government document.

References

Anbe, Brent, and Kathryn Xian. 2001. *Ke Kūlana He Māhū: Remembering a Sense of Place*. Film. Zang Productions.

Bérubé, Allan. 2010. *Coming Out under Fire: The History of Gay Men and Women in World War II*. Raleigh/Durham: University of North Carolina Press, 2010.

Boyce, Bret. 2015. "Sexuality and Gender Identity under the Constitution of India." *Journal of Gender, Race & Justice* 18(1): 21.

Cooper's Donuts. N.d. "Paper." http://cdonuts1959.weebly.com/paper.html.

Das, Debjani. N.d. "Bahuchara Mata and the Hijras." https://debjani11.wordpress.com/bahuchara-mata-and-the-hijras/.

Denny, Dallas. 2014. "The Historical Roots of Casa Valentina." *Chrysalis Quarterly*. May 10, 2014. http://dallasdenny.com /Chrysalis/2014/05/10/the-historical-roots-of-casa-valentina/.

Filice, Michelle. 2015. "Two-Spirit in Historical Canada." November 26, 2015. http://www.thecanadianencyclopedia .ca/en/article/two-spirit/.

Forbes, James. 1813. *Oriental Memoirs: Selected and Abridged from a Series of Familiar Letters Written during Seventeen Years Residence in India: Including Observations on Parts of Africa and South America, and a Narrative of Occurrences in Four India Voyages*. Vol. 2. London: White, Cochrane, and Co., 62.

Goodman, Elyssa. 2018. "Drag Herstory: This Drag Queen Was Once the Highest Paid Actor in the World." *Them*. April 6, 2018. https://www.them.us/story /julian-eltinge-drag-queen-history.

Harten, Duke. 2017. "This Nonbinary Lesbian Ruled the Harlem Renaissance." *OMG Facts*. https://omgfacts.com /this-nonbinary-lesbian-ruled-the-harlem-renaissance/.

James, Sandy E., Jody L. Herman, Susan Rankin, Mara Keisling, Lisa Mottet, and Ma'ayan Anafi. 2016. *The Report of the 2015 U.S. Transgender Survey*. Washington, DC: National Center for Transgender Equality.

Kinsey Institute. N.d. "Dr. Alfred C. Kinsey." https:// kinseyinstitute.org/about/history/alfred-kinsey.php.

Kukla, Rabbi Elliot. 2006. "Terms for Gender Diversity in Classical Jewish Texts." *TransTorah*. (Educational flyer).

Laqueur, Thomas. 1990. *Making Sex: Body and Gender from the Greeks to Freud*. Cambridge, MA: Harvard University Press.

Loguidice, Rosie. 2014. "Male Impersonators." *LGBT History Project*. February 16, 2014. http://lgbthistoryproject .blogspot.com/2014/02/male-impersonators.html.

Meerwijk, Esther L., and Jae M. Sevelius. 2017. "Transgender Population Size in the United States: A Meta-Regression of Population-Based Probability Samples." *Am J Public Health* 107(2): e1–e8.

Parkinson, R. B. 2013. *A Little Gay History: Desire and Diversity across the World*. London: British Museum Press.

PBS. 2015. "A Map of Gender-Diverse Cultures." August 11, 2015. www.pbs.org/independentlens/content /two-spirits_map-html.

PBS Hawai'i. 2015. *A Place in the Middle*. Nov. 12, 2015. http://aplaceinthemiddle.org/.

Rivera, Sylvia. 1998. "I'm Glad I Was in the Stonewall Riot." Interview in Leslie Feinberg, *Trans Liberation: Beyond Pink or Blue*. Boston: Beacon Press.

Rivera, Sylvia. 2007. Speech to the Latino Gay Men of New York. June 2001. *Centro Journal* 19, 1.

Roberts, Monica. 2007. "The 1965 Dewey's Lunch Counter Sit-In." *TransGriot*, October 18, 2007. http://transgriot .blogspot.com/2007/10/1965-deweys-lunch-counter-sit-it .html.

Sax, Leonard. 2002. "How Common Is Intersex? A Response to Anne Fausto-Sterling." *Journal of Sex Research*, *39*(3), 174–178.

Skiba, Bob. 2013. "Dewey's Famous." Philadelphia Gayborhood Guru. January 28, 2013. https:// thegayborhoodguru.wordpress.com/2013/01/28 /deweys-famous/.

Stryker, Susan, and Victor Silverman. 2005. *Screaming Queens: The Riot at Compton's*. Film. Frameline.

Wilson, Kathleen. 2004. "Thinking Back: Gender Misrecognition and Polynesian Subversions aboard the Cook Voyages." In *A New Imperial History: Culture,*

Identity, and Modernity in Britain and the Empire, 1660–1840, ed. Kathleen Wilson, 358–359. Cambridge: Cambridge University Press.

Woolf, Virginia. 1928. *Orlando: A Biography.* Reprint. London: Hogarth, 1933.

Introduction

This chapter focuses on problems, controversies, and solutions regarding various issues faced by trans, non-binary, and Two-Spirit communities. From terminology that changes rapidly, and can be confusing, to the issues that face trans, non-binary, and Two-Spirit students as they access K–12 education, this chapter explains some of the problems and controversies and gives some examples of solutions.

Transgender Terminology

While the words *transgender* or *trans* are widely used today, the meaning of these words has been in flux and debated for decades. Various formulations that are similar to the term transgender can be traced as far back as 1915 in English-language newspaper articles describing people who lived as a gender other than the one they were assigned at birth. The pioneering German Jewish sexologist Magnus Hirschfeld published what was probably the first scientific article using a German variant term (*seelischer transsexualismus*), and the word

Taken from the title of the 1955 song and film, "Love Is a Many Splendored Thing," this Miami Beach LGBT Pride parade participant's sign says that gender can be diverse and that love is not just for heterosexual or cisgender people. (Olga Kulakova/Dreamstime.com)

transgenderism was first used in a psychology journal in 1965. From then until now, it has remained unclear exactly who was meant to be included in these and many other terms used over the years (Williams 2017).

From the beginning, some people wanted to have separate words for various types of people who had different ways to understand, or to show, that they did not feel entirely at home in the sex or gender that was assigned to them at birth. Many different words were suggested. Some caught on for a while and then faded from use. Some are still with us today, although they don't always mean the same thing now as they once did. Similarly, some of the words we consider correct today will no longer be popular, or even acceptable, a few years from now. However, social change is uneven. Old words, and old ways of understanding them, remain in use and coexist with new words and with new interpretations of old words. As a result, miscommunications and disagreements abound about who is or is not trans and about whether trans is even the right word to use any more.

The words trans and transgender are commonly used today as umbrella terms to include anyone whose gender identity does not match their assigned sex in a stereotypical way. In its broadest interpretation, it may include a range of gender-diverse and gender-nonconforming people, such as transsexual, non-binary, genderqueer, queer, gender-fluid, pangender, agender and Two-Spirit people; cross-dressers and people who identify as autogynephilic; drag queens and kings; eunuchs; and intersex people. Most trans people prefer that the word trans be used as an adjective (e.g., trans people), which recognizes that being trans is just one aspect of who a person is. Most feel that it should not be used as a noun (e.g., they are transgenders), which can imply that being trans is the totality of who someone is, nor as a verb (e.g., they transgendered to another gender), because it can imply either that being trans is something that happened *to* someone rather than how a person *is*, or that a person is not trans unless they do something (such as surgery) to make it happen.

Transsexual people are those who fully identify as the sex and gender "opposite" to the one they were assigned at birth. Generally, they make as many social and physical changes as they feel are necessary to bring their gender expression and the sex of their bodies into alignment with traditional versions of men/males and women/females. There are a variety of terms used to describe transsexual people. Some of them are more widely accepted by transsexual people than others. Older terms that are still used by some people but that are no longer appreciated by most transsexual people include pre-op, post-op, and non-op; MTF and FTM; and tranny.

Most transsexual people consider that they have always been the sex and gender with which they identify. They generally feel that their gender identity, not their bodies, is the core determiner of who they are, and that they want to be known for their gender, not for the private matter of what their primary and secondary sex characteristics look like. If surgical status is discussed, most transsexual people prefer to talk about gender confirmation or affirmation procedures rather than sex reassignment surgeries. In addition, because those procedures are complex and often require many steps over a number of years, most transsexual people disdain being known as pre-, post-, or non-op, terms that imply that a person's legitimate claim to a gender and sex depends on whether or not they have had maximum genital reconstruction surgery.

MTF means male-to-female; FTM means female-to-male. These terms are often used in medical and professional literature but are no longer widely used by trans people. They have the drawback of emphasizing an originally incorrect sex and gender assignment both by mentioning it at all, and by making it the first thing said. When this information needs to be discussed, many trans people prefer to use more neutral acronyms such as AFAB (assigned female at birth) or AMAB (assigned male at birth). But better terms emphasize people's identities rather than their originally incorrect assignments. People often think of themselves as being on the transmasculine spectrum or transfeminine spectrum, as affirmed males or affirmed females, or as trans men or trans women—written as two words so as to indicate that being trans is simply one of many attributes, not a defining feature. Similarly to how the term *queer* has been adopted with pride by contemporary sexual minority people, some transgender people would like to reclaim the term *tranny*, which in the past has largely been used as an insult to transgender women who are homeless or do sex work.

Some transsexual people object to being considered transgender because they feel that their specific uniqueness disappears when they are lumped in with everyone else who is gender different. They feel that being transsexual requires a more intense commitment than people who are more partial in their gender changes. One way to keep everyone under the umbrella is to shorten transgender to trans (sometimes written as trans*). That way, it can be seen to include both transsexual and transgender people without specifying or excluding one or the other.

However, some people don't like the term trans in any form. Alternative terms that are sometimes used are gender nonconforming, gender variant, and gender diverse. These terms describe groups that overlap in some ways with trans, but are not exactly the same groups as trans. A person can be gender nonconforming and still identify very strongly as the sex and gender assigned to them at birth. For example, many feminists and gay people are gender nonconforming and not at all trans in their gender identities.

Some people dislike the term gender nonconforming because it can be interpreted to imply that there is something abnormal or negative about some kinds of gender expression. Many of the people who dislike the term gender nonconforming prefer the ideas expressed in the words gender variant. They prefer to think of various gender identities and gender expressions as simply part of a healthy natural variation. Hence, they would rather use gender variant than gender nonconforming to describe the full range of genders because they see it as less judgmental. Some people don't like gender variant either, because they feel that it implies that there is a correct kind of gender to vary from. Gender diverse is generally seen as the most nonjudgmental of these terms.

Other people object to the term trans because they feel that trans implies movement from one point on a gender binary to another, and that it therefore reinforces a heteronormative system of gender and does not properly represent the experiences of people who feel that binary ideas about gender such as male/female and man/woman do not describe their gender identities and/or gender expressions. Some people might feel partially like a man and partially like a woman at any one time; they might look or feel like a man sometimes and like a woman sometimes; or they might never feel like a man or a woman. In each case they may or may not express that to others. Such people describe themselves using a range of self-descriptive terms that collectively can be called either gender non-binary or genderqueer. Often, gender non-binary people use gender-neutral pronouns such as they (singular) or ze or hir.

Terms that genderqueer and gender non-binary people prefer include bi-gender (being both a man and a woman); pan-gender (being all genders, including more than two); agender, null gender, neutrois (having no gender); and gender creative or gender fluid (continuing to explore and change gender identity and expression), which are used by both adults and children but are more commonly used to describe children so as to avoid prematurely imposing a gender on them.

Many Indigenous peoples around the world have terms in their own languages that describe people whom some would consider to be trans. While each Indigenous community and language confers a culturally specific meaning to their own kinds of gender variance, people from North American Indigenous communities in the 1990s adopted the English-language term Two-Spirit as a kind of umbrella term to describe some commonalities among traditional North American Indigenous

understandings of gender variance. Two-Spirit people were traditionally recognized as having some mixture of the spirits of
both men and women, which was demonstrated by their gender variance in social interactions, often including sexual expression consistent with their gender. Thus, Two-Spirit people are
often thought of as lesbian, gay, or bisexual, whereas in traditional understandings, the gender(s) of a person's spirit take pri-
macy over the sex of their body in understanding who a person
is. Two-Spirit people are neither trans nor lesbian nor gay in the
sense that these terms are used in English.

Some people who do drag consider themselves to be trans,
while others do not. Many people who are cisgender intermittently also adopt an expression of another gender. They may
be heterosexual, or lesbian, gay, bisexual, or queer. Some gay
men and lesbian women do drag performances where they
dress as exaggerated versions of glamorous women or macho
men. While their gender expression may cause others to pre-
sume that they are trans, many continue to solidly identify
with their gender assigned at birth. While many people enjoy
doing and watching drag performances, there are many people
who take offence at them. Some people object to what they
perceive as disrespectful parodies of other people's gender
expressions. Some people feel that drag trivializes the difficulties that some trans people have with gaining acceptance of
their gender expressions. At the same time, some drag kings
and queens do drag as a way to express trans, non-binary, or
Two-Spirit identities.

A mostly underground population of heterosexual men periodically dresses in women's clothing for short spans of time.
During the twentieth century, the term transvestite was most
commonly used to describe these men. Today, most prefer to
be known as cross-dressers or non-binary. Some men cross-
dress entirely in secret. Some go out in public, but do not join
with others. Some are engaged in communities of like-minded
people. Most start by wearing one or two items of women's
clothing and find it both highly sexually arousing and very

shameful. Some men continue to escalate over many years until they have acquired a complete wardrobe and a feminine name and persona. Shame may abate or continue. If it continues, it is most often accompanied by a periodic purging of all things feminine and an unsuccessful dedication to never dress as a woman again. Over time, some people who fit this pattern will shift their gender identities to become transsexual women and pursue gender affirmation.

The term *autogynephilia* has been used to describe men who are sexually aroused by dressing in women's clothing. Autogynephilia comes from Latin and means "love of oneself as a woman." The word is considered, by those professionals who use it, to describe a sexual fetish or paraphilia rather than a gender identity. Some men who cross-dress find this term useful and embrace it as descriptive of themselves. Some consider themselves to be trans; some do not (Lawrence 2013). Most transsexual women who followed this pattern prior to transition find the term highly offensive because it does not recognize their gender identity as women and instead implies that they are men with a sexual obsession. Many of them consider anyone who uses the term to be transphobic.

Eunuchs are another group of people assigned male at birth who may consider themselves as gender diverse. A contemporary eunuch is a male-bodied person who has been castrated (either through chemical treatment, usually for prostate cancer, or by the physical removal of the testicles). Most are men who have been castrated as treatment for disease, and although castration may cause them to harbor insecurities about their masculinity, they continue to be completely cisgender men. Some cisgender men voluntarily become eunuchs because they are unhappy living under the influence of the amounts of testosterone secreted by their testicles. Some men have their testicles removed as part of their sexuality and continue to identify fully as cisgender men (Wassersug, McKenna, and Lieberman 2012). A small number of castrati identify as male-to-eunuch, a nonbinary gender identity between male and female. They recognize themselves as less male and more female than they were before their castration. They may continue to present themselves in public as men, or as an agender person. They do not see themselves as women (Vale et al. 2010), but as people who identify as non-binary, they may consider themselves to be part of the larger trans family.

Intersex people (also known as people with differences of sex development, or DSD) include individuals whose bodies are such that it is not immediately obvious to doctors what sex should be assigned to them at birth. An older term that is still sometimes used is hermaphrodite; however, this term is considered pejorative by most intersex people. Normal medical procedures are to assign a sex at birth based on best clinical judgment even when the evidence is not entirely clear. Some people who are easily assigned to a sex at birth are discovered, often around puberty, to have *differences of sex development (DSD)*. In either case, a person with DSD may conclude that the wrong sex and gender was assigned to them and they may request gender-affirming procedures. Some people with DSD who adopt a different gender later in life identify themselves as trans; some do not. Other than in these instances, people with DSD are not usually included under the trans umbrella. However, scientific evidence and opinion is mounting that rather than people with DSD being a kind of trans people, trans people may well be a kind of DSD condition wherein a person's primary and secondary sex characteristics appear in congruence with the binary sex/gender assigned at birth while their brain structures and functions are closer to those of the other binary sex/gender.

Is Gender Identity the Same as Sexual Orientation?

Today, most people familiar with trans and non-binary people are careful to acknowledge that knowing someone's sex doesn't tell you anything about what their gender might be, and knowing their gender doesn't tell you anything about what their sexuality will be. However, many people in the general public do not make this separation in their thinking. Throughout most of human history, gender diversity was not separated from sexual diversity.

Until very recently, sexual interests were always seen as part of a person's gender expression, and gender expression was always seen as part of a person's sexuality. In fact, the original use of the concept of being "trapped in the wrong body" was first used in the nineteenth century by Karl Heinrich Ulrichs, who described homosexual or bisexual men as female souls in male bodies (*"anima muliebris virile corpore inclusa"*) (Ulrichs 1994, 289). Then, sex and gender and sexuality were all thought of as part of the same thing. "Normal" people were expected to be what we would now call heteronormative, and many variations were thought of as gender done backward, or as "inversion." Through this lens, people who were not heterosexual, and people who were gender atypical, and people who crossdressed, and people who were interested in changing their sex and gender were all considered to be people who turned "normal" gender on its head, that is, inverts (Chauncey 1983).

Today, we have built alliances among LGBTQ2+ people. While people within these communities and their allies recognize that sex and gender and sexuality need not combine in any particular way, many people in the broader public still think in ways not that different from the ideas of the nineteenth and twentieth centuries. They very often think of a wide range of people as being part of one big group whom they see as varieties of homosexuals. To this kind of thinking, anyone who is not heteronormative has *perverted*, rather than *inverted*, the proper natural order of humanity. Thus, while many people in LGBTQ2+ communities might think of their various members as having productively *queered* sex, gender, and sexuality to varying degrees, those who misunderstand or disapprove of them often think of trans, non-binary, and Two-Spirit people as more radical forms of being gay or lesbian, or as people who have taken being gay or lesbian to the extreme.

The commonplace practice of speaking of LGBTQ2+ people all in one acronym in some ways adds to the ongoing public habit of thinking of trans, non-binary, and Two-Spirit people as a kind of most-extreme homosexuals. The public became accustomed to the terms lesbian and gay being combined (both homosexual). Then a B was added for bisexual people (who were often seen by members of the public as partly homosexual). Then a T was added for trans people (often seen by members of the public as homosexuals gone too far). Then a Q for queer and a 2 for Two-Spirit were added along with many other letters to expand the acronym to be as inclusive as possible (seen by many people as all sharing some taint of "perversion"). LGBTQ2+ people have learned to work together to improve society because homophobia and transphobia, and all the other phobias associated with LGBTQ2+ people, share a common origin—they are all hostile reactions to people who do not conform to gender expectations as shaped by heteronormativity. Vestiges of the idea of inversion remain strong in public thought.

Is Trans a Disease or a Natural Variation?

The question of whether gender variance is part of nature's diversity or is a diseased condition has not yet been fully settled in the context of Western medicine. Starting in the nineteenth century, some prominent sexologists argued that gender variance was a mistake of nature that needed to be avoided if possible and corrected if it could not be averted (Krafft-Ebing 1965). This way of thinking about gender variance is based on heteronormative assumptions about the ways that people's bodies are presumed to dictate how they experience and express gender and sexuality, and it is still ascribed to by many people today. This heteronormative belief system can be summed up as follows:

• Sex is an intrinsic biological characteristic. There are two and only two sexes: male and female. Everyone is either one sex or the other. Normally, no one can be neither; no one can be both.

- Genders are the social manifestations of sexes. There are two and only two genders: men and women (boys and girls). All males are supposed to be either boys or men. All females are supposed to be either girls or women. Everyone is supposed to be one gender or the other. Normally, no one can be neither; no one can be both.

- Gender role styles are culturally defined expressions of sex and gender. There are two main gender role styles: masculinity and femininity. Normally, males are heterosexual and masculine men, and females are heterosexual and feminine women.

- Any variation from these patterns is caused by biological or mental pathology.

From this perspective, any variation in gender identity or gender expression that is not heteronormative is seen as abnormal and pathological. Many people who subscribe to this point of view also consider any form of sexuality or sexual orientation other than strict heterosexuality to be a diseased condition. Therapies that attempt to cure people of gender or sexual variance are offered under a variety of names, which are often collectively called reparative or conversion therapies (i.e., they are meant to repair a damaged condition). In recent years, many jurisdictions and professional associations have passed laws or otherwise made official statements condemning such practices as unethical and damaging to LGBTQ2+ people. Such laws and policy statements implicitly support the idea that gender and sexual diversity is an intrinsic part of natural human variation.

This concept of gender diversity, while gaining prominence in recent years, is not new. There were also nineteenth-century sexologists who argued that gender diversity was part of nature's plan and should be fully accepted. At that time, as remains true today, many saw same-sex sexuality as a relatively mild form of gender diversity, whereas the wish to live as another gender was seen as an extreme manifestation of gender diversity. Karl Heinrich Ulrichs described gay men using a "wrong body" concept (a female psyche confined in a male body) that today is commonly used to describe transsexual people. Similarly, early in the twentieth century, Edward Carpenter considered homosexual people to be "an intermediate sex" (Carpenter 1952). Magnus Hirschfeld was the first to distinguish between sexual orientation diversity and gender diversity when he described "transvestites" as a separate type of person who may, or may not, also be homosexual (Hirschfeld 1991).

In the middle of the twentieth century, Harry Benjamin published *The Transsexual Phenomenon*, which popularized the idea that homosexuality, cross-dressing, and transsexualism were different phenomena. He wrote that gender variance was part of all humans, and he recognized that there were no effective ways to change a person's sense of themselves as properly belonging to a gender, even when that gender identity was apparently at odds with a person's physical body. He proposed that treatment with hormones and surgery were the correct approaches for transsexual people whose identities differ from their assigned sex and gender. Benjamin's approach, which in an updated form remains the accepted approach today, construed transsexualism as a naturally occurring phenomenon that nonetheless required medical diagnosis and treatment— thus also implying that it was a diseased or pathological condition (Benjamin 1966).

One of the arenas in which the question of disease versus natural variation becomes critical is when trans, non-binary, and Two-Spirit people wish to engage medical professionals to assist them in finding a satisfying physical manifestation of their gender identity. Many trans, non-binary, and Two-Spirit people believe that being trans, non-binary, and Two-Spirit is no more than a natural human variation and that treatment should be freely available at the discretion of each individual, that is, should not require a diagnosis. However, other trans, non-binary, and Two-Spirit people live in circumstances such that access to medical procedures would be impossible without a diagnosis because of regulatory and/or financial barriers.

In most cases, reputable medical professionals will not provide treatment unless they are able to diagnose an individual as having a bona fide medical condition. Widely recognized and accepted diagnostic categories are found either in the *Diagnostic and Statistical Manual* (DSM) of the American Psychiatric Association or in the *International Statistical Classification of Diseases and Related Health Problems* (ICD) of the World Health Organization. In the United States and Canada, the DSM is almost exclusively used to diagnose trans, non-binary, and Two-Spirit people who request medical attention. The ICD is much more widely used in the rest of the world (Winter et al. 2016).

The DSM, last revised in 2013, continues to include trans as a mental health diagnosis. Version 5 has shifted from a diagnosis of "Gender Identity Disorder" to one of "Gender Dysphoria," which "refers to the distress that may accompany the incongruence between one's experienced or expressed gender and one's assigned gender . . . and focuses on dysphoria as the clinical problem, not identity per se." It further provides for "posttransition" support such as lifelong hormone treatments (American Psychiatric Association 2013). The inclusion of gender dysphoria as a mental health diagnosis is consistent with a view of trans, non-binary, and Two-Spirit people as having a pathological condition despite the expressed wish of the DSM authors to reduce the stigma associated with a diagnosis of gender dysphoria (Drescher 2013).

The *International Classification of Diseases* (ICD) is published by the United Nations' World Health Organization and used by governments and health care service providers throughout most of the world. Drafts of Version 11, published in 2018, have similarly attempted to reduce the stigma associated with a diagnosis while continuing to provide diagnostic codes that allow professional service providers to be paid by government and private health insurance programs. ICD-10 diagnoses of "Transsexualism" and "Gender Identity Disorder of Childhood" are slated to be replaced in ICD-11 with "Gender Incongruence of Adolescence and Adulthood" (GIAA) and "Gender Incongruence of Childhood" (GIC). These diagnoses are to be moved out of a chapter called "Mental and Behavioural Disorders" and into a separate chapter called "Conditions Related to Sexual Health," thus shifting the focus from disorders to health, despite the fact that a diagnosis still exists in a manual for classification of diseases. This move can be seen as supporting the idea that one can be gender diverse and healthy. However, the placement in a chapter on *sexual* health contributes to the widespread conflation of gender identity and sexual orientation (World Health Organization 2018).

Trans as an Innate Condition

While the debate has not been entirely settled in Western societies about whether trans, non-binary, and Two-Spirit people feel the way they do because of something in their biology, most trans, non-binary, and Two-Spirit people, and most experts, tend to believe that being trans, non-binary, and Two-Spirit is innate. As with many other innate characteristics, there are many ways that people choose to respond to those parts of who they are. Some people may prefer to ignore or repress or hide those parts of themselves. Other people may feel that the best course of action for them is to fully express themselves. Still others will take intermediate paths.

A number of studies have been done over the years attempting to find a genetic explanation for how people come to know themselves as trans, non-binary, and Two-Spirit. The majority of studies concerned with possible biological explanations for people experiencing themselves as trans, non-binary, and Two-Spirit have been done with transsexual people. The logic underlying this approach is that transsexual people represent the most pronounced form of trans, non-binary, and Two-Spirit experience and can provide the clearest examples of phenomena that would be more difficult to recognize in less binary people.

One avenue of study has been to look at sets of twins in which one twin identified as transsexual and underwent transition from one binary sex to the other. Among identical twins, who share as many genes as two people can possibly share, one study found that in 20 percent of cases, both twins identified as transsexual and underwent transition. This was more common among twins who were transsexual women than among twins who were transsexual men. Interestingly, there were even three sets of identical twins who were separated at birth and both twins identified as transsexual and transitioned sex and gender. However, among nonidentical twins it was extremely rare that both twins transitioned (0.34 percent) (Diamond 2013).

Another approach to the question of whether there is a genetic basis for transsexualism is to investigate how common it is that two nontwin siblings are both transsexual. A study conducted in Spain found that 12 nontwin siblings of 995 transsexual people were also transsexual, which was much higher than would be expected based on the occurrence of transsexualism in Spain. The probability that a nontwin sibling of a transsexual woman would also be transsexual was 0.6 percent, whereas the probability that a nontwin sibling of a transsexual man would also be transsexual was only 0.14 percent (Gomez-Gil et al. 2010).

Together, this evidence would seem to imply that there may well be a genetic component to transsexualism. At the same time, it is important to keep in mind that, even among identical twins, not *all* transsexual twins had a twin or sibling who was also transsexual. Thus, genetics alone cannot provide a full explanation for transsexualism. Furthermore, existing twin studies do not tell us anything about other types of trans, non-binary, and Two-Spirit people.

Evidence is mounting that being trans may be a kind of difference of sex development wherein some parts of the body are consistent with what is more typical of one binary sex and other parts of the body are more consistent with what we usually see in the other binary sex. Currently, some of the strongest evidence for this position comes from studies of the brains of transsexual people. A variety of brain features have been found to differ between cisgender men and women. Some of these differences have also been found in transsexual women and men wherein the brains of transsexual women and men, even prior to hormonal treatments, in some ways resemble those of the sex that they feel themselves to be. More specifically, parts of the brains of transsexual women who are attracted to men, and knew themselves to be transsexual from an early age, have been found to be demasculinized. (Note that demasculinized is not the same thing as feminized. There are some aspects of human brains that are common to males that have been found to be less masculine in trans women while not approximating patterns of females.) Similarly, parts of the brains of transsexual men who are attracted to women, and knew themselves to be transsexual from an early age, have been found to be masculinized; they approximate the patterns commonly seen in males (Kreukels and Guillamon 2016; Guillamon, Junque, and Gomez-Gil 2016).

Many trans, non-binary, and Two-Spirit people make use of hormonal treatments to assist them in changing their bodies so that they more accurately reflect the sex and gender that they feel themselves to be. While such hormonal treatments are sought precisely because they will affect various parts of the body, including brain structures, there is evidence to suggest that trans, non-binary, and Two-Spirit people's physical selves may have already been affected by hormones circulating through their bodies during their prenatal months (Bao and Swaab 2011). At least some of the preexisting masculinization of the brains of transsexual men and demasculinization of the brains of transsexual women have been found to subsequently become amplified by the hormonal treatments that many transsexual people undergo (Kranz et al. 2017).

Other evidence that contributes to the idea that gender diversity may be prompted by innate dispositions comes from studies of human features that are presumed to be caused by genetic or prenatal hormonal influences. Autism spectrum disorders, gendered relative finger length, and otoacoustic emissions have been hypothesized to be the result of relative amounts of prenatal androgen exposure at critical periods of brain organization. Autism spectrum disorders have been found to occur more frequently among people diagnosed with gender dysphoria than in the general population (Van Der Miesen, Hurley, and De Vries 2016); the relative length of gender diverse people's second and fourth fingers have been found to resemble the patterns found in cisgender people with their same gender identities (Kraemer et al. 2009; Hisasue et al. 2012); and sounds produced by the inner ear (otoacoustic emissions) in male (but not female) children diagnosed with gender dysphoria have been found to be intermediate between those typical of cisgender girls and boys (Burke et al. 2014). While there has been some evidence to suggest that transsexual women who are sexually attracted to men (androphilic) are more often born as younger brothers who have more older brothers than sisters (Green 2000), it seems most likely that this is related to their being androphilic rather than their being transsexual (Semenyna, VanderLaan, and Vasey 2017).

Treatment Issues

Informed Consent

The international authority on transgender health, the World Professional Association for Transgender Health (WPATH), publishes a set of guidelines that are used around the world for the treatment of trans, non-binary, and Two-Spirit people. The *Standards of Care for the Health of Transsexual, Transgender, and Gender-Nonconforming People, Version 7* (Coleman et al. 2012) recognizes that trans, non-binary, and Two-Spirit people may desire to exercise a wide range of options to allow them to live well in a gender appropriate for them. Some trans, non-binary, and Two-Spirit people will require no medical or psychological assistance at all, whereas others may wish to make use of counseling, hormonal treatments, and surgeries.

One of the issues that continues to be debated among interested people is what level of informed consent should be required for trans, non-binary, and Two-Spirit people to access medical services to assist them in adjusting their genders from what was assigned to them at birth to what they feel is correct for them. Version 7 of the WPATH *Standards of Care* specifies that individuals who wish to start taking gender-affirming hormones, or to have masculinizing chest surgeries, should have a psychosocial assessment conducted by a trained physician or mental health care professional. The *Standards of Care, Version 7* further requires that people who wish to undergo gender-affirming genital surgeries must be first assessed by two mental health professionals and live in their felt gender for at least one year before being able to access surgical care. Many people see requirements for assessment letters as reflecting a distrust of trans, non-binary, and Two-Spirit people's ability to make normal adult judgments about their health care needs, and discouraging honest dialogue between patients and health care providers.

An alternate informed consent approach that is being increasingly adopted by service providers assumes that trans, non-binary, and Two-Spirit adults and their physicians can jointly determine the best course of action. In this model of informed consent, physicians ensure that patients fully understand and explore their options and patients make their own determinations about what care is best for them (Cavanaugh, Hopwood, and Lambert 2016).

Gender Transitions for Children and Youth

Families, schools, medical professionals, social institutions, and communities are seeing increasing numbers of young people proclaiming themselves to be trans, non-binary, or Two-Spirit. Many members of the public wonder whether young children or teens actually have the ability to correctly understand themselves in this way. People who are skeptical in this way are reluctant to provide support for what they imagine may be a temporary state of mind in a young person. However, most who live or work with gender-diverse prepubertal children or teens acknowledge that young people should be allowed to explore gender options without medical interventions. Many gender-diverse children thrive after socially transitioning to live as their felt gender (Olson et al. 2016).

Opinion is somewhat divided about the age at which adolescents should be permitted to make independent decisions about gender-affirming medical interventions. The WPATH *Standards of Care, Version 7*, recommends a staged approach beginning with a fully reversible regime of puberty-blocking treatments around the age of nine to twelve years, to allow the individual further time to explore gender options and to reach greater decision-making maturity. In most jurisdictions, consent for such treatments is required from parents or guardians. The second stage recommended by the WPATH *Standards of Care* is treatment with hormones to stimulate the desired puberty. Some of the effects of this kind of treatment are reversible, some are not. The final stage involves generally irreversible surgical interventions. In most countries, adolescents of age sixteen and older may make their own medical decisions for stages two and three independently of their parents. However, parents and guardians can also consent to stages two and three when their children are at younger ages, where there are physicians who are willing to comply and laws that allow such interventions.

A minority view is that many young people are getting swept up in a social-psychological epidemic of teens and preteens erroneously believing themselves to be trans, non-binary, or Two-Spirit. Those who see things in this way argue that it is incorrect to offer social and medical transition to young people for two reasons. In the first place, they believe that there is some evidence that the majority of young people who question their assigned gender prior to puberty will eventually resolve their gender issues in favor of their originally assigned gender, if they are not locked into transition too soon. According to this view, some of those who do transition at a young age will transition back a few years later after having undergone irreversible medical procedures, which cause considerable disfiguration in relation to the gender that was originally assigned and later returned to. The second argument against supporting staged transitions for young people is based on the belief that the currently prevailing attitude among therapists dealing with young people is that very little therapy is required to reach an accurate diagnosis of gender dysphoria. Those who oppose transition for young people maintain that gender dysphoria can come in varying degrees that can often be resolved through therapy or a range of social adjustments well short of gender transition (Marchiano 2017). However, many jurisdictions now outlaw attempts to actively attempt to alter a young person's gender identity or sexual orientation.

Fertility and Reproduction

Until very recently, and still in many places, trans, non-binary, and Two-Spirit people have been required to verify that they had been rendered unable to have children before they would be allowed to legally change their sex and gender on their government-issued identification papers. Increasingly, this requirement has come to be seen as both unnecessary and an abuse of government powers. In 2010 the World Professional Association for Transgender Health issued a statement in support of activists' efforts to abolish such requirements: "No person should have to undergo surgery or accept sterilization as a condition of identity recognition. If a sex marker is required on an identity document, that marker could recognize the person's lived gender, regardless of reproductive capacity" (WPATH 2010).

In the United States, birth certificates and the identification papers that depend upon them are issued by states. As of the end of 2017, four U.S. states refused to issue new birth certificates to trans, non-binary, and Two-Spirit people who had changed gender. The majority of those states that do issue corrected birth certificates require some form of proof of surgical sex-changing procedures, which usually means sterilization (Lambda Legal n.d.). In Canada, birth certificates are issued by provinces. All provinces in Canada issue corrected birth certificates. None requires surgical procedures. In 2017, the European Court of Human Rights declared it a human rights violation to require sterilization as a precondition for legal gender change. At least twenty-two European nations were affected by this ruling (Mohdin 2017).

Many trans, non-binary, and Two-Spirit people voluntarily make use of hormone replacement therapies and surgical procedures that can affect fertility and the ability to have genetically related children. For this reason it is important that people considering taking these steps seriously consider fertility questions. Over time, transfeminine people who take feminizing hormones will have diminished ability to get erections and produce sperm, culminating in infertility. However, sperm production can become revitalized if feminizing hormones are stopped. Similarly, masculinizing hormones will cause the cessation of menses within a few months of reaching full dosage, thereby rendering individuals infertile. As with sperm production, menses will resume after the cessation of masculinizing hormonal treatment, and fertility can become restored.

For those who would like to retain the possibility of having genetically related children at a later date, there are a number of options available. Transfeminine people can preserve sperm relatively easily at sperm banking facilities that exist in most cities. Preserved sperm can later be used to inseminate a person who wishes to bear a child. Things are a bit more complicated for transmasculine people. Harvesting of eggs is a fairly complex, intrusive, and expensive matter. Storage of human eggs is also more complicated, prone to failure, less widely done, and expensive. An alternative that is being used by a small but growing number of post-transition transmasculine individuals is to pause masculinizing hormone treatments long enough to resume menstruation, become pregnant, and give birth to healthy children. Many of the men who have exercised this option have already had upper chest surgeries and have nonetheless been able to go on to breast feed their babies. Thus, the people who have done this have been pregnant, birthing, and lactating men who became fathers to the children to whom they gave birth. This phenomenon has challenged the previously seemingly unassailable idea that all who bear, birth, and breastfeed babies can only be females, women, and mothers.

Individualized Treatment Pathways

Many people who identify as trans, non-binary, or Two-Spirit people do not wish to transition at all. Most people who do undertake some sort of gender transition do not desire to effect a complete surgical realignment (James et al. 2016), and some people do not wish to transition into a standard man or woman gender. Some people prefer a gender expression that mixes genders. Other people prefer to express their gender as typical-looking men or women, but not to stay in one or the other gender expression all the time. Thus, there are a very wide range of social and physical gender expressions that are desired and enacted by trans, non-binary, and Two-Spirit people. Some of what people need to do to effectively express their gender identities can be done nonmedically or without enlisting the aid of health care professionals. Some people turn to black market sources for hormones, or make use of the services of unlicensed self-taught surgeons. When hormonal or surgical interventions by trained professionals are desired, the WPATH *Standards of Care* are generally called upon for guidance.

While Version 7 of the *Standards of Care* allows flexibility in the provision of hormonal and surgical care for trans, non-binary, and Two-Spirit people, many practitioners are unaware of this. It is not uncommon for service providers to rely on earlier versions of the *Standards of Care,* which were designed specifically with transsexual people in mind, or to reference their own sense of binary gender and demand that individuals seeking care commit to a full binary transition in what was previously known as the triadic sequence: psychotherapy first, followed by hormonal care, culminating in full genital surgery. Non-binary people have often found that it is difficult for them to convince physicians to prescribe hormones for them at all, or in nonstandard doses, when they do not wish to transition from one binary gender to the other, and/or have no interest in genital surgeries. Similarly, people who do not describe themselves as having felt that they were trapped in the wrong body for as long as they can remember sometimes find that it is difficult to convince health care practitioners to provide them with the transition services that they desire.

Trans, Non-Binary, and Two-Spirit Inclusion in Health Care

Jamison Green, who is a former president of the World Professional Association for Transgender Health (WPATH), said the following in an interview with Andrea Jenkins of the Transgender Oral History Project:

> The intersection of law and medicine is where we are most oppressed and it's also where we're most vulnerable. It's also where we need the most support in order to find our place in society and to be healthy. Without health care you're not a human being. (Green 2016)

Green's statement about vulnerability echoes the findings of the National Center for Transgender Equality's (NCTE) 2015 *Report of the Transgender Survey* in the United States:

> One-third (33%) of respondents who had seen a health care provider in the past year reported having at least one negative experience related to being transgender, such as verbal harassment, refusal of treatment, or having to teach the health care provider about transgender people to receive appropriate care. (James et al. 2016)

One-third is a large percentage of people seeking basic medical care and finding either a hostile environment or an environment where they have to educate health care providers on trans, non-binary, or Two-Spirit issues before they can get care. And for many, surmounting these obstacles can often feel completely humiliating and dehumanizing. The quality of basic medical care for people who are trans, non-binary, or Two-Spirit varies widely depending on location and how well the people at a medical facility have been educated in matters of primary care for the trans, non-binary, and Two-Spirit people.

For trans people who identify within the gender binary—that is, who identify as a man or as a woman—there are obstacles regardless of whether or not a person has had any gender-affirming procedures. Many trans men and women do not want any sort of medical gender affirmation procedures. For many of those who do, gender affirmation procedures and hormones may not be possible based on financial concerns, particularly in places where gender affirmation is not covered by insurance plans or national health plans. There are also many health reasons why a trans person may be unable to move forward with gender affirmation procedures. Even for trans men and trans women who have been able to access gender affirmation procedures, the doctor's office can still be a hostile environment. A trans man, for example, might be persistently questioned about the scars on his chest from top surgery even though his medical issue might be bronchitis. These types of situations can be frightening and alienating for trans people.

Non-binary people (as well as people with differences of sex development) often find that medical care facilities force them to choose either "male" or "female" for their sex or gender designation on intake forms. So, before they even see a health care provider, they may have already experienced what feels like an erasure of their identity. In some cases, non-binary people may circle both choices, or make a note that explains that they are neither gender. However, depending on their health care provider, this can also create problems. Non-binary people are often treated with confusion and are still referred to as "sir" or "ma'am" by nurses and doctors. Each time this sort of interaction happens, non-binary people may feel that their health care providers see them as being difficult or as too complicated to treat, and a non-binary person can feel forced to choose an identity within the gender binary.

For Two-Spirit people, the interlocking oppressions of racism and transphobia can add another complex layer to getting much-needed health care. For example, Eileen Chester, who is a Two-Spirit First Nations person from the Nuu-chah-nulth Territory on Vancouver Island in British Columbia, Canada, recalls:

> I have been harassed and discriminated against for simply being myself, even in exclusively First Nations treatment centers. . . . I was harassed and discriminated against for being transgender or a cross-dresser, although I identify myself as a Two-Spirited person of the First Nations. (Chester, forthcoming)

Indigenous-focused treatment centers are well versed in the needs of Indigenous communities and the ways that these communities have been vulnerable to and often not served well by Western and Eurocentric health care models. Indigenous-focused clinics, though, as exemplified by Chester's statement above, may not be prepared to work with the Two-Spirit people within their communities, because many colonial religious stereotypes about gender-diverse people remain. Likewise, many mainstream LGBTQ+ focused clinics do not have the cultural competence needed to work with Two-Spirit people. In their 2010 health care needs assessment focused on Two-Spirit people in New York State, M. Somjen Frazer and Harlan Pruden noted the following:

> Because of these key differences in LGBT and two-spirit experiences, health and human services designed for the

wider LGBT population may not serve two-spirit needs: either because of outright experiences of racism or a failure to provide culturally sensitive services owing to lack of knowledge or experience with this population. Because some Native communities may hold homophobic and/or transphobic attitudes toward two-spirit and LGBT people, they also do not provide all needed services for this population. (Frazer and Pruden 2010)

In life-threatening situations, emergency room care for trans, non-binary, and Two-Spirit people may not be sensitive to issues surrounding gender identity, gender expression, and cultural practices. In some cases, trans, non-binary, and Two-Spirit people who have sought medical care for life-threatening conditions have died because medical systems did not treat them properly.

It is crucial that health care facilities work within models of cultural competency and cultural humility when working with trans, non-binary, and Two-Spirit people. In order for a medical care facility to show cultural humility, it often takes a group of people working together who embrace the notion that doctors and nurses are not the only experts when it comes to health care; rather, a more holistic approach that includes members of the trans, non-binary, or Two-Spirit community is vital.

The Need for Trans-Inclusive Clinics and Hospitals: The Case of Robert Eads (1945–1999)

In January 1999, Robert Eads, a fifty-three-year-old trans man from Toccoa, Georgia, died of ovarian cancer. When he initially transitioned from female to male, the doctors encouraged him not to have a full hysterectomy since he was already in his forties. Later, Eads would say that "the last part of me that is female is killing me" (Davis 2000). When Eads first became sick in 1996, he encountered over fifteen different doctors and practices that "refused to treat him fearing that taking him on as a patient might harm their practice" (Riverdale 2015). Eads needed to be cared for by a gynecology/oncology doctor; however, many of the clinics were unwilling to have a trans man in their waiting rooms and on their examination tables. Of course, gynecologists are trained to care for and treat people who have a vagina, cervix, and ovaries; however, the underlying assumption for these clinics was that they were there to work with cisgender women only. When Eads finally found a doctor who would administer treatment, the cancer had already spread throughout his body. January 17 is now Robert Eads Day in the United States, when his memory is honored during Cervical Health Awareness Month. Robert Eads Day is meant to help raise "awareness for preventative care and early detection of cancer and HPV in trans men" (Riverdale 2015).

In the case of Robert Eads, he sought medical care shortly after he started having symptoms of the cancer; however, many trans, non-binary, and Two-Spirit people do not seek medical attention as soon as they feel sick because they fear discrimination. From medical facilities that deny services outright, to clinics that make gendered assumptions about language on forms, on signs, and in the ways that medical care staff approach each patient individually, the health care field can be a very insulting and intimidating place for trans, non-binary, and Two-Spirit people.

Medical facilities can make small changes to ensure that all people are welcome in their clinics. One of the ways a medical practice can make their practice open and accessible for trans, non-binary, and Two-Spirit people is to reconsider their basic assumptions about who will need what sort of test, and the language used in the clinic. Small changes to words on forms and signs in the bathroom can make a much safer environment for all people. For example, because there are trans, non-binary, and Two-Spirit people who might need a pap smear but who do not identify as women, a sign in the bathroom stating that women do not need to give a urine sample should actually say that if someone is there for a pap smear, then they do not need to give a urine sample.

Educational Access for Trans, Non-Binary, and Two-Spirit Students

What makes an educational environment accessible for *all* students—not just cisgender students? In the United States, trans, non-binary, and Two-Spirit students face numerous challenges within the K–12 educational system. There are several aspects to consider when looking at educational access for trans, non-binary, and Two-Spirit students. In the K–12 system, for example, how often do teachers have activities that ask the girls to be on one side of the room and the boys on the other? What happens, then, to students who do not fit within this binary, or who go to the "wrong" side? These types of situations can become dangerous because such students will be more likely to face harassment.

What happens in school settings where there are only boys' and girls' bathrooms? In the United States, even for trans students who identify within the binary, there has been heated debate about bathroom use. Often, trans, non-binary, and Two-Spirit students in K–12 try not to go to the bathroom for the entire school day, which can lead to negative health effects. As with health care, educational access and full acceptance within an educational setting often depends on school location and the community of teachers, parents, counselors, and peers attached to a specific school or school district.

For trans, non-binary, and Two-Spirit students in the United States who enter trade schools, college, or a university, often the situation only gets marginally better because they may often face the same challenges that they did in K–12. And many students who are harassed in K–12 may miss the full curriculum and learning possibilities because it is much more difficult to concentrate on educational materials when there are larger issues of harassment and bullying that loom over the classroom.

K–12 in the United States

The National Center for Transgender Equality's (NCTE) 2015 *Report from the U.S. Transgender Survey* found that throughout K–12, 77 percent of trans, non-binary, and Two-Spirit students and students *perceived* to be trans had been harassed, bullied, or suffered physical violence at school. They also found that 52 percent of students who were either out as trans, or were perceived that way, had attempted suicide. Forty percent of these same respondents were more likely to be homeless (James et al. 2016, 132). Ninety-two percent of respondents who identified as Indigenous and Two-Spirit, or were perceived to be Two-Spirit, were verbally or physically attacked. In fact, in all cases of students of color who were perceived to be trans, the percentage of people experiencing verbal abuse and/or physical abuse was consistently over 80 percent, which underscores the ways that intersecting identities and oppressions can also feed transphobia (James et al. 2016, 132–135).

Bathrooms and/or locker rooms are among the most dangerous places for trans, non-binary, and Two-Spirit students in K–12. In many U.S. states, trans students who identify along the gender binary may not be able to go to the bathroom according to their gender identity. In June 2017, the Texas state legislature had a heated debate between Republicans, some wanting to make sure that single-user restrooms in schools were available for trans, non-binary, and Two-Spirit students and others urging "that the House pass a bill with stronger language that more clearly bars transgender students from using the bathroom of their choice" (Burnette 2017). Other states that have had high-profile cases since 2016 are North Carolina, Virginia, and Wisconsin. As of fall 2018, these states had bathroom laws that were not inclusive of trans people; Texas, in particular, has suggested that students who report trans students using the "wrong" bathroom will receive a $2,000 reward. When legislation happens like these bathroom laws that openly discriminate against trans, non-binary, and Two-Spirit students, it becomes about much more than using a toilet. Often, laws like these work on multiple levels to underscore the idea that it is okay not only to discriminate against, but also to bully and harass trans, non-binary, and Two-Spirit students. Often, teachers, parents, and peers who want to be supportive of gender-diverse people in their communities face an uphill battle against legalized hate.

Conversely, in 2000, the California state legislature passed the California Student Safety and Violence Prevention Act (Assembly Bill 537), which added protections that cover sexual orientation and gender identity. The state superintendent of public instruction wrote the following upon the bill's passage:

ONE OF OUR SCHOOLS' MOST important jobs is to ensure that all students are offered equal protection from potentially violent discrimination and harassment, which not only disrupt learning but also can leave lifetime scars. . . . The new law has added the provision that all students and staff in public education facilities have the same right to a safe learning environment, regardless of their sexual orientation or gender identity. . . . Successful implementation of the law will help ensure that schools provide a safe, supportive environment for all students. (Eastin 2001)

While the passage of AB 537 did not automatically mean that all trans, non-binary, and Two-Spirit students were suddenly free of harassment and violence, it did set a standard that protection of trans, non-binary, and Two-Spirit students is what is expected, and it did create a law so that students who were harassed and bullied based on sexual orientation or gender identity could lodge a formal complaint against a school or a school district. Laws do not, singlehandedly, change social and cultural attitudes overnight; however, the passage of fully inclusive laws begins to pave the way for full access and inclusion for trans, non-binary, and Two-Spirit students. Similar laws have been enacted throughout Canada and much of Europe.

Vocational School, College, and University Settings

Trans, non-binary, and Two-Spirit people who continue in their education after high school still struggle with harassment and discrimination, although the incidence is lower than in the K–12 setting. NCTE's 2015 survey notes that 24 percent of trans, non-binary, and Two-Spirit students were harassed verbally, physically, or sexually. And, again, just as in K–12, Indigenous students had the highest rate of harassment at 37 percent (James 2016, 136). Among vocational school or college students surveyed, who were out as trans to their classmates, 56 percent reported that they did have support from their peers.

In the United States, public vocational schools, colleges, and universities often do not have the same strict guidelines that K–12 public schools have to follow. For religious and/or private schools that are either K–12 or in higher education, the acceptance of, and access for, trans, non-binary, and Two-Spirit students is completely dependent on the governing body of the institution. Historically, some private universities like Stanford University and Columbia University, for example, have had very progressive and open policies toward trans, non-binary, and Two-Spirit students. Many public universities throughout the United States, Canada, and Western Europe have also included gender identity and gender expression in their nondiscrimination policies, have put preferred or chosen name (the name the student wants to be known by as opposed to name given at birth) policies for trans, non-binary, and Two-Spirit students into place, and have also made sure that their campuses include numerous fully accessible all-gender bathrooms for students, faculty, and staff.

Title IX and Accessibility

Title IX was originally signed into law by U.S. president Nixon in 1972 as one of a number of amendments to the Higher Education Act of 1965. Title IX "prohibits sex-based discrimination in schools and other education programs that receive federal funding. Given that the vast majority of schools receive some form of federal funding, Title IX's reach is wide" (FindLaw n.d.). In 2013, the U.S. Department of Education began looking to Title IX to see if it could be interpreted in a way that would help protect transgender students. By November 2016, under the Obama administration, "the U.S. Department of Education . . . issued guidelines clarifying that Title IX's prohibition against sex-based discrimination extends to claims of discrimination based on gender identity" (FindLaw n.d.). Under this interpretation of Title IX, trans, non-binary, and Two-Spirit students were legally protected in all educational settings that received any federal funding. This not only included classroom protections and protections on school sports teams, but also extended to school clubs and groups such as school bands. In 2017, however, the Trump administration rescinded the protections for trans, non-binary, and Two-Spirit students. As of July 2018, many states across the United States were in flux where Title IX protections are concerned. Some states such as California had already made statewide laws that ensured the protection of trans, non-binary, and Two-Spirit students. Other states, though, such as Texas, took the opportunity to make more stringent statewide laws that will ensure trans, non-binary, and Two-Spirit students do not have protections in educational settings that receive federal funding. In all cases, private and/or religious schools do not necessarily need to follow these laws if they receive absolutely no federal monies.

Title IX laws cover K–12 schools as well as institutions of higher education. Even in states that have put laws into place that help protect trans, non-binary, and Two-Spirit students, studies have found that transgender students of all sexual orientations have major mental health disparities when compared to cisgender students. Generally speaking, LGBTQ2+ students have only recently been tracked by health and wellness surveys at colleges and universities. In 2018, the Cooperative Institutional Research Program's Freshman Survey, which is the "oldest and largest" in the United States, found that out of 6,976 trans-spectrum students surveyed,

> reported feeling depressed (48.6 percent) at four times the frequency of non-transgender peers (12.1 percent). . . . When asked to appraise their emotional health, nearly half (49.6 percent) rated themselves as below average/lowest 10 percent, compared to just 15.8 percent of non-transgender students. (Greathouse 2018)

The findings of this report conclude with the recommendations that college and university settings need to have LGBTQ2+ outreach and resource centers that offer counselors who work within the LGBTQ2+ community and who are clearly sensitive to the differences in the issues faced by cisgender, gay, lesbian, and bisexual students and those faced by trans, non-binary, and Two-Spirit students who identify all across the sexual orientation spectrum. It is also crucial to have faculty and staff mentors who are out as trans, non-binary, and Two-Spirit, and to have a robust peer group program such as a social club.

Possible Solutions for Full Accessibility in School Settings

In Stockholm, Sweden, a preschool has been experimenting with ways to make the learning environment completely accessible and open for all students of all genders. Since preschool is one of the first places that binary gender stereotypes are put into place socially and culturally, the preschool Egalia has chosen to eliminate books, toys, and games that reinforce gender stereotypes and the gender binary. Egalia has garnered international and national attention in Sweden for their best practices guidelines. What had started as preschool policy is now national policy. In large part because of the work of Egalia and the success of this school as a safe place for children of all gender identities and gender expressions, Sweden has adopted a gender-neutral pronoun, *hen*, which is used on educational and state documents throughout the country.

In reality, the majority of schools do not approach accessible education in the ways that Egalia in Sweden has done. There are countries like Sweden and Canada that have put protections in place that help trans, non-binary, and Two-Spirit students. In the United States, though, while the Department of Education fluctuates on Title IX policies and the coverage of trans, non-binary, and Two-Spirit students in institutions that receive federal funding, finding a trans, non-binary and Two-Spirit welcoming educational setting can be a challenge. With "states' rights" in place in the United States—meaning that not all states are mandated by the federal government to have the same laws—trans, non-binary, and Two-Spirit students remain vulnerable. The best policy for trans, non-binary, and Two-Spirit students who are looking for a safe place to go to trade school, college, or university is to learn about the laws of the state where the institution is located to see if the state government has a policy in place protecting students based on gender identity and/or gender expression. On a more micro-level, students should also research a school's mission statement and nondiscrimination policies to get an idea about the campus climate and attitude toward trans, non-binary, and Two-Spirit students. Alternatively, students can opt to study in another country whose laws and practices are more hospitable to trans, non-binary, and Two-Spirit students.

Sports Rules and Access for Trans, Non-Binary, and Two-Spirit People

The iconic South African human rights and anti-apartheid activist Nelson Mandela said about sport: "It is more powerful than governments in breaking down barriers. It laughs in the face of all types of discrimination" (Mandela 2015). Mandela, who spent much of his adult life imprisoned for fighting against the violence of British colonial rule in his home country of South Africa, viewed sports as a powerful universal language of solidarity in the face of adversity. Sports can be found in every country and at all levels of competition: from the world stage like the Olympics, the Paralympics, or the World Cup, to various local community sports events.

Famous athletes are celebrities and have the opportunity to influence social and cultural perceptions, which is why trans athletes, for over four decades, have led the fight for trans, non-binary, and Two-Spirit acceptance in the world of athletics. Cisgender people who might otherwise not be exposed to trans, non-binary, or Two-Spirit people often become more accepting of gender-diverse people when they see them performing as successful athletes. At the same time, many nationally sanctioned amateur and professional sporting organizations throughout the world often struggle with issues about how to categorize and work with trans, non-binary, and Two-Spirit athletes.

This section focuses on athletes who are, or were, publicly out as trans, non-binary, or Two-Spirit (and, in one case, one athlete who identifies as intersex) and who have pushed athletic associations around the world—from small-town competitions to the international competitive stage—to find ways to include them in sports.

Renée Richards and the United States Tennis Association

In 1976, at the age of forty-two, Renée Richards, an American trans woman and professional tennis player who was living in La Jolla, California, was banned by the United States Tennis Association (USTA) from playing in the U.S. Open as well as in international tournaments like Wimbledon and the Italian Open. With encouragement from several people in her community, she filed a lawsuit against the USTA. A New York Supreme Court judge ruled in Richards's favor, saying that USTA was guilty of gender discrimination (Holter 2015). Richards played in the U.S. Open in 1977, where she made it to the finals in women's doubles; she retired from professional tennis at the age of forty-seven in 1981.

After undergoing gender affirmation procedures, Renée Richards, who is an ophthalmologist, did not necessarily want to be the poster person for trans activism in sport. In the 1970s, cisgender women were also being told that they could not participate in sports because of their gender identity. Richards, however, like so many women in sports in the 1970s, got tired of the injustice of being told that she could not participate in a sport *because* of her gender. At many points in her journey to play professional tennis on the women's circuit, Richards considered quitting. In the following statement, though, it is clear that Richards understood the fight was larger than one person:

I was getting a lot of calls from people who were downtrodden, who were part of sexual minorities, who were part of ethnic minorities. And they said, Renée, you've got to go and do this. You've got to take up this fight. You can't just take what they say and go back and lead a private life. (Richards 2007)

Renée Richards recognized that being out as a trans woman in the sports world went beyond her own personal fight, and that she was also fighting for the rights of many other marginalized groups of people.

The year 2017 marked the fortieth anniversary of Renée Richards's historic walk onto the tennis court for the U.S. Open. In commemoration of this anniversary, sportswriter Steve Tignor wrote:

As Renée Richards walked through the winding, Tudor-lined lanes of Forest Hills, people from the neighborhood gathered around her to wish her luck. After seeing the ophthalmologist's picture in the newspapers for months, the locals of Queens knew where she was going—the West Side Tennis Club—and the magnitude of what she was about to do. (Tignor 2017)

Richards has noted that playing in the U.S. Open, with all of the press and notoriety, was like "playing in a fish bowl."

More importantly, though, Richards received so much support from people from all walks of life who recognized the true significance of this event. When Renée Richards walked onto the court, she was playing a game of tennis at the highest level of the sport. When Renée Richards walked onto the court in 1977, she not only set a precedent for trans, non-binary, and Two-Spirit athletes, but she helped pave the way for the advocacy of numerous marginalized communities in sport. Her courage to sue the U.S. Tennis Association has served as a model for athletes for over forty years. Because of Richards's example, for instance, Lana Lawless, a trans woman and professional golf player, sued the LPGA in 2010 to allow *all* people who identify as women to play in the LPGA, not just women assigned female at birth.

Caster Semenya and the Problems with Binary Sex Designations

In 2009, at the World Championships of track and field, Caster Semenya, a black South African track star, won the eight-hundred-meter event. Many of her competitors from South Africa and other countries, most of whom were white, had complained that either Semenya was "too masculine" or that she was not a "real woman." There were enough complaints from her peers that, just before the event, she was "subjected to genetic, gynecological, psychological, and endocrine 'gender verification' testing to determine her eligibility to compete as a woman" (Swarr 2009). During these invasive tests, it was discovered that Semenya has relatively high levels of naturally occurring testosterone, which put her into a category of someone who has differences of sex development (DSD), also known as being intersex. Semenya refers to herself as being intersex. She identifies as a woman. She also identifies as a lesbian.

Almost every governing body for every sport in the world asks competitors to enter as either male or female—men or women. Athletic governing bodies have made the assumption that there are only two sexes and, therefore, only two genders, but Semenya's case brought an important question to light: how can the world of athletics be inclusive of people of all sexes as well as all genders? It is also important to note that although Caster Semenya does not have a strict binary definition of her sex, she does not identify as transgender. Her case, though, has certainly had ramifications for trans, non-binary, Two-Spirit, and other athletes who identify outside of the cisgender boxes.

Once Caster Semenya's case was publicized, two South African groups that work on intersex/DSD and transgender rights—Intersex South Africa and Gender DynamiX—began advocating on her behalf. Their efforts to bring international attention to what they could see were intersecting bases for oppression—Semenya's being intersex as well as Semenya being a black South African from a rural area—helped force the International Association of Athletics Federations (IAAF), the governing body of track and field, to reconsider her suspension from her sport. During the time that the IAAF was reassessing, they continued to put Semenya through humiliating tests, as she explains:

> I have been subjected to unwarranted and invasive scrutiny of the most intimate and private details of my being. Some of the occurrences leading up to and immediately following the Berlin World Championships have infringed on not only my rights as an athlete but also my fundamental and human rights. (Young 2018)

Even with the advocacy of Intersex South Africa and Gender DynamiX, as well as athletes from various sports around the world who have spoken out about the ways that Semenya has been, and continues to be, discriminated against, in 2018, the IAAF once again reset their rules for levels of naturally occurring testosterone in women athletes, and once again, Semenya does not pass this test. In 2018, she began another legal battle to be able to compete in the middle distance competitions that she so loves. While the IAAF continually changes the rules and continues to enforce a sex binary and a gender binary, in large part because of Semenya's struggle, in 2016, the governing body of the Olympics ruled that athletes can participate in Olympic sports according to their gender identity regardless of any sort of hormone treatments or gender affirmation procedures. This is particularly excellent news for trans athletes who do identify as either male or female. However, this new Olympic policy does not necessarily cover Caster Semenya's situation. What happens to athletes who do not identify within the gender binary? How can the sports world accommodate all people who would like to compete?

LGBT International Powerlifting Championships and MX Category

In late 2016, Chris Morgan, a British white cisgender gay man who is an eight-time world champion powerlifter and Gay Games Ambassador for the sport of powerlifting, was notified that the 2018 Gay Games in Paris, France, were not going to include powerlifting on their roster of sports. Powerlifting, which consists of three progressive areas of competition—squat, bench press, and deadlift—was one of the original sports in the first Gay Games in 1982 in San Francisco. Since then, the Gay Games have become a huge international sporting event with upwards of 10,000 athletes competing over 10 days.

The Gay Games notified Morgan that it was not cost effective to drug test all of the powerlifters, and that there needed to be a unified governing body for the sport. Other controversies that have arisen over the years have included the fact that the Gay Games has said it is meant to be a sporting event inclusive of all people; however, many trans athletes and athletes who take HIV medications have failed the drug testing and have not been allowed to compete in their sport. After several discussions with powerlifters who had competed in past Gay Games, Morgan and a core group of powerlifters decided to hold a separate annual LGBT International Powerlifting Championship (IPC) outside of the Gay Games.

In 2017, the historic Bethnal Green Weightlifting Club in London, established in 1926, held the inaugural LGBT IPC. The athletes and officials at the competition on July 29 also formed an LGBT powerlifting union, which met as a governing body the day after the competition. Athletes at this inaugural event came from Australia, Belarus, Canada, France, Germany, Iceland, Ireland, the United Kingdom, and the United States.

One of the lifters, Charlotte Wareing, is a white trans woman in her fifties who works nights as a mental health nurse. She came to the sport of powerlifting after she came out as a trans woman. Morgan had already worked with Wareing after she had encountered a few incidents of transphobia in various European lifting competitions prior to the London event. Overall, though, Wareing had found that she had many more allies in the lifting world than enemies. Wareing has steadily helped change the face of powerlifting during her years in the sport as an out and proud trans woman. She discusses how powerlifting and being out has empowered her:

> Powerlifting gave me the opportunity to compete for my country, I've won 7 world powerlifting titles and hold 41 world records. Powerlifting has also accepted me, as me. I have been involved in writing trans-inclusive rules and in refereeing at national and international level[s]. One of my proudest moments occurred last year when, at the LGBT International Powerlifting Championships, I was awarded the "LGBT IPC Spirit Award" for courage and commitment to LGBT Sports. (Morgan 2018, 36)

At the union meeting, Morgan and many other members of the newly formed union were ready to discuss the group's need to support transgender athletes who identify as either male or female in powerlifting. The group, the majority of whom were cisgender gay and lesbian lifters, agreed that they all needed to be allies and advocates. Once it was clear that there did not need to be further discussion about advocating for trans athletes who identify as either male or female, Ardel Haefele-Thomas, a white non-binary trans person in their fifties who has been a competitive powerlifter for twenty years, noted that the group of lifters who needed to be acknowledged and supported were people with differences of sex development (or intersex) and lifters who identified as non-binary, agender, genderqueer, or any other gender identity or sex status outside of a binary. Haefele-Thomas explained that they never felt like a man or a woman, but that, having been assigned female at birth, they were always put into a women's category at sporting events, which always felt very uncomfortable. The newly formed union agreed unanimously that an open gender category needed to be created for the 2018 LGBT IPC, and Haefele-Thomas was selected as the international non-binary and intersex representative to the union.

Their decision was to create an MX category that is open to people of all genders who will simply compete against one another using weight classes, as opposed to gender, as the dividing line. With that decision, the LGBT powerlifting union made international history in sports. Press releases about this decision were sent out to LGBT news agencies around the world, and the magazine *Transliving*, which does not usually cover sports, thought it was important to have a feature article on this historic decision. Haefele-Thomas said the following about their experiences in lifting:

> Powerlifting has always given me such a positive outlet. I have been powerlifting for over twenty years now, but I have never been more proud than I was in 1998 . . . in Amsterdam, Netherlands at my first Gay Games when I won the gold medal in my weight class. For those moments up on the stage, my gender did not matter. What mattered was the chalk, the weights, and the sheer joy of being able to participate. (Morgan 2018, 37)

This joy of being able to participate is what sports should be about. There are still many struggles ahead for trans, non-binary, and Two-Spirit athletes, but in the past four decades since Renée Richards sued the United States Tennis Association, there have been many positive changes around the world.

People in Institutions

Many people live in institutional settings such as long- or short-term mental or medical health care facilities, jails and prisons, or military bases. An issue that frequently arises is where to house trans individuals when living arrangements in a facility are segregated according to sex. Until very recently, the most common approach was to house people in accordance with the state of their genitals—in other words, on the basis of the presence or absence of a penis. More recently, many jurisdictions in the United States, Canada, and the European Union have enacted legal decisions that establish that people in institutions must be housed on the basis of their gender identities, irrespective of either their genitals or their official legal status. In a minority of cases, unsuccessful attempts have been made to block progress on trans rights by creating laws prescribing that people must use public facilities only in accordance with the sex on their birth certificates. In all instances, such efforts have either failed to pass a ratifying vote, or have been struck down by courts.

However, it remains a common occurrence that decision-makers in many institutional settings feel either unable or unwilling to provide transition-related services. In some cases, this may be due to religious or moral objections to gender transitions. In other instances, care may be denied due to assertions that costs would be excessive (Dais and Cooper 2017). Sometimes people refuse to provide care because they feel that specialized knowledge is required that is beyond their capabilities, and they are unwilling or unable to acquire the requisite knowledge and skills (Bauer et al. 2009).

The WPATH *Standards of Care* explicitly specify that "Health care for transsexual, transgender, and gender-nonconforming people living in an institutional environment should mirror that which would be available to them if they were living in a non-institutional setting within the same community. . . . Access to these medically necessary treatments should not be denied on the basis of institutionalization or housing arrangements" (Coleman et al. 2012, 67). Furthermore, when a trans person is in an institution due to a mental or physical health issue, once that condition is stabilized, all other treatments should proceed as they would outside of an institutional setting.

Legal Issues

Trans Rights Are Human Rights

Human rights refers to the idea that there are certain freedoms and ways of being that every person should always have just because they are human beings. In 1948, most of the nations of the world agreed to the United Nations' Universal Declaration of Human Rights, which, among other things, included the following statements:

- Recognition of the inherent dignity and of the equal and inalienable rights of all members of the human family is the foundation of freedom, justice and peace in the world;
- All human beings are born free and equal in dignity and rights;
- Everyone has the right to life, liberty and security of person;
- No one shall be subjected to torture or to cruel, inhuman or degrading treatment or punishment;
- Everyone has the right to recognition everywhere as a person before the law;
- All are equal before the law and are entitled without any discrimination to equal protection of the law;
- No one shall be subjected to arbitrary interference with his [sic] privacy, family, home or correspondence, nor to attacks upon his [sic] honour and reputation;

- Men and women [*sic*] of full age, without any limitation due to race, nationality or religion, have the right to marry and to found a family;
- Everyone has the right of equal access to public service;
- Everyone has the right to a standard of living adequate for . . . health and well-being. (United Nations 1948)

Building on this, in 2013, the Office of the United Nations High Commissioner for Human Rights (OHCHR) specifically took up a campaign for trans human rights as part of a UN public information campaign called "Free & Equal," which focuses on equal rights and fair treatment of LGBTQ2+ people. In 2017, this campaign connected with 2.4 billion social media feeds worldwide (United Nations n.d.). That same year, the Yogyakarta Principles +10 "on the application of international human rights law to sexual orientation, gender identity, gender expression, and sex characteristics" were adopted by a group of international experts. These widely acclaimed principles, among others, proclaim that:

- Everyone has the right to legal recognition without reference to, or requiring assignment or disclosure of, sex, gender, sexual orientation, gender identity, gender expression or sex characteristics.
- Everyone has the right to obtain identity documents, including birth certificates, regardless of sexual orientation, gender identity, gender expression or sex characteristics.
- Everyone has the right to change gendered information in such documents while gendered information is included in them.
- No one shall be subjected to invasive or irreversible medical procedures that modify sex characteristics without their free, prior and informed consent, unless necessary to avoid serious, urgent and irreparable harm to the concerned person . . . forced, coercive and otherwise involuntary modification of a

person's sex characteristics may amount to torture, or other cruel, inhuman or degrading treatment

- [Governments shall] ensure that requirements for individuals to provide information on their sex or gender are relevant, reasonable and necessary as required by the law for a legitimate purpose in the circumstances where it is sought, and that such requirements respect all persons' right to self-determination of gender;

- [Governments shall] ensure that changes of the name or gender marker, as long as the latter exists, is not disclosed without the prior, free, and informed consent of the person concerned, unless ordered by a court. (Grinspan et al. 2017)

The rights to choose one's own gender markers, to change them on official government identification papers, the right to privacy, and the right to live free of discrimination are all fundamental human rights. However, in many places around the world, access to these rights are either unavailable or only available under conditions that violate some core principles of basic human rights. Many legal jurisdictions force persons wishing to change their gender markers to satisfy some or all of the following requirements: be legally adult, be diagnosed as having a pathological mental disorder, not be married, not have dependent children, or have sterilization surgeries that render them permanently unable to have children. Each of these requirements may violate the human rights of trans, non-binary, and Two-Spirit people.

The United Nations Children's Fund's (UNICEF) Convention on the Rights of the Child states that children have a right to have their identities respected (UNICEF 1989). The requirement that a person must be an adult in order to change their gender does not allow children and youth to have their identities respected. The requirement that a person who changes their gender must have themselves diagnosed as having a mental illness, even though they may feel entirely healthy, can be a violation of the human right not to be forced to undergo "cruel, inhuman or degrading treatment." Requiring sterilization as a prerequisite for gender change amounts to forced sterilization and, as such, involuntarily eliminates the human right to "marry and to found a family." It has been found by the European Court of Human Rights to be a violation of human rights and, in 2013, the UN Special Rapporteur on Torture called upon all countries to outlaw forced sterilization as a prerequisite for trans people to access legal gender change (Chiam, Duffy, and Gil 2017). Likewise, the requirement to not be married and to not have children is also a violation of the human right to "marry and to found a family" (IGLA Europe 2017).

The World Professional Association for Transgender Health issued a statement in November 2017 that is consistent with human rights principles:

> *The World Professional Association for Transgender Health (WPATH) recognizes that, for optimal physical and mental health, persons must be able to freely express their gender identity, whether or not that identity conforms to the expectations of others. WPATH further recognizes the right of all people to identity documents consistent with their gender identity, including those documents which confer legal gender status. Such documents are essential to the ability of all people to enjoy rights and opportunities equal to those available to others; to access accommodation, education, employment, and health care; to travel; to navigate everyday transactions; and to enjoy safety. Transgender people, regardless of how they identify or appear, should enjoy the gender recognition all persons expect and deserve.*
>
> *Medical and other barriers to gender recognition for transgender individuals may harm physical and mental health. WPATH opposes all medical requirements that act as barriers to those wishing to change legal sex or gender markers on documents. These include requirements for diagnosis, counseling or therapy, puberty blockers, hormones, any form of*

surgery (including that which involves sterilization), or any other requirements for any form of clinical treatment or letters from doctors. WPATH argues that marital and parental status should not be barriers to recognition of gender change, and opposes requirements for persons to undergo periods living in their affirmed gender, or for enforced waiting or "cooling off" periods after applying for a change in documents. Further, court and judicial hearings can produce psychological, as well as financial and logistical barriers to legal gender change, and may also violate personal privacy rights or needs.

WPATH advocates that appropriate gender recognition should be available to transgender youth, including those who are under the age of majority. . . . WPATH urges governments to eliminate barriers to gender recognition, and to institute transparent, affordable and otherwise accessible administrative procedures affirming self-determination, when gender markers on identity documents are considered necessary. These procedures should be based in law and protect privacy. (WPATH 2017; used by permission)

Legal Name and Gender Identity Changes

As of 2017, in most states in the United States, it is possible to change one's gender identity, although it is often administratively very difficult to do so, and it usually involves several of the above requirements. In four U.S. states, it remains impossible for anyone to change their legal gender (Transgender Law Center n.d.). In most U.S. states a legal name change is less difficult to accomplish, but it most often requires a public disclosure of that name change (Chiam, Duffy, and Gil 2017), in violation of the Yogyakarta Principles + 10. In Canada, all provinces and the federal government permit name and gender identification changes without any requirement of gender-affirming surgeries. Eight countries in Europe do not allow a legal gender or name change at all, while twenty-eight European countries still require forced sterilization as a prerequisite for a legal gender change, and only six countries do not require a mental health diagnosis (IGLA

Europe 2017). Most countries in South America permit legal gender changes, generally without a requirement for medical interventions. Most Asian nations permit trans people to legally change their names, while a change of legal gender is less commonly allowed and generally requires significant medical interventions. A similar situation exists in Australia and New Zealand. Information about the situation in Africa is difficult to obtain (Chiam, Duffy, and Gil 2017). Trans activists and their allies continue to fight for basic human rights to self-determination for trans, non-binary, and Two-Spirit people.

In a number of parts of the world, sex or gender markers other than the typical male and female designations are starting to become available. Although it has been argued that gender identity should be treated as a private matter and not displayed on publicly facing identification documents at all, so long as such identification documents are required by governments and international agencies, options beyond M (male) and F (female) are seen by many trans, non-binary, and Two-Spirit people and their allies as progressive. However, some people are concerned that any gender marker other than M or F on a public document makes the bearer of that document vulnerable to increased gender-based discrimination (Gender-Free ID Coalition n.d.; Devor 2017; Young, 2017).

As of early 2018, some form of non-binary gender is permitted on government-issued identification in Malta, Denmark, Scotland, Germany, Canada, Nepal, Australia, New Zealand, Pakistan, and India, and in the United States alternative genders can be chosen on identification documents in California, New York, Oregon, Washington State, and Washington, DC (Transgender Europe 2017; Fine Gael LGBT 2018).

Marriage and Family Rights

In many places around the world, marriage and parental rights for trans, non-binary, and Two-Spirit people are tied to social attitudes toward homosexuality and the legal status of same-sex marriages. Where same-sex marriages are not legally permitted, already heterosexually married people who wish to legally change their gender will create a same-sex marriage by doing so. Therefore, such jurisdictions require divorce prior to legal recognition of gender changes. Where legal gender changes are not permitted, people who socially transition to another gender may create the appearance of being in a same-sex marriage while being legally heterosexually married. For example, thirty European countries require divorce as a prerequisite for granting a legal gender change (IGLA Europe 2017).

Similar issues are invoked concerning parental rights where homosexuality or being transgender is either illegal or socially condemned. In such places, laws, policies, and procedures are structured so as to deny parental custody and adoption rights to those people who are perceived to be in homosexual relationships either by virtue of their originally assigned sexes or, where gender change is legally recognized, by virtue of their affirmed genders.

In the United States and Canada, child custody cases are usually decided by judging what circumstances are considered to be "in the best interests of the child." In some cases, judges have accepted arguments that a parent's transition can cause children to suffer from shame and harassment and that therefore custody should be awarded to cisgender parents. In other cases, arguments have been successfully made that supporting a transgender child in a social transition constitutes child abuse and that such children should be removed from the care of supportive parents. However, there are also many cases where parents come to amicable custody arrangements, or where courts reject transphobic arguments and fairly award custody in families with transgender members (American Civil Liberties Union n.d.; LGBTQ Parenting Network n.d.).

Law Enforcement and Corrections

Trans, non-binary, and Two-Spirit people, like other people, have many reasons to come into contact with law enforcement officers. In many instances, trans, non-binary, and Two-Spirit people are victims of crimes and need law enforcement personnel to protect them and to pursue perpetrators. Trans, non-binary, and Two-Spirit people also suffer disproportionately from harassment and assault. For example, in the United States, 46 percent of trans, non-binary, and Two-Spirit people reported that they had been verbally harassed and 9 percent said that they had been physically attacked because of being transgender within the last year. Ten percent said that they had been sexually assaulted in the past year and nearly half (47 percent) reported that they had been sexually assaulted at some point in their lifetime (James et al. 2016, 3). Yet, due to apprehensions about, or past experiences with, police mistreatment, 57 percent of trans, non-binary, and Two-Spirit people feel uncomfortable seeking police assistance (James et al. 2016, 12).

In their interactions with police, 58 percent of trans people report being verbally harassed or called by wrong pronouns, and 14 percent report being physically or sexually assaulted by police (Redfern 2013). Furthermore, many trans, non-binary, and Two-Spirit people, especially people of color, poor, and homeless people, have experienced mistreatment by police who assumed them to be engaged in illegal sex work. Fully 86 percent of trans, non-binary, and Two-Spirit people who either were doing sex work, or who police *thought* were doing sex work, report being attacked, sexually assaulted, or mistreated by police (James et al. 2016, 12). The term "walking while trans" has been coined to describe being targeted as criminal by police in this way.

When trans, non-binary, and Two-Spirit people are accused or convicted of violating the law, they may be incarcerated in jails, prisons, or other kinds of detention centers. When this occurs, there are a number of contentious questions that need to be resolved and are handled in a variety of ways in different locations. At the core of these issues is the fact that penal institutions are organized on the basis of binary sexes and that, in most cases, prisoners are categorized on the basis of their genitals. Considering that in the United States only 2 percent of trans, non-binary, and Two-Spirit people originally assigned female, and only 10 percent of those originally assigned male, have had genital reconstruction surgery (James et al. 2016, 101–102), the vast majority of trans, non-binary, and Two-Spirit people are liable to be incarcerated in institutions incongruent with their gender identities.

In the United States, while policies vary state by state, for the most part this means that they will likely be misgendered during the entirety of their incarceration, often by name and almost always by pronoun. They will be clothed in prison uniforms of a wrong gender, and only permitted to access personal care items of a wrong gender. They will be observed in public and private moments, handled and body searched, by guards of a wrong gender. They are often subjected to harassment, ridicule, and sexual assault both by prison personnel and other inmates. In most instances, they will be denied access to transgender health care. And because of the higher rates of incarceration of trans women of color, these individuals also suffer the most detrimental effects of these policies (Reisner, Bailey, and Sevelius 2014; Oparah 2010).

Canadian policies concerning trans, non-binary, and Two-Spirit prisoners now accept prisoners' self-definitions of their genders "regardless of their anatomy (sex) or gender on their identification documents, unless there are overriding health or safety concerns which cannot be resolved" (Canadian Human Rights Commission 2018). However, practices take considerable time to become well aligned with policies, and Canadian trans, non-binary, and Two-Spirit prisoners remain vulnerable to many of the same problems as in the United States (Rose 2018).

The Middle East, Iran, and Israel

Most of the countries that comprise the Middle East are dominated by Sunni Islamic perspectives and rely heavily on legalistic religious interpretations of the Qur'an as the basis for legislation, public policies, and social mores. With a couple of notable exceptions, they are almost entirely inhospitable to trans, non-binary, and gender-diverse people. The Qur'an recognizes five gender types: males, females, castrated men (eunuchs), effeminate men (*mukhannathun*), and intersex people. In addition, the statement in the Qur'an that God "created everything in pairs" has been consistently interpreted to mean that intersexed or otherwise ambiguously gendered people (known as *khuntha*) must have a "hidden" sex, which can be discovered. Traditional teachings also hold that the founder of Islam cursed effeminate men and mannish women. These teachings have been used as the basis for an almost total rejection of any kind of non-binary or nonheteronormative gender expression. The level of intolerance of gender variance is such that cross-dressing, name changes, and gender changes are largely illegal. Thus, every person may be, and must be, assigned to one of the two binary sexes, and must behave in accordance with the expectations of the corresponding gender. Fines, incarcerations, profound abuse, even murder of gender-nonconforming people are, to a large degree, socially acceptable.

Where some progress has been made in Islamic countries, it has largely been on the basis of interpreting transgender people as a kind of psychological *khuntha* whose "true sex" can only be uncovered by gender transition surgeries. However, these interpretations hinge on such surgeries being necessary and not a matter of complying with a nonintersex person's "wish" to be another sex. Furthermore, such interpretations leave no room for trans, non-binary, or other gender-diverse people who may wish to live in another gender without a complete physical transition. Such gender expressions would be understood as cross-dressing and remain completely unacceptable in most of the Middle East (Whitaker 2016).

One Islamic country of the Middle East that has legalized gender-affirming medical procedures is Iran, a predominantly Shi'a Muslim country. In 1986, after many years of lobbying and many injustices and abuses along the way, a trans woman named Maryam Khatoon Molkara led a campaign that convinced the then religious leader of Iran, Ayatollah Khomeini, to issue a religious verdict (a *fatwa*) that declared gender affirmation medical procedures religiously acceptable. It has been reported that almost as many gender-affirming surgeries are done in Iran as in Thailand, and that Iran's two clinics performing the surgeries are heavily in demand from both Iranian citizens and from people who travel from other Middle Eastern and Eastern European countries. Iranian government statistics report that almost 1,400 people made such requests in the eight-year period between 2006 and 2014. Genital surgeries are required for name and gender changes on identification documents, and non-binary statuses are forbidden.

However, just because transition is possible in Iran, it does not mean that it is socially accepted. Iranian trans people still have no human rights protections at all. They are frequently disowned by their families, unable to find work or fired when the fact that they are trans becomes known, refused or evicted from housing, and subjected to ridicule, abuse, and violence. Furthermore, Iran remains a deeply gender divided society. There are strictly enforced laws against cross-dressing and very narrow definitions of what constitutes acceptable dress codes and behaviors for men and women.

While it is legal to be transsexual in Iran, it is illegal to be homosexual. Male homosexuality is punishable by death. Female homosexuals are subject to lashings. Thus, any trans, non-binary, or gender-diverse person who has not been officially designated as a transsexual is liable to be deemed to be homosexual, and it could cost them their life, or they could be severely whipped. This danger has caused an unknown number of people to register themselves as transsexual for reasons of self-preservation, some of whom have proceeded with physical transformations that otherwise they would not have chosen to do (Bagri 2017).

The situation for trans, non-binary, and gender-diverse people in Israel is quite different from the other countries in the Middle East and bears many similarities to what can be found in Europe and North America. While Israel is a predominantly

Jewish country (approximately 75 percent Jewish, 21 percent non-Jewish Arabs), the Jews of Israel hail from a wide range of cultures: 44 percent from Israel, 26 percent from Europe, 14 percent from Africa, 11 percent from Asia, and 5 percent from the Americas or Oceania. The religiosity of the populace is much lower than in the rest of the Middle East (43 percent call themselves "secular") (Central Bureau of Statistics Israel 2017). Only the most conservative religious elements completely oppose gender changes, and those who are most religiously conservative can only influence the public legal system through the mechanisms of a European-style democracy.

In Israel, name and gender changes are permitted and surgery is not required. Gender-affirming treatments are funded by the public health system under a relatively conservative interpretation of the World Professional Association for Transgender Health's *Standards of Care*. Transgender rights are enshrined in antidiscrimination legislation and trans advocacy organizations thrive in the major cities, where some of them receive government funding for their work (Transgender Europe 2018; Equaldex n.d.). The Tel Aviv Pride celebrations are the largest in Asia, and in 2015 the official theme was Trans Pride, the first time that a Pride celebration anywhere had been so designated (Beyer 2017). Trans, non-binary, and other gender-diverse people are welcome to serve in the Israeli military in accordance with their gender identities, regardless of surgical status. Full medical transition services are available to military personnel as needed. Since 2016, a corporately funded scholarship program is in place for trans, non-binary, and other gender-diverse students. Social attitudes and transphobic discrimination show a range of expression similar to that in most Western countries (WDG 2017).

References

American Civil Liberties Union. N.d. "Know Your Rights: Transgender People and the Law." https://www.aclu.org /know-your-rights/transgender-people-and-law.

American Psychiatric Association. 2013. "Gender Dysphoria." https://doi.org/10.1176/appi.books.9780890425596 .dsm14.

Bagri, Neha Thirani. 2017. "'Everyone Treated Me Like a Saint'—In Iran, There's Only One Way to Survive as a Transgender Person." *Quartz,* April 19, 2017. https:// qz.com/889548/everyone-treated-me-like-a-saint-in-iran -theres-only-one-way-to-survive-as-a-transgender-person/.

Bao, Ai-Min, and Dick F. Swaab. 2011. "Sexual Differentiation of the Human Brain: Relation to Gender Identity, Sexual Orientation and Neuropsychiatric Disorders." *Frontiers in Neuroendocrinology* 32: 214–226.

Bauer, G., R. Hammond, R. Travers, M. Kaay, K. Hohenadel, and M. Boyce. 2009. "'I Don't Think This Is Theoretical; This Is Our Lives': How Erasure Impacts Health Care for Transgender People." *JANAC—Journal of the Association of Nurses in AIDS Care* 20: 348–361.

Benjamin, Harry. 1966. *The Transsexual Phenomenon.* New York, NY: Julian Press.

Beyer, Dana. 2017. "Israeli Trans Rights and 'Pinkwashing'—A Disconnect Grounded in Bad Faith." *Huffpost,* December 6, 2017. https://www.huffingtonpost .com/dana-beyer/israeli-trans-rights-and_b_7640382.html.

Burke, Sarah M., M. Willeke, Peggy T. Menks, Daniel T. Cohen-Kettenis, and Julie Bakker Klink. 2014. "Click-Evoked Otoacoustic Emissions in Children and Adolescents with Gender Identity Disorder." *Archives of Sexual Behavior* 43: 1515–1523.

Burnette II, Daarel. 2017. "Cyberbullying, Transgender-Student Rights Among K–12 Issues Tackled in Texas." *Education Week* 36, no. 34 (June 6, 2017): 17. https:// www.edweek.org/ew/articles/2017/06/07/a-roundup-of -texas-legislatures-k-12-action.html.

Canadian Human Rights Commission. 2018. "Joint News Release—Changes to the Way Transgender Offenders Are Accommodated in Canada's Federal Prison System." January 31, 2018. https://www.chrc-ccdp.gc.ca/eng /content/joint-news-release-changes-way-transgender -offenders-are-accommodated-canadas-federal-prison.

Carpenter, Edward. 1952. *The Intermediate Sex: A Study of Some Transitional Types of Men and Women*. London: George Allen & Unwin.

Cavanaugh, Timothy, Ruben Hopwood, and Cei Lambert. 2016. "Informed Consent in the Medical Care of Transgender and Gender-Nonconforming Patients." *AMA Journal of Ethics* 18(11): 1147–1155.

Central Bureau of Statistics Israel. 2017. *Israel in Figures.* http://www.cbs.gov.il/reader/publications/israel_fig _e.htm.

Chauncy, George, Jr. 1983. "From Sexual Inversion to Homosexuality: Medicine and the Changing Conceptualization of Female Deviance." *Salmagundi* no. 58/59 (Fall 1982–Winter 1983): 114–146.

Chester, Eileen. Forthcoming, 2019. "Healing," in Ardel Haefele-Thomas, *Introduction to Transgender Studies.* New York: Harrington Park Press/Columbia University Press.

Chiam, Zhan, Sandra Duffy, and Matilda González Gil. 2017. *Trans Legal Mapping Report 2017: Recognition before the Law.* Geneva: International Lesbian, Gay, Bisexual, Trans and Intersex Association.

Coleman, Eli, Walter Bockting, Marsha Botzer, Peggy Cohen-Kettenis, Griet DeCuypere, Jamie Feldman, Lin Fraser, Jamison Green, Gail Knudson, Walter J. Meyer, Stan Monstrey, Richard K. Adler, George R. Brown, Aaron H. Devor, Randall Ehrbar, Randi Ettner, Evan Eyler, Rob Garofalo, Dan H. Karasic, Arlene Istar Lev, Gal Mayer,

Heino Meyer-Bahlburg, Blaine Paxton Hall, Friedmann Pfäfflin, Katherine Rachlin, Bean Robinson, Loren S. Schechter, Vin Tangpricha, Mick van Trotsenburg, Anne Vitale, Sam Winter, Stephen Whittle, Kevan R. Wylie and Ken Zucker. 2012. *Standards of Care for the Health of Transsexual, Transgender, and Gender-Nonconforming People, Version 7*. WPATH.

Dais, Julie Hirschfeld, and Helene Cooper. 2017. "Trump Surprises Military with a Transgender Ban." *New York Times*, July 27, 2017. Section A, p. 1. https://www.nytimes .com/2017/07/26/us/politics/trump-transgender-military .html.

Davis, Kate. 2000. *Southern Comfort* (film). Docudrama.

Devor, Aaron. 2017. "Opinion: The Negative Impacts of Forced Gender Identification." *Vancouver Sun* (December 10, 2017, updated December 13, 2017), http:// vancouversun.com/opinion/op-ed/opinion-the-negative -impacts-of-forced-gender-identification.

Diamond, Milton. 2013. "Transsexuality Among Twins: Identity Concordance, Transition, Rearing, and Orientation." *International Journal of Transgenderism* 14: 1, 24–38.

Drescher, Jack. 2013. "Controversies in Gender Diagnoses." *LGBT Health* 1, no. 1.

Eastin, Delaine. 2001. "A Message from the State Superintendent of Public Instruction." *Assembly Bill 537 Advisory Task Force Report: California Student Safety and Violence Prevention Act of 2000*. Sacramento: CDE Press, v.

Equaldex. N.d. LGBT Rights in Israel. https://www.equaldex .com/region/Israel.

FindLaw. N.d. "Title IX Protections for Transgender Students." https://education.findlaw.com/discrimination -harassment-at-school/title-ix-protections-for-transgender -students.html.

Fine Gael LGBT. 2018. "Submission to the Review of the Gender Recognition Act 2016." (February 5, 2018). https://www.welfare.ie/en/downloads/Sub056-GRA2015 .pdf.

Frazer, M. Somjen, and Harlan Pruden. 2010. "Reclaiming Our Voices: Two Spirit Health & Human Service Needs in New York State." Albany, NY: NYS DOH AIDS Institute. https://www.health.ny.gov/diseases/aids/providers/reports /native_people/docs/reclaiming_our_voices.pdf.

Gender-Free ID Coalition. http://gender-freeidcoalition.ca/.

Gomez-Gil, Esther, Isabel Esteva, M. Cruz Almaraz, Eduarado Pasaro, Santiago Segovia, and Antonio Guillamon. 2010. "Familiality of Gender Identity Disorder in Non-Twin Siblings." *Archives of Sexual Behavior* 39: 546–552.

Greathouse, Maren. 2018. "It Doesn't Always Get Better for Queer-Spectrum and Trans-Spectrum College Students." *Higher Education Today*, June 6, 2018. https://www .higheredtoday.org/2018/06/06/doesnt-always-get-better -queer-spectrum-trans-spectrum-college-students/.

Green, Jamison. 2016. Interview with Andrea Jenkins for the Transgender Oral History Project as part of the Jean-Nickolaus Tretter Collection in Gay, Lesbian, Bisexual and Transgender Studies at the University of Minnesota, March 20, 2016. https://www.lib.umn.edu/tretter /transgender-oral-history-project

Green, Richard. 2000. "Birth Order and Ratio of Brothers to Sisters in Transsexuals." *Psychological Medicine* 30, no. 4: 789–795.

Grinspan, Mauro Cabral, Morgan Carpenter, Julia Ehrt, Sheherezade Kara, Arvind Narrain, Pooja Patel, Chris Sidoti, and Monica Tabengwa. 2017. "The Yogyakarta Principles Plus 10." http://yogyakartaprinciples.org /principles-en/yp10/.

Guillamon, Antonio, Carme Junque, and Esther Gomez-Gil. 2016. "A Review of the Status of Brain Structure Research in Transsexualism." *Archives of Sexual Behavior* 45: 1615–1648.

Hirschfeld, Magnus. 1991. *Transvestites: The Erotic Drive to Cross-dress.* Trans Michael A. Lombardi-Nash. Buffalo, NY: Prometheus Books.

Hisasue, Shin-ichi, Shoko Sasaki, Taiji Tsukamoto, and Shigeo Horie. 2012. "The Relationship between Second-to-Fourth Digit Ratio and Female Gender Identity." *Journal of Sexual Medicine* 9: 2903–2910.

Holter, Lauren. 2015. "Renee Richards Is a Transgender Sports Icon Who Paved the Way for Caitlyn Jenner with a Game-Changing Lawsuit Back in 1975." *Bustle,* June 4, 2015. https://www.bustle.com/articles/88119-renee-richards-is-a-transgender-sports-icon-who-paved-the-way-for-caitlyn-jenner-with-a

IGLA Europe. 2017. "The Trans Rights Europe Map & Index." https://tgeu.org/trans-rights-map-2017/.

James, Sandy E., Jody L. Herman, Susan Rankin, Mara Keisling, Lisa Mottet, and Ma'ayan Anafi. 2016. *The Report of the 2015 U.S. Transgender Survey.* Washington, DC: National Center for Transgender Equality.

Kraemer, Bernd, Thomas Noll, Aba Delsignore, Gabriella Milos, Ulrich Schnyder, and Urs Hepp. 2009. "Finger Length Ratio (2D:4D) in Adults with Gender Identity Disorder." *Archives of Sexual Behavior* 38: 359–363.

Krafft-Ebing, Richard von. 1965. *Psychopathia Sexualis: With Especial Reference to the Antipathetic Sexual Instinct.* Trans. Franklin S. Klaf. New York: Stein & Day.

Kranz, Georg S., Rene Seiger, Ulrike Kaufmann, Allan Hummer, Andreas Hahn, Sebastian Ganger, Martin Tik, Christian Windischberger, Siegfried Kasper, and Rupert Lanzenberger. 2017. "Effects of Sex Hormone Treatment on White Matter Microstructure in Individuals with Gender Dysphoria." *Neuroimage* 150: 60–67.

Kreukels, Baudewijntje P. C., and Antonio Guillamon. 2016. "Neuroimaging Studies in People with Gender Incongruence." *International Review of Psychiatry* 28: 1, 120–128.

Lambda Legal. N.d. "Changing Birth Certificate Sex Designations: State-by-State Guidelines." https://www .lambdalegal.org/know-your-rights/article /trans-changing-birth-certificate-sex-designations.

Lawrence, Anne A. 2013. *Men Trapped in Men's Bodies: Narratives of Autogynephilic Transsexualism.* New York, NY: Springer.

LGBTQ Parenting Network. N.d. "Trans Parenting." http://lgbtqpn.ca/trans-parenting/.

Mandela, Nelson. 2015. Speaking at the Laureus World Sports Awards, 2000, quoted in Jeff Sheng, *Fearless: Portraits of LGBT Student Athletes.* Los Angeles: Somebody Books, 2015, n.p.

Marchiano, Lisa. 2017. "Outbreak: On Transgender Teens and Psychic Epidemics." *Psychological Perspectives* 60: 3, 345–366.

Mohdin, Aamna. 2017. "In Many European Countries, Transgender People Who Update Their Driver's License Have to Be Sterilized First." Quartz online. April 18, 2017. https://qz.com/957752/in-a-slew-of-european-countries -transgender-people-who-update-their-drivers-license-have -to-be-sterilized-first/.

Morgan, Chris. 2018. "Grace, Grit, and Glory." *Transliving* 59, March 2018.

Olson, Kristina R., Lilly Durwood, Madeline DeMeules, and Katie A. McLaughlin. 2016. "Mental Health of Transgender Children Who Are Supported in Their Identities." *Pediatrics* 137, no. 3: e20153223.

Oparah, Julia. 2010. "Feminism and the (Trans)Gender Entrapment of Gender Nonconforming Prisoners." *UCLA Women's Law Journal* 18: 239–271.

Redfern, J. 2013. "Best Practices to Improve Police Relations with Transgender Individuals." *Journal of Law Enforcement* 3, no. 4. https://www.researchgate.net /publication/260122015_Best_Practices_to_Improve _Police_Relations_with_Transgender_Individuals.

Reisner, Sari, Zinzi Bailey, and Jae Sevelius. 2014. "Racial/ Ethnic Disparities in History of Incarceration: Experiences of Victimization, and Associated Health Indicators among Transgender Women in the U.S." *Women & Health* 54: 750–767.

Richards, Renée. 2007. "The Second Half of My Life," interview by Neal Conan on *Talk of the Nation*. National Public Radio, February 8, 2007. www.npr.org/templates /story/story.php?storyId=7277665.

Riverdale, Joshua. 2015. "Robert Eads Day—January 17." *Trans Guys*, January 12, 2015. https://transguys.com /features/robert-eads-day.

Rose, Rebecca. 2018. "Selection of Prison Based on Gender Identity a Victory, but Alternatives to Incarceration Still Needed, Says Advocate." *The Nova Scotia Advocate*, February 7, 2018. https://nsadvocate.org/2018/02/07 /selection-of-prison-based-on-gender-identity-a-victory -but-alternatives-to-incarceration-still-needed-says -advocate/.

Semenyna, Scott W., Doug P. VanderLaan, and Paul L. Vasey. 2017. "Birth Order and Recalled Childhood Gender Nonconformity in Samoan Men and Fa'afafine." *Developmental Psychobiology* 59, no. 3: 338–347.

Swarr, Amanda Lock, with Sally Gross and Liesl Theron. 2009. "South African Intersex Activism: Caster Semenya's Impact and Import." *Feminist Studies* 35, no. 3: 658.

Tignor, Steve. 2017. "40 Years Later, Renée Richards' Breakthrough Is as Important as Ever," *Tennis*, September 20, 2017. http://www.tennis.com/pro-game/2017/07/40 -years-later-renee-richards-breakthrough-important -ever/68064/.

Transgender Europe. 2017. "Third Gender Marker Options in Europe and Beyond." https://tgeu.org /third-gender-marker-options-in-europe-and-beyond/.

Transgender Europe. 2018. "Legal Gender Recognition: Change of Name." https://transrespect.org/en/map /legal-gender-recognition-change-of-name/.

Transgender Law Center. N.d. "State-by-State Overview: Rules for Changing Gender Markers on Birth Certificates." https://transgenderlawcenter.org/resources/id/state -by-state-overview-changing-gender-markers-on-birth -certificates.

Ulrichs, K. H. 1994. *The Riddle of "Man-Manly" Love: The Pioneering Work on Male Homosexuality.* M. Lombardi-Nash, Trans. Buffalo, NY: Prometheus Books. (Original work published 1864–1880).

UNICEF. 1989. The Convention. https://www.unicef-irc.org /portfolios/crc.html.

United Nations. 1948. "Universal Declaration of Human Rights." http://www.un.org/en/universal-declaration -human-rights/.

United Nations. N.d. "About UN Free & Equal." https:// www.unfe.org/about/.

Vale, Kayla, Thomas W. Johnson, Maren S. Jansen, B. Keith Lawson, Tucker Lieberman, K. H. Willette, and Richard J. Wassersug. 2010. "The Development of Standards of Care for Individuals with a Male-to-Eunuch Gender Identity Disorder." *International Journal of Transgenderism* 12, no. 1: 40–51.

Van Der Miesen, Anna I. R., Hannah Hurley, and Annelou L. C. De Vries. 2016. "Gender Dysphoria and Autism Spectrum Disorder: A Narrative Review." *International Review of Psychiatry* 28 :1, 70–80.

Wassersug, Richard J., Emma McKenna, and Tucker Lieberman. 2012. "Eunuch as a Gender Identity after Castration." *Journal of Gender Studies* 21, no. 3: 253–270.

WDG. 2017. "Being Transgender in Israel: Current State." *A Wider Bridge.* December 1, 2017. http://awiderbridge .org/being-transgender-in-israel-current-state/.

Whitaker, Brian. 2016. "Transgender Issues in the Middle East." February 8, 2016. http://al-bab.com/blog/2016/02 /transgender-issues-middle-east-1.

Williams, Cristan. 2017. "Tracking Transgender: The Historical Truth." http://www.cristanwilliams.com/b /tracking-transgender-the-historical-truth/#27.

Winter, Sam, Griet De Cuypere, Jamison Green, Robert Kane, and Gail Knudson. 2016. "The Proposed ICD-11 Gender Incongruence of Childhood Diagnosis: A World Professional Association for Transgender Health Membership Survey." *Arch Sex Behav* 45: 1605–1614.

World Health Organization. 2018. "ICD-11 for Mortality and Morbidity Statistics (draft)." https://icd.who.int /dev11/l-m/en#/http://id.who.int/icd/entity/411470068.

WPATH. 2010. "WPATH Identity Recognition Statement." June 16, 2010. https://www.wpath.org/policies.

WPATH. 2017. Identity Recognition Statement. November 15, 2017. https://www.wpath.org/policies.

Young, Dennis. 2018. "The Only Point of Track's Dumb New Testosterone Rules Is to Make It Illegal to Be Caster Semenya." *Deadspin*, April 26, 2018. https://deadspin.com /the-only-point-of-track-s-dumb-new-testosterone-rules-i-1825546141.

Young, Leslie. 2017. "Canadians Travelling with Gender-Neutral Passports Could Face Problems Abroad." *Global News,* August 25, 2017. https://globalnews.ca /news/3696784/gender-neutral-passport-canada -travel-problems/.

Introduction

This chapter includes writing from people around the world who have various experiences in transgender studies. These profiles include a personal essay by Jo Clifford, an award-winning playwright from Scotland whose plays have been staged all over the world; Harlan Pruden's writing about Two-Spirit conversations and work; and a personal essay by Tru Wilson, a trans teen who took her Canadian Catholic middle school to court for full access for trans, non-binary, and Two-Spirit students, among others.

Sixty Years of Transgender Culture and Care in the Netherlands
Alex Bakker

For a small country, the Netherlands have a remarkable transgender history and a lively transgender present. Holland has been a guiding nation in transgender care. A high number of clients over the past sixty years has allowed for a substantial quantity and quality of scientific research and medical care.

Trans bodybuilder Cody Harman is an out and proud trans man. (Adam Gray / Barcroft Images / Barcroft Media via Getty Images)

The Fifties: Refuge for American Trans Women

The famous case of Christine Jorgensen in 1952 had a huge impact on trans women all over the world. The clinic in Copenhagen, Denmark, received hundreds of requests from transgender people, mostly from the United States where gender-reaffirming surgery was not allowed. Soon, the Danish doctors had to decide to refuse treatment to foreign trans women. American sexologist Harry Benjamin contacted his Dutch colleague Coen van Emde Boas for help, hoping that the Netherlands were as liberal as Denmark.

During the years 1954–1956 Harry Benjamin sent approximately thirty American trans women to the Netherlands. They were clinically examined and psychologically tested for a few hours a day over a period of several months. With much effort, Van Emde Boas managed to find a plastic surgeon in a small private clinic who was willing to do gender-affirming surgeries under the radar. This is how the first transgender medical care in Holland was provided. It stopped when the hospital director found out, and threw the surgeon and his patients out.

Life in the Shadows of Society

In Dutch society, there was simply no place for trans persons, especially for trans women. If you wanted to live openly as a female, there was only one way to go: into the subculture of prostitution and cabaret night life.

Getting hormones was not very difficult. There was an outlaw doctor in the red light district of Amsterdam (an area of legal prostitution) who was happy to help, if you just gave him some money. For surgery, you had to save money and go to Dr. Georges Burou in Casablanca, Morocco. Only some trans women were willing to live such a life. More bourgeois trans people stayed in the closet.

1959: First Transgender Surgery out in the Open

The first official transgender surgery in Holland took place in 1959. An anonymous thirty-four-year-old trans man got a phalloplasty. When this became known, it led to lots of commotion in the medical field and in public opinion. The national government started an investigation because many people thought that this type of surgery should be banned from medical care. After five years they released a statement saying that trans persons should only be treated psychologically, never medically. Being transgender was called "a dangerous delusion." This kept doctors away from even trying to help transgender people. General imagery in the mass media labeled trans people as having psychiatric problems or as perverted people, or both.

Dutch Gender Foundation: The Spirit of the Sixties and Seventies

The social changes of the late sixties created new values. An unorthodox and outspoken doctor, Otto de Vaal, took an interest in the fate of trans people. He felt that the help so far was outrageous, with all the talking in endless psychoanalyses, and no real help. De Vaal started the Dutch Gender Foundation. Important values at the foundation included no unnecessary psychiatric therapy; a focus on medical help, including hormones and surgery; accepting that trans people could self-diagnose.

The Gender Foundation tried to find practical solutions for the problems that transsexuals faced: negative stigma; problems with jobs, housing, family, the law: and a need for surgery. Again, there was only one plastic surgeon willing to perform gender-affirming surgeries. He had the capacity of doing one or two surgeries a month, so it took lots of time to get through the waiting list.

An important part of Dutch transgender history that emerged in the seventies was self-help groups of trans people to support and educate one another. Also at this time, a new generation of trans women who had previously been invisible came out: persons with steady jobs, with wives and children.

Academic Environment: A Crucial Turn

The Gender Foundation tried to find hospitals and surgeons to gain more capacity, but only one institution wanted to take it on as a structural commitment, the VU (Free University) hospital in Amsterdam, a university clinic with a traditional Protestant Christian identity. This surprising turn can only be explained by the leading role of a few doctors and ethicists who stated that caring for people in need was the meaning of true Christian compassion.

From the mid-seventies on, the gender clinic of the VU hospital grew into the biggest multidisciplinary academic team in the world. The highly respected academic VU hospital made transgender care acceptable for politicians, and for public health insurance to pay for the costs of treatment. The fact that it became part of regular health care is a key factor. It allowed a large population of trans people to seek and receive treatment, which made more research possible, which led to more expertise.

Meanwhile the Dutch government had published a new report that condoned the medical treatment of transsexuals (1977), and devised a transgender law so people could change their birth certificate (1985).

Emancipation in the Eighties

In the 1980s, the image of trans people in media changed from "psychiatric and/or perverted freaks" to "people with a serious problem who need understanding and compassion." Hateful or demeaning depictions became very rare. Media representation had been mostly focused on trans women but, in the eighties, trans men started to get into the picture.

1999: Panic around Trans Children

The eighties and nineties for Dutch trans people were years of growing acceptance and emancipation. Mass media were mostly helpful in spreading awareness and tolerance. Strong public controversy was only aroused in 1999 over a news article about treatment for trans adolescents. All nuances got lost in the upheaval and the caregivers were heavily under attack.

It took a few years before the outrage subsided. By then, there was room for arguments and scientific data. Plus, the appearance of transgender children on television and in magazines made the public more aware that they needed help, and that help should be given in a secure and safe way. Currently, dozens of clinics around the world are following "the Dutch protocol" for the treatment of trans children and youth.

Twenty-First-Century Communities

The last fifteen years have been characterized by much more and stronger community building than before. During this time the T got integrated into LGBT. In the Netherlands, trans people had never been part of gay and lesbian political movements. Most trans persons did not recognize being trans as an identity and did not feel the need to make themselves known as trans people in society.

Connected with stronger communities is a new phase in emancipation. Trans people are becoming less dependent on health care providers, and there is more public attention on ensuring transgender rights.

Gender Diversity and a New Law

There is also an increasing understanding of the broad range of transgender diversity. Medical treatment, supervised by the Dutch Health Inspection, did not officially allow for so-called partial treatment until ten years ago. This caused some clients to lie about their needs and wishes. Now clients can make their own choices about hormones and surgery that better fit non-binary identities.

New times are also reflected in the new law from July 1, 2014. The thirty-year-old law had become quite outdated and, as Human Rights Watch pointed out, Holland was falling behind other countries such as Argentina, Denmark, and Malta. Nowadays, it is no longer required to have medical treatment before changing your birth sex on your identity documents.

A High Tide

As in many countries in the Western world, today the transgender phenomenon is having its definitive breakthrough. Visibility is unprecedentedly high with a transgender item on national television at least once a week. New role models appear frequently, and sometimes it even seems hip to be trans in Holland.

Although transgender identities that do not require medical care are better understood now, at the same time, the number of persons who come to the gender clinic has exploded. In 2016 it was around 1,000, ten times what it used to be. The fact that the Amsterdam gender clinic and the smaller Groningen gender clinic are currently more or less the only caregivers is not ideal, and efforts are being made to expand gender care around the country. The Dutch government is now a firm believer in securing and promoting trans rights.

Dutch historian and writer Alex Bakker specializes in transgender issues. In 2018 he published Transgender in the Netherlands, *the first history book on this topic. Bakker works as a researcher and writer for documentary films (*Transit Havana, *2016). In 2014 he published his autobiography,* My Untrue Past.

The Tortuous Path to Creative Liberation
Jo Clifford

I couldn't stop myself being a writer any more than I could stop myself being trans.

And I became aware of both more or less at the same time. I had to read a book called *The Outsider* by a French writer called Camus and I loved the book, mainly because I felt so much like an outsider myself.

My French teacher told us Camus used to write in a notebook every day and I began to do the same.

I must have been about thirteen then. And I still do.

I was in a boys' boarding school in England, and around then I was asked to play girls' parts in the school plays. I felt so at home in the rehearsal room and on stage, and so at home being a girl too.

It's clear I discovered my vocation then; but the sad thing was that, it being the sixties, and transphobia being so unquestioned and universal, I felt so terribly frightened and ashamed of being a girl, and there was no option open to me then but try to suppress it.

My vocation as a theater artist got all tangled up in the same profound fear and shame, and so I lost my vocation as soon as I found it.

What I didn't lose, though, was my sense of being a writer. And because that gave me a sense of being someone worthwhile, it saved my life.

I spent the next fifteen years trying to become a novelist and getting nowhere. I was never a novelist. I couldn't be bothered describing places or people, and all the stories I wrote turned into dialogue. And I got bored trying to find different ways of saying "he said" and "she replied."

I really should have known I was a playwright. But I didn't, because the shame and fear were still too strong. Somehow I needed to work in the theater, though without understanding why, and the only way that I could safely do it was through academic research. So I became an expert on seventeenth-century Spanish drama, and it was through translating the play that was the subject of my thesis that I accidentally met someone who wanted to direct one of my translations.

We put on a seventeenth-century comedy by Calderon that I'd translated. There I was, thirty years old, carrying my first child on a sling and watching my translation on stage in the Edinburgh Fringe. I wish I could say it was a big success, but it wasn't. Audiences were tiny. But the ones that came laughed.

I was so happy with my daughter, and so happy with the laughs that I had helped create. And that was how I discovered I was a playwright.

Five years later, my second daughter was born and I was cradling her as I watched the rehearsals for my first original play to be professionally staged. It was 1985, twenty years after the trauma that made me lose my vocation and almost made me lose my voice. The play was called *Losing Venice*. It was also being put on in the Fringe, and rehearsals were going terribly wrong.

It was horribly difficult being in rehearsal. I hated what I'd written and I had no idea to how help the actors perform it. There was something very different about how I wrote; and eventually the director, too, burst into tears and said she couldn't direct the play. Somehow we all hung on, and somehow the play got performed, and somehow it became an enormous success. And that was how my career started.

I worked out that to earn as much as a schoolteacher, I needed to write five plays a year. And that's what I set out to do. It was hard, especially because I could only write half time. I was working as a parent the other half of the week. Those years, I wrote everything: stage plays, translations, adaptations of novels, radio plays, the words for operas, puppet plays, children's plays, film and TV scripts. And that's why, if you go to my website where they're all listed, you'll find about eighty-five titles.

I made a woman the central character whenever I could, and I tried to make sure there were equal number of parts for female and male actors, and because to write a play I have to become the characters, I learned to explore the woman inside me without shame.

And I discovered that what made my writer's voice so special was not just my old obsession with the theater of seventeenth-century Spain, but the fact that I wasn't a male writer, and I wasn't a female writer. I was a trans writer. And that was something to celebrate.

And I also discovered that as I wrote, I wasn't just the character in my imagination. I was the actor, or the actress, too. And I knew if a line was good or not through my old instincts as a performer. Which meant they hadn't disappeared.

By that time I knew I had to write about being trans. It was the 1990s and there were no trans actresses anywhere. But I had a sense I could write for myself. So I wrote and performed *God's New Frock*, about the suppressed trans-ness of God. And the suppressed trans-ness of me. And that's how I came out.

Eventually I wrote and performed a play called *The Gospel According to Jesus Queen of Heaven*, which imagines Jesus coming back to earth in the present day as a trans woman. Many outraged Christians demonstrated against me in the street. I'd always been afraid, way back when I first performed, that if I played female parts people would find out about and hate me. And that week in 2009, my nightmare had come true. The demonstrators in the street, and hundreds of thousands of people online, did know about me. And did hate me. But their hatred couldn't destroy me. And that gave me strength.

I still perform that play, and it's been touring Brazil for a year, where it's transforming attitudes to trans people and affirming everyone's right to live a life free of prejudice.

In 2017, I performed my new play, *Eve*. Again in the Fringe, again in the Traverse. Produced by the National Theatre of Scotland.

I describe it as a manifesto. A manifesto for freedom, and a life free of shame. Which is exactly what it is. I know theater can be a powerful force for human liberation. I know it because creating it has set me free.

Jo Clifford is a playwright, poet, performer, father, and grandmother. She is author of about ninety plays seen all over the world. In 2018, her works were performed in Argentina, Brazil, Japan, Scotland, England, and Uruguay. Her plays include Eve, Gospel According to Jesus Queen of Heaven, Anna Karenina, Losing Venice, Five Days Which Changed Everything, *and a queer adaptation of* The Taming of the Shrew. *Her website is* www .teatrodomundo.com.

An Accidental Activist
Dallas Denny

Imagine this: You are thirteen years old, with an awakening and urgent realization that all is not right with gender, and, specifically, with *your* gender. You have discovered a single pubic hair and know it's a sign of a puberty you don't want, and it fills you with dread. You want the puberty of the *other* sex, not the one you were born with.

Now, if you can, imagine this: There is absolutely no one you can talk to about what is going on with you, and absolutely nowhere to go for information. Telling your parents would result in a freakout that might get you beaten, hospitalized, medicated, or expelled from the family home. There are no LGBT liaisons, no savvy counselors in your school.

There are no obviously gender-variant people at your school, and if there were, even speaking to them would make you a target for harassment and ridicule. There are no community organizations that might help you, no physician or hospital, no gender clinics, no psychologist or social worker, no sympathetic member of the clergy, nor is there anything you can do to educate yourself. You can find no books or magazines, and, since it is 1963, the Internet has not been invented yet. There are no cell phones, no tablets, or home computers. Computers are huge, fill entire rooms, and cost millions of dollars.

There are no television shows or radio programs or movies that speak seriously about gender. When gender variance is treated at all, it is used as a comic plot, or, as in Alfred Hitchcock's 1960 film *Psycho*, as murderous and maniacal.

You know there must be others like you somewhere, but they are as invisible to you as the information you so desperately need and cannot find.

That's pretty much how it was for me in 1963, when I was thirteen.

The puberty I dreaded arrived, and I was forced into an adolescence, and then an adulthood, I didn't want.

By the time I was in graduate school, things had changed, but not much. Transsexuals Jan Morris, Renée Richards, and Canary Cohn were being interviewed on TV. There was a network of gender clinics around the United States and Canada, but they rejected most applicants. There was some press about the clinics, and about people who changed their sex, and there were smutty magazines sold in adult bookstores. Small numbers of gender-variant people were meeting in big cities, but they were invisible to me. Short of traveling to a gender clinic and applying for sex reassignment, there was nothing I could do.

And so that's what I did. When I discovered Nashville's Vanderbilt University had a gender program, I went there, and gave them a lot of money, only to be told I was not screwed up enough to be transsexual. The clinics viewed transsexuals as mentally ill, and because I had graduated from college, had a job, had been married, and wasn't suicidal, I was told I was unsuitable for sex reassignment.

I spent the next couple of months at Vanderbilt's medical library, looking up and reading everything I could about gender variance. What I found was almost entirely about transsexualism, which described me well, but confirmed what I had been told at Vanderbilt: I wasn't screwed up enough to qualify for sex reassignment.

Faced with a body that was becoming more masculine in appearance, desperate for resolution of my gender issue, and with no legal way to get estrogen, I did something that would normally have been unthinkable to me—I researched hormones and their dosages and forged a prescription. At age twenty-nine, I was on hormones. At the time it was a bold and necessary thing that I did. As soon as I was able to find a physician to prescribe hormones, I immediately put myself under his care. Important note: Don't do what I did. Times have changed, and sympathetic physicians will help you. Human sex hormones can have serious health effects. DO NOT TAKE HORMONES WITHOUT MEDICAL SUPERVISION!

The knowledge that my masculinization had been halted and my body would slowly feminize was a huge psychic relief, but expressing myself as female was still a challenge. It would be years before I found the support to transition.

In the fall of 1988, I ambivalently joined the Society for the Second Self, an organization for cross-dressers. I say ambivalently not because I have a problem with cross-dressers, but because transsexuals were excluded from membership and I was forced to misrepresent myself as a cross-dresser to gain membership.

My hope was that by joining I would finally find the information and support I needed, and that's exactly what happened. In early 1989 a trans woman named Jessica Britton showed me a magazine called *TV/TS Tapestry Journal*; in the back was a list of supportive organizations. One, the Montgomery Medical and Psychological Institute, was in Atlanta, a reasonable drive from my home in Greeneville, Tennessee.

Despite its fancy name, the Montgomery Institute was a support group for transsexuals, and there, twenty-five years after I first looked for support, I finally reached my goal of finding community and getting the information and support I needed to change my gender.

I soon parted ways with the Montgomery Institute, and the separation was not a pleasant one. The split happened for several reasons, but primarily because I had come to embrace transgender as an umbrella term and to advocate new and developing trans identities. The founders of the institute had not.

My goal had been to find the information and obtain the support I needed to transition. I had found it, and I had transitioned. What I was then supposed to do, according to the wisdom of the day, was to disappear into the larger society and have a wonderful life and pretend I wasn't trans. To my surprise, I discovered I didn't want to lie and become invisible about who I was. No, not again.

Over the preceding year and a half I had somehow, accidentally become a leader in the trans community. I say accidentally because that was never my intention. I had been drafted to direct the Montgomery Institute because my undergraduate and graduate degrees are in psychology, and because I was licensed to practice psychology in Tennessee.

I was writing prolifically about trans issues and I liked and sympathized with the trans people I had met. Most were in the same desperate and generally fruitless quest for information and support as I had been, and I was now able to give them the information and support they needed to make sense of their lives. I decided I liked doing that, and that I was good at it. And so I founded a national nonprofit corporation and a local support group: the American Educational Gender Information Service and the still-existent Atlanta Gender Explorations support group.

The next twenty years of my life were consumed by transgender people, transgender policy, and transgender community. I slowed down a bit when I reached age sixty, but I continue to advocate on behalf of trans and non-binary and gender-nonconforming people. I continue to write, and I continue my involvement with trans community organizations and conferences. It's been a great experience and one I could, and probably will, write a book about.

Dallas Denny has been a leader in the transgender rights movement since the 1980s. Her work as advocate, writer, editor, speaker, and community builder played a significant role in the advancement of rights for transsexual and transgender people in North America and around the world. Her website is http://dallasdenny.com.

Transgender and Jewish
Joy Ladin

As long as I can remember, I knew that I was Jewish and what we now call "transgender," though I didn't learn that word until my mid-forties.

My family wasn't religious, but being Jewish was important to us. We belonged to a synagogue, had seders, fasted on Yom Kippur, and made sure that others knew that we were Jews. Even as a small child, I knew I had to hide the fact that I wasn't the boy everyone thought I was, but I was proud to identify as a Jew. Even though there weren't many Jews where we lived, being Jewish connected me to Jews around the world as well as to millennia of history and culture.

But being transgender, which in my case meant feeling that I was really female even though I had been born and lived as a male, didn't seem to connect me with anyone or anything. Until I was ten, I didn't know there was anyone else like me. I thought that being human meant fitting into the binary gender categories of male and female, and even when I learned that there were other transsexuals—that's the word for people who feel the way I do—I didn't feel connected to them. They were different in the same way I was different, but unlike being Jewish, as far as I could tell, that difference didn't give us a common history or culture.

So instead of looking to other transgender people to understand being different, I looked to Jewishness and Judaism. (I describe my experience of growing up transgender and Jewish in my memoir, *Through the Door of Life: A Jewish Journey Between Genders*, published in 2010 by University of Wisconsin Press.) I learned about Jewish children who had to pretend not to be Jewish in order to survive the Holocaust. Like them, I knew I had to hide who I was in order to survive. By the time I was in first grade, I had trained myself not to sit, act, talk, or do anything that might reveal that I wasn't the boy everyone thought I was. I was afraid of everyone, even my own parents.

I survived—sort of. My female gender identification—my strange, unshakable sense that despite my male body and life, I was really a girl—was the part of me that felt true, real, alive. Hiding who I really was meant that even when I was a young child, I felt fake, hollow, numb, more like a ghost than a person. My name wasn't my real name (I didn't have a real name then); my face wasn't my face; my body wasn't my body; no one who looked at me was really looking at me, because there was nothing of me that was visible. Like many trans children and adults, I tried to kill myself more than once, and thought about suicide all the time.

Even though I felt completely cut off from the human world, I wasn't alone. Like many children, I had a strong sense that

God was there, a living presence. Like many queer children who grow up hiding who we are, I felt that God was the only one who knew who I really was, who knew my loneliness and pain. Because my family wasn't religious, I didn't have anyone to teach me that I was wrong about God, that God would never talk to a kid like me. To me, there was no conflict between being religious and being transgender. From the time I started reading the Torah, the Hebrew Bible, when I was six or seven, I saw it as a book about someone like me: someone (God) who didn't have a body that fit into human gender categories, or the world that was based upon them. Even though everyone, including the Torah, referred to God as "He," I knew that God couldn't be male (or female, for that matter) because God was not human. God, like me, existed outside of gender, invisible and incomprehensible to the human beings God dwelt among and loved. (I discuss how I read the Torah as a trans child, and how I read it now, in *The Soul of the Stranger: Reading God and Torah from a Transgender Perspective*, published by Brandeis University Press in 2018.)

When I started living as myself—living as a woman—I was a tenured professor at Orthodox Jewish Yeshiva University. That was a decade ago, but I am still at Yeshiva—and still the only openly transgender employee of an Orthodox Jewish institution. As both a child and an adult, my life as a transgender person is inseparable from my life as a Jew.

Many people think of those identities as mutually exclusive, but I've spent much of the last ten years thinking, speaking, and writing about how trans and Jewish identities can connect and intertwine. Being transgender has made me a more spiritually alive and engaged Jew, leading me to the Torah when I was a child, and inspiring me to probe Jewish conceptions of God and humanity to this very day. And being Jewish has taught me a lot about being transgender. It has taught me how to be out and proud about being different; that being a minority can connect me to, as well as separate me from, others; and that no matter how different we seem to those around us, we, like them, are created in the image of God. Both as a trans person and a Jew, I have learned that whether or not our identities reflect the bodies and lives we were born to, what matters is that they enable us to express who we truly are, and to become the best version of ourselves we can be.

Joy Ladin is Gottesman Chair in English at Yeshiva University and author of a memoir of gender transition, National Jewish Book Award *finalist* Through the Door of Life, *nine books of poetry, and* The Soul of the Stranger: God and Torah from a Transgender Perspective.

Parental Research and Advocacy in Canada: One Mother's Journey
Kimberley Ens Manning

In June 2017, Bill C-16, a bill designed to protect gender identity and gender expression in the Canadian Human Rights Code and Criminal Code, was ushered into law. It was a moment that trans activists and allies in Canada had long struggled for, a true victory overcoming what, at times, had felt like an insurmountable series of setbacks and transphobic backlash.

Although there were many reasons for the 2017 victory, emerging research played a significant role. Indeed, between 2010, when my daughter, Florence, first began her social transition, and today, we have acquired compelling quantitative and qualitative data that is at long last beginning to grapple with the diversity and complexity that is trans experience in Canada (Scheim, Bauer, and Pyne 2014; Veale et al. 2015).

I stumbled into this world of emerging scholarship and advocacy by way of my daughter. As a political scientist with a particular focus on gender in revolutionary China, I was initially unsure how I could contribute to the conversation. But I also knew that new approaches were urgently needed. In 2011 and 2012, Annie Pullen Sansfaçon, also a parent of a transgender child, at the University of Montreal; Elizabeth Meyer, now at the University of Colorado, Boulder; and I received grants from the Social Sciences and Humanities Research Council of Canada (SSHRC) to undertake social action research with parents and educators. In 2012, our team held Canada's first national conference on trans kids and their families and developed a website for Canadian parents. Our three pilot studies later produced a number of scholarly publications, including *Supporting Transgender Children and Their Families* (now in its second edition) (Meyer and Sansfaçon 2017).

My original pilot study was focused on the emergence of parents advocating on behalf of their transgender children. At the time we started there were less than a handful of parent advocates in Canada. In fact, when Annie and I applied for our grant, neither of us considered ourselves as "parent advocates." Our initial work thus focused on mobilizing others through social action research, but not on ourselves. I, myself, did not begin to conduct qualitative interviews with parents until the fall of 2013 when a few Canadian parents, often working closely with their children, began to lobby for legislative changes.

What Annie and I had not realized when we began this work was how much our new investment in social action research would challenge our conceptions of ourselves as scholars and as parents. As we became rapidly aware of the needs of our children, and of other families, we too became activists (Manning et al. 2015). Alongside some of the parents who had participated in Annie's original social action research group, for example, Annie and I became founding board members of Gender Creative Kids Canada. We also began to provide training in schools, advocate for legislative change, and speak with the media. Annie and her daughter, Olie, made national history when they, alongside several other families, were featured in a 2014 major national newsmagazine story about transgender children. Two years later, Annie and Olie worked successfully with members of the Québec legislature to change laws that had previously prevented children and youth from changing their sex markers on their documents.

Florence and I also became involved in legislative work in 2015, advocating for the passage of Bill C-279 (an earlier version of C-16), and again in 2017 when I appeared before the Senate's Legal and Constitutional Affairs Committee. In the meantime, my ongoing research with, and writing about, parent advocacy was helping me to see and articulate how race, class, and other social structures of oppression shape the capacity of parents, including myself, to be public advocates. I began to read more work by trans and queer scholars of color who challenge white, cis, heteronormative assumptions about safety, identity, and resistance in the settler society that is Canada. This scholarship and the generous input of trans scholars and community leaders deeply informed an article that I published in the summer of 2017 (Manning 2017). It also influenced my advocacy in support of Bill C-16.

As many have remarked, the passage of Bill C-16 into law is only one step on a very long road. The new law will not directly produce safe employment and housing, nor will it enable refugees and migrants to change their identity documents. For that to happen, we need more research, advocacy, and public policy reform that is grounded in radically inclusive and transformative approaches. To this end, many new research projects focused on trans youth and their families are already underway, all of which take the ethical challenge of intersectionality to heart. It is because of this, and because of the ongoing struggle of so many trans people and their allies, that I ultimately feel hopeful that the next five years will prove even more trans-affirming than the hard-won victories of the last five.

References

Manning, Kimberley Ens. 2017. "Attached Advocacy and the Rights of the Trans Child." *Canadian Journal of Political Science/Revue canadienne de science politique* 50, no. 2: 579–595.

Manning, Kimberley Ens, Cindy Holmes, Julie Temple Newhook, Annie Pullen Sansfaçon, and Ann Travers. 2015.

"Fighting for Trans* Kids." *Studies in Social Justice* 9, no. 1: 118–135.

Meyer, Elizabeth, and Annie Pullen Sansfaçon (eds.). 2017. *Supporting Transgender and Gender Creative Youth: Schools, Families, and Communities in Action.* New York: Peter Lang. (Second edition, forthcoming 2018.)

Scheim, Ayden, Greta Bauer, and Jake Pyne. 2014. "Avoidance of Public Spaces by Trans Ontarians: The Impact of Transphobia on Daily Life." *Trans PULSE E-Bulletin* 4, no. 1.

Veale, J., E. Saewyc, H. Frohard-Dourlent, S. Dobson, B. Clark, and the Canadian Trans Youth Health Survey Research Group. 2015. *Being Safe, Being Me: Results of the Canadian Trans Youth Health Survey.* Vancouver, BC: Stigma and Resilience Among Vulnerable Youth Centre, School of Nursing, University of British Columbia.

Kimberley Ens Manning is principal of the Simone de Beauvoir Institute and associate professor of political science at Concordia University, Montreal. A founding board member of Gender Creative Kids Canada, Kimberley conducts social action research in support of gender-nonconforming children and their families and teaches and researches about gender and politics in the People's Republic of China.

Transgender Care Program at Quest Community Health Centre
Carys Massarella

When I first opened the Transgender Care Program in 2011 I never imagined we would end up as busy as we find ourselves now. We are a transgender health clinic in the Niagara Region of Southern Ontario within a community health center setting.

We have never advertised our presence or actively sought clients. Indeed, most of our patients have come through word of mouth via the transgender community, or through publicity from news and information outlets.

When I envisioned this clinic back in 2010, the goal was to create a fair and equitable space for transgender patients to access informed-consent transition health care. This was how I had been treated in my transition, and it seemed to be the best answer for most transgender-identified patients.

In fact, if we are ever to break the endless cycle of patholo-gizing trans bodies, we need to pursue our work in this way. In essence, by using an informed-consent approach we were say-ing that transgender people understand who they are and need appropriate expert medical care rather than to be subjected to endless interrogation about the reality of their existence. The facts are that transgender people exist and have a right to access health care in a supportive and meaningful way.

So that's exactly what we did, and by any measure we have been wildly successful. Today, our clinic sees transgender-identified patients of all ages using an informed-consent model of care.

I would say the biggest surprises have been that the demand for our services has far exceeded our initial expectations, and that there have been a large number of younger people who are accessing transgender care. It has been a worldwide phenome-non that patients are coming out at much younger ages and are seeking transition-related care. There is no consensus as to why this is happening, other than that there is now greater aware-ness, meaningful legal protections, and increasingly supportive parental and public support for transgender people.

We have seen this reflected in our clinic, where we have experienced a huge surge in youth referrals. Parents no longer see a transgender identity as a one-way ticket to personal obliv-ion, but rather as a meaningful identity in a more inclusive society. This, of course, is a good thing, and it is a future that we can all look forward to.

I think that the next few years may be a minefield for trans-gender people as the movement to refute transgender identities continues to smolder, particularly in more conservative areas. Nonetheless, the medical work will continue and the momentum of history is on our side.

The next evolution is of non-binary identities, a broader and less well-defined category that can be a challenge for health care providers. But we can listen, engage, and be ready to meet the needs of this population if we remind ourselves that identity is not a simple binary but rather complex and fluid in the context of our work.

I have great hopes for the next generation of medical providers. They have demonstrated a great interest in trans health care and a willingness to learn about the care and treatment of transgender and non-binary patients. I think it will be much easier for trans-identified individuals to access expert care in the future that is supportive and nonpathologizing.

For those of us engaged actively in this work, it is both gratifying and exciting to be part of a new way of doing health care. The worldwide community of health care providers who do this work are a close-knit group who care deeply about the community we serve. In the future, I hope to see more transgender health care providers doing this work supporting the community both medically and as part of an important social movement.

Medicine is conservative and changes slowly, but we have shown that a small number of dedicated people can change the conversation and improve the care provided to a vulnerable population.

I only ever look forward, and I see a bright future.

Carys Massarella, MD, FRCPC is the lead physician at the Quest Community Health Centre's Transgender Care Program and an assistant clinical professor at the Degroote Medical School in St. Catharines, ON. She was the world's first trans teaching hospital medical staff president, one of the Huffington Post's World's 50 Transgender icons, *and was a YWCA woman of distinction in 2017.*

Two-Spirit Conversations and Work: Subtle and at the Same Time Radically Different
Harlan Pruden

A great place to begin our conversation is: "What and who is Two-Spirit?" Although this seems like a straightforward and simple question, the answer is somewhat complex and nuanced.

Two-Spirit is a way for Two-Spirit communities to organize; in other words, a way to identify those individuals who embody diverse (or non-normative) sexualities, genders, and gender expressions and who are Indigenous to Turtle Island. This statement requires some qualification as it is intentionally nuanced. The first part is positioned so that it does not use or affirm Western frameworks, concepts, or identities of LGBTQ+. Instead, it is descriptive: "who embody diverse (or non-normative) sexualities, genders, and gender expressions." And the statement concludes with "Turtle Island," which is harkening to some of the first peoples' creation stories (Anishinaabe, Lenepe, to list a few) and is used to name the land that we have come to call North America. The name Turtle Island is used to reference this land mass while not affirming or recognizing the two nation states of Canada or the United States of America.

Two-Spirit is a placeholder of sorts. When individuals show up at a (Two-Spirit) gathering or some other indigenous event, the first question that is often asked is, "What Nation are you?" If the individual is male-assigned and is Anishinaabe, then we gift and/or honor them their word *agokwe*; if the individual is female-assigned, we would use the word *okitcitakwe*—if these individuals do not know these words already. Thus, "Two-Spirit" is a community organizing strategy or tool and not an identity. Although it is often positioned as an identity, it is neither an end-point nor an identity. When treated and positioned as an identity, it becomes highly problematic.

There are about 130 terms within our own languages that name, account, and identify these other genders—these words are Nation specific. As a result, Two-Spirit will mean something slightly different depending on the individual's Nation affiliation and therefore, there is no one definition of Two-Sprit to be offered.

There are many words in Cree for Two-Spirit. The following Cree words were validated by twenty-one Cree elders (and speakers); these elders were the advisory council for the Alberta Aboriginal Association of Friendship Centre: *napêw iskwêwisêhot* (nu-PAYO ihs-gwayo-WIH-say-hoht), a man who dresses as a woman; *iskwêw ka napêwayat* (ihs-GWAYO ga nu-PAYO-wuh-yut), a woman dressed as a man; *ayahkwêw* (U-yuh-gwayo), a man dressed/living/accepted as a woman; *iskwêhkân* (IS-gwayh-gahn), literally "fake woman," but without negative connotations; *napêhkân* (NU-payh-gahn), literally "fake man," again without negative connotations. It must be noted that the above translations are approximations and not direct translations, as English is limiting when it comes to many Indigenous languages and concepts.

After individuals have received their word in their own language, along with a framework to understand it and to (re)learn this almost lost history and tradition(s), these individuals come to an awareness, or an awakening, and begin the "coming in" process. "Coming in does not centre on the declaration of independence that characterizes 'coming out' in mainstream depictions of the lives of LGBTQ+ people. Rather, coming in is an act of returning, fully present in ourselves, to resume our place as a valued part of our families, cultures, communities, and lands, in connection with all our relations" (Wilson 2015). Expanding upon the above Anishinaabe example, this awakening is marked when the individual begins a self and communal discovery: "What does *okitcitakwe* mean? Who is *okitcitakwe* and what is my role and purpose as an *okitcitakwe* for my Anishinaabe people?" Thereby, *okitcitakwe*, a female-assigned Anishinaabe (Two-Spirit) person, will have different socially defined or expected role(s) than someone who is *iskwêhkân*, a female-assigned Cree (Two-Spirit) person.

Within a non-Indigenous Western context, there is often an overemphasis or prioritization of binary stories and experiences (whether cisgender or transgender) to the exclusion and invisibility of non-binary people. However, the work with, and for, the Two-Spirit community is about the reclaiming and restoring of our traditional and Indigenous ways in which many first peoples had more than two genders; thereby, this work challenges this Western dualistic construct. For example, the Cree people had four accepted and honored genders, an ontological example of the transcending of this Western binary.

This framing makes the work and conversation(s) of "Two-Spirit" subtle and at the same time radically different from that of the LGBT/queer movement, where that work is often asking/demanding new rights and privileges or an expansion of rights and privileges within a Western/colonial framework. A good example is the U.S. Supreme Court ruling of *Loving v. Virginia* (1967) that granted the right for African Americans to marry anyone they want irrespective of the race of their spouse. Then the gay community followed suit and stated: "We want that right," so LGBTQ used a social justice/human rights and/or a civil rights framework as they advocated for and won that right. This is not a criticism of this good and necessary work that has been, and continues to be, done by, for, and within LGBTQ+ communities, but simply an observation that allows us to see the fuller picture of Two-Spirit as having its own meaningful history and cultural context that predates colonial contact.

For us within the Two-Spirit community, we are not asking for anything new. Where we begin the conversation is "Remember when?"—Remember when Two-Spirit people were honored and respected and had full equality and citizenship within their respective nations—where *agokwe, okitcitakwe,* or *ayahk-wêw, napêhkân* meant something, and these individuals had a specific and honored role(s) within their societies, communities, and Nations.

If there is a Native person doing language work, include us, the Two-Spirit community, as we were included before. If a person is doing some ceremonial or cultural work, include us as we were included before. At the heart of this work is the reclaiming and restoring of a place of honor and respect for Two-Spirit persons within our Nations—a calling home of their Two-Spirit people.

In summary, Two-Spirit, the intersection of those who embody diverse sexualities, genders, and gender expressions, and who are indigenous to Turtle Island, is a community organizing tool and not an identity. It is going to mean something different depending on what Nation an individual is from and a member of. Two-Spirit refers to history/tradition that predates Western and colonial notions and concepts of LGBTQ+ and thereby is about reclaiming and restoring a place of honor and respect within the individual's Nation. This work is deep decolonizing work that calls Two-Spirit people home and is thereby a mending of the sacred hoop (Gunn Allen 1986).

References

Gunn Allen, Paula. 1986. *The Sacred Hoop*. Beacon Press.

Wilson, A. 2015. "Our Coming In Stories: Cree Identity, Body Sovereignty and Gender Self-Determination." *Journal of Global Indigeneity*, 1(1).

Harlan Pruden, First Nation Cree, works with and for the Two-Spirit community locally, nationally, and internationally. Harlan is a PhD student at UBC and an educator at the BC Center for Disease Control's Chee Mamuk program. Harlan is also the managing editor of TwoSpiritJournal.com.

(In)visible Transgender Bodies: A View from Tamil Nadu, India
Shabeena Francis Saveri

Within an Indian context, the *hijra* community is a closed community with a rich religious-cultural-historical background.

The *hijra* identity is unique because of its "third-gender" identity acceptance and *jamaat* subculture (a community system). Since antiquity, *hijra* people have been considered a part of Indian society. However, they were, and still are, deprived of many fundamental rights. Recently there has been a rise in *hijra* and LGBT activism in India.

In the late 1990s, when I got involved in an HIV/AIDS intervention program among the *hijra* population in Mumbai, the term "eunuch" was used for *hijras*, and they were considered men who have sex with men (MSM). However, over a period of time, the term *hijra* has become used along with the Western term "transgender," and *hijra* and transgender people are no longer thought of as MSM.

There is a significant difference between current issues and those addressed two decades ago. We started with HIV/AIDS awareness and prevention activities, which later took the shape of highlighting transgender rights issues, and now we have transgender individuals in various professions such as education, law, nonprofit, the beauty industry, and so on, and a few corporations have opened their doors for employment. Though my own professional journey began as a community organizer, I gradually reached my goal to achieve my doctorate and lead a more mainstream life. It is amazing to see the changes that have taken place in these last two decades.

One of the most important changes is the use of the Western term transgender for *hijra* people and various other male-to-female (MTF) transgender identities/categories in India. Though *hijra* people fall under the Western definition of the term transgender because of their gender transition, what differentiates them from Western transgender/transsexual people is the traditional *hijra jamaat* subculture and preference for a "third-gender" identity.

Within an Indian context the term transgender/transsexual is often confused with MTF bodies, ignoring various other identities/categories within the larger transgender umbrella. People in India do not always use the term transgender because until recently the *hijra* identity was the only visible identity. However, the term is gaining popularity.

There is a dearth of literature on transgender people in India. The available literature is mostly within a religious-cultural context, with an emphasis on the socioeconomic and political situation of the *hijra* and MTF transgender populations. Transgender people other than the *hijra* are not adequately discussed in the available literature, and the general public does not differentiate between *hijra* and other MTF people.

My doctoral research was focused on the *hijra* population in the state of Tamil Nadu in India, where the term *aravani* is used for *hijras*. The term *aravani* literally means one who worships Lord Aravan and does not have a direct relation with sex/gender. It signifies the act of marrying a god. It does not have any traditional and historical significance within the *hijra* or transgender communities in the Western and North Indian states and neighboring south Indian states.

The various trans(gender) identities that exist in Tamil Nadu can be broadly classified in the following two categories: *aravani* and MTF transgender/transsexual (those who prefer to be identified as a woman). The latter prefer to use terminologies such as transgender, transsexual, transgender (woman), transsexual (woman), or just woman.

In both categories, urban (city and big towns) people are more likely to have the advantages of education; they may be involved in transgender activism; they may have alternative sources of livelihood, for example, working in NGOs (nongovernmental organizations) or CBOs (community-based organizations); they may have IGPs (income-generation programs); and they may have a liberalist, individualistic, and independent perspective toward transgender welfare and development.

Likewise both *aravani* and MTF women in rural (small towns and villages) areas share some similarities. They are more likely to be disadvantaged; they may have little education; they may have an affiliation with the *aravani jamaat*; they may be engaged in a traditional *aravani* occupation such as begging or sex work; they may be involved in IGPs or work in NGOs/ CBOs; and they may also be engaged in transgender activism.

My research revealed that the family is often the first place of violation of transgender rights, violence, and discrimination. When a person comes out as transgender, parents and family members often disown their child because of the stigma attached to transgender identities. In the absence of their family's support, many young *aravanis* migrate to other Indian states for gender transition, and to join the *hijra* community. Without education and unable to find other employment, they often end up in sex work, or begging, or in other professions followed by *hijra* people, such as *badhai* (traditional dancing). Thus, the *hijra* community becomes a safe haven for gender transition, security, and alternative sources of livelihood.

Aravani people face difficulties in their everyday lives within the larger society. *Aravani* and MTF transgender people are prohibited from using ladies' restrooms, and on trains, women do not allow *aravani* people to travel in the ladies' compartment, while men don't like them in the gentlemen's compartment. However, women have slowly started accepting their presence in the ladies' compartment.

Aravani-phobia (transphobia) mostly exists within the middle class and upper class. *Aravani* people are often unable to rent an apartment. So *aravani* and transgender people often live in slums where there is much less discrimination against them.

The *hijra/aravani* identities in India help us to understand that a "third gender" does exist there, but it is understood mainly within a religious-cultural context. Issues faced by the *aravanis* or other MTF trans(gender) people are similar. Transgender activists are striving hard to get equal recognition, opportunities, and space in mainstream society.

Shabeena Francis Saveri received her PhD from Tata Institute of Social Sciences, Mumbai, in 2013. She has presented her research at national and international conferences and facilitated LGBT consultations both in and outside of India working with nongovernmental organizations and nonprofit organizations. She has also worked as a full-time lecturer in sociology in a college in Mumbai.

Pressing for Change: The Foundation Stone of a Gender-Queer Europe
Stephen Whittle

In 1992, as Sandy Stone sat in the California sun writing "The Empire Strikes Back," in which she called for trans activists and scholars "to speak from outside the boundaries of gender, beyond the constructed oppositional nodes which have been predefined as the only positions from which discourse is possible" and to reclaim our histories (Stone 1992), I cannot imagine she thought a small group of trans people in the United Kingdom would be the first to step up to the mark.

February 1992: Rain in icy daggers was sleeting down onto the dark London streets when half a dozen transsexual people—Mark Rees, David McDermott, Mjka Scott, Krystyna Sheffield, Linda, and I—walked into the entrance to the Houses of Parliament. It was a monumental moment in so many ways, but largely because it was the first time ever that we had walked as a herd, we three very tall women and three very short men. That had never previously happened because there had always been concern that if seen together, we would be recognized for what we were: transsexual people. On this occasion, we were prepared to take that risk because we had very little to lose.

Mark was unemployed. Years earlier he had been thrown out of the Women's Royal Naval Service after admitting that he had never kissed, never mind slept with a woman whom he had found very attractive. David, a high school gym teacher, had been hounded out of his job when he had told them he was receiving successful treatment for a health condition and growing a beard. Mjka, a rather successful actor, was now struggling to get any auditions. Krystyna, a successful airline pilot, had been sacked for wearing her uniform correctly. I was self-employed in the building trade, after years of being sacked from too many jobs had left me depressed and demoralized. Linda was working as a temporary receptionist, despite her extensive engineering career. We really were the lowest of the low, the sexual perverts of the sensationalist press. We were simply not persons enough to have any protection under the law; we were transsexual people. But we had been promised a meeting with a member of Parliament, Alex Carlile. The police officers on duty who searched our bags looked very closely at us, but we had made sure that we were dressed in our "Sunday best," and we were very polite. As we walked past the Victorian Gothic splendor of the St. Stephen's entrance lobby into the history of the eleventh-century Westminster Hall, we knew their eyes were still on us.

Our meeting with Alex Carlile inspired us. He gave us cups of tea and three key pieces of advice: go across Parliament Square into Granny's Café and organize ourselves; write a letter on no more than one side of a sheet of paper and send it with a glossy leaflet to every new and returning member of Parliament in the forthcoming election; and finally, get a name for our organization that didn't include the "T" word if we wanted our letters to be read.

We had not realized that we were an organization until that moment. Over in the café, we put our hands into our pockets and between us managed to come up with enough money to buy whatever was needed for the letters and glossy "brochure." The name was brainstormed; this was about change, particularly the need for the press to start writing about us in a respectful and realistic manner. The law had to change; there was the work we would do to change things; and of course, it was about our "sex changes." By 5:30 p.m. we had become Press for Change (PFC).

Over the next ten years we became accidental autoethnographers, repeatedly telling the story—our stories—that challenged the view that gender is only binary. PFC was the start of what Stone had demanded: a new political trans movement, not just in the United Kingdom, but globally. We were reclaiming not just our history, but also our right to be full citizens of our country and the world. It was our ideas, our writing, our educational and social projects, and our challenges to legislators and the judiciary that became trans activism. And it was our use of new technologies. PFC's website was, in 1995, the biggest political website in the world, through which we developed a new sense of purpose and a new way of fighting for thousands of trans people throughout the world.

PFC's campaigning went beyond the medical trope within which we were sentenced to existing as mentally ill perverts, as lesser beings. PFC demanded our human rights, including those of nondiscrimination and equality in employment, and when accessing housing, goods, and services. PFC also demanded relationship recognition rights. Nobody was insisting on marriage then, just to be "next of kin" at a dying partner's bedside. PFC also insisted that trans people were entitled to safety in both public and private domains, and fought for access to medical gender reassignment for those who wanted it. PFC became, almost certainly, the most successful and effective national (or international) transgender activist group in the world. With the success of its campaigns, using political lobbying, social education, and legal case work, PFC successfully pushed cases through both the Court of Justice of the European Union and the European Court of Human Rights. By the early 2000s, PFC had successfully campaigned for gender recognition under the law, without prior medical requirements, to be enshrined in the United Kingdom's Gender Recognition Act of 2004.

PFC provided an effective model of how to campaign for legal and social change. That model has now been adopted by many other national and international transgender groups. The wider trans community in Europe, in particular Transgender Europe, has organized following PFC's working model. This has enabled them to bring further successful claims to Europe's courts, including demands for inclusion in antidiscrimination legislation, spousal and family rights, adoption rights, an equal right of access to health care, and other forms of social entitlement that are afforded to heterosexual, gender-normative people in Europe (Whittle 2002).

The transgender activist movement has very effectively engaged with the European institutions, leading to significant reports and publications to come from the Fundamental Rights Agency of the European Union, the European Commission, and the office of the Council of Europe's Commissioner for Human Rights, which has funded new research into health care, and ensured full trans inclusion in new LGBT social and legal research (Hammarberg 2009). In 1990, the European transgender movement was lagging far behind the LGB rights movement. PFC's work enabled trans activism to catch up and, as a result, Europe is now very gender-queer.

References

Hammarberg, Thomas. 2009. *Human Rights and Gender Identity.* Strasbourg: Commissioner for Human Rights.

Stone, Sandy. 1992. "The Empire Strikes Back: A Posttranssexual Manifesto. The Authorized Version." *Camera Obscura: Feminism, Culture, and Media Studies* 10 (2: 29), pp. 158–176.

Whittle, Stephen. 2002. *Respect and Equality: Transsexual and Transgender Rights.* London: Cavendish.

Stephen Whittle, a law professor at Manchester Metropolitan University, is a world expert on transgender law. He is a past president of the World Professional Association for Transgender Health (WPATH), a past chair of Transgender Europe, a founder of the UK's FTM Network, and a founder and, for more than twenty-five years, a co-chair of Press for Change. Whittle's work has been recognized: Human Rights Award, Officer of the Order of the British Empire (OBE), Sylvia Rivera Award for Transgender Studies, Virginia Prince Lifetime Achievement Award, Lambda Literary

*Award, US LGBT Bar Association's Frank Kameny Award, Fellow
of the Academy of Social Sciences, and National Transgender Lifetime Achievement Award.*

A Trans Youth at Catholic School
Tru Wilson

I have had a lot of experiences in my life. The majority of my
experiences were normal teenage things like my first crush and
my first time skipping school. But that's not what we're here
to talk about now, is it? This essay is me telling you (the reader)
all about my achievements, experiences, and hopes for the
LGBTQ2+ community. Specifically, my experience with the
Catholic school district of Vancouver, Canada. And the human
rights complaint I filed against them a few years ago.

When I was a little boy I was very feminine. At playtime I
would always run to the princess dress and fairy wings, or the
dollhouse. My parents were a bit worried at first, but the teacher
told them not to worry. "Kids experiment with all sorts of
things to figure out what they like," she told them. "Eventually
he'll start drifting over to the boy's side of the playroom." Boy,
were they wrong. As time went on my parents were starting to
realize that my feminine qualities were not fading quickly. In
fact, they weren't fading at all. So my mom started researching.
She found a study that showed that 75 percent of boys who like
girl things turned out to be gay. There was the off chance that
your child was transgender, but that was highly unlikely. So,
for a while, my mom just assumed I was gay.

By this time I was at a Catholic school. I had made a large
group of friends consisting mainly of girls. And when I went
home I would dress up in some of my mom's old dresses and
throw on a wig. My dad would come home from a long day of
work and see his oldest son running up to him in fairy wings
and a prom dress. My dad was getting worried because as a kid
he was bullied for his skin being darker than the kids at his

school. He didn't want his son to suffer the same fate of being bullied for being different from the other kids.

Meanwhile, my mom started researching what it meant to be transgender. She found a documentary about transgender children and wanted to show it to me. So one fateful night my mom, dad, and I sat down on the couch and my mom pulled the documentary up on the TV. After it was over, I broke down into tears and, in between sobs, I said, "That's me, I'm transgender." Immediately after that my mom took me to the store. I got my first feminine T-shirt, skirt, tights, headband, everything. We started going to see counselors as a family. Then just me. The counselor we were seeing recommended we take the summer to just let me be me, and see how it goes. My parents and I agreed.

After what my family called "the summer of Trey," I had fully transitioned in everything. I had transitioned at home, in sports, at my dance school, everything. There was just one target left, school. Keep in mind this was a semi-private Catholic school. My parents already knew it wasn't going to be easy. And they were right. The school wouldn't budge. Even after showing them letter after letter after letter from multiple doctors saying that my parents were doing the right thing, they weren't convinced. Then they started recommending their own doctors to give me assessments. Soon my parents realized that they weren't going to get anywhere with the school, and we left.

Not long after we left, my parents and I filed a human rights complaint against the Catholic school district of Vancouver. And halfway through, my mom told me that I had a choice. I could either accept the progress we had made, and I could live my life incognito. Or I could go public with it and press further to have the policy how I wanted it. And I told her that it would be nice to live life as a "normal" girl, but if I could stop a child from having to go through the horrors I went through at that school, then it was worth it. So we were able to get a policy made that allows all children to use their preferred bathrooms, uniforms, names, and pronouns. Believe me, it's not a perfect policy, but at least it's a start.

Since then my advocacy has grown. I have been on panels, given presentations at universities and schools, been on the cover of *Vancouver* magazine, and named one of the most powerful people in Vancouver, and now I get the chance to do a TEDxEastVan presentation that I am stoked for! But I don't advocate because I want to be in magazines and newspapers. I mean, it's not the worst thing to get the publicity, but that's not why I do it. I do it because it's important to be visible as a trans person so that other youth know that they are not alone.

I was so fortunate to be born into a family built on love and acceptance. But there are so many youth out there who are stuck in homes that treat them like garbage. They are forced to live their lives lying to everyone about who they really are. As they go through puberty, their body turns against them and their reflection becomes a stranger. It is the worst feeling knowing you are becoming the exact person you fear the most, and knowing you can do nothing about it. They fall deeper and deeper into a never-ending hole where their screams and cries for help are silenced. I have chosen to be the voice for those who don't have one. And I solemnly swear that, like a child in a candy store, I won't stop screaming until I get what I want. What I need. Heck, what we all need. Love. That's it. I want my children to be born into a world where you can be whoever you are. With no limitations, no holes, no lying to yourself about who you are on the inside. I want to see a world where no one is afraid anymore. A world where everyone has a voice. A world of love.

Tru Wilson is an articulate and bold fourteen-year-old transgender advocate from Vancouver, BC. Tru first made headlines when she filed a human rights complaint against her local Catholic school board for not supporting her transition, which resulted in the first known policy in any Catholic school in North America supporting a child's transition. Since then, Tru has become a popular speaker for trans rights. In 2015 Tru was recognized by Vancouver *magazine as one of the city's fifty most powerful and influential people. In 2016, she was named Options for Sexual Health's Sexual Health Champion, and in 2017 her entire family was nominated to be grand marshals in the Vancouver Pride Parade.*

WHO, the ICD, and the Young Children
Sam Winter

The World Health Organisation (WHO) is responsible for publication and periodic update of the *International Classification of Diseases and Related Health Problems* (ICD) (World Health Organization 1990). By the time you read this, WHO's governing body, the World Health Assembly (WHA), probably will have approved the eleventh edition, the first revision in over a quarter century. The ICD is used by doctors, researchers, health care planners and funders, and governments in the provision of health care services across the globe. Psychiatrists use the ICD's chapter on "Mental and Behavioural Disorders" more than they use the American Psychiatric Association's higher-profile DSM (the *Diagnostic and Statistical Manual of Mental Disorders*) (American Psychiatric Association 2013). So the ICD-11 matters a lot for people around the world.

Since 1990, trans people's access to gender-affirming care has been through diagnoses such as "Transsexualism," "Gender Identity Disorder of Childhood," and other "Gender Identity Disorders." These diagnoses are located in the ICD's "Mental and Behavioural Disorders" chapter in a subsection on "Disorders of Adult Personality and Behaviour."

The classification of trans people's experiences as mentally disordered has long been a matter of concern to trans people (and many of their health care providers) and has had terrible consequences for trans people. First, it has undermined their hopes for gender identity recognition. When transgender (wo)men are seen as mentally disordered people, they are likely to be seen as mentally disordered (wo)men. Second, it has undermined their access to health care. It has caused insurance coverage problems because policies often don't cover mental illness. Arguably, it also has undermined patient autonomy, because health care providers who see their patients as mentally disordered are less confident in their patients' ability to make decisions about their health care.

As I write, big changes are in store for the ICD-11. A WHO Working Group on Sexual Disorders and Sexual Health (of which I was a member) made several proposals relevant for trans people and their health care providers. First, that all the old trans diagnoses should be replaced with just two: "Gender Incongruence of Adolescence and Adulthood" (GIAA) and (for children below the age of puberty) "Gender Incongruence of Childhood" (GIC). Second, that these diagnoses should be taken out of the "Mental and Behavioural Disorders" chapter and placed in an entirely new one concerned with sexual and gender health—a chapter that attempts to do justice to the importance and complexity of sexuality and gender in all of our lives.

These are transformative proposals. As I write, the key players in WHO appear to have accepted our proposals. By the time you read this, the key diagnoses employed to facilitate trans people's access to health care should be in that new chapter, and the trans experience should no longer be regarded as a mental disorder. Go to the ICD-11 on the Web and check. If these proposals have not been incorporated, it will likely be because conservative thinking in WHO got the better of the decision makers.

While you are on the ICD-11 site, be sure to also check if the "Gender Incongruence of Childhood" (GIC) diagnosis is there. This diagnosis for young children below the age of puberty was by far the most controversial recommendation to come out of the Working Group.

Few questioned the need for a GIAA diagnosis in the ICD-11. For many trans adolescents and adults, gender-affirming health care can change, even save, their lives. Across the world, in both public and insurance-funded health care systems, any substantial or continuing health care is contingent on the person concerned having such a diagnosis.

But GIC is a bit different. Those opposed (and I am one of them) argue that the proposed diagnosis is unnecessary. Gender-diverse children under the age of puberty don't need medical interventions. The GIC diagnosis pathologizes diversity; it perpetuates stigma, promotes noninclusive policies in schools, and promotes repressive "treatment" approaches, all without any redeeming purpose (Winter 2017). Those in favor argue that the diagnosis can provide a focus for research on childhood gender diversity and the development of health care services for such children (Drescher, Cohen-Kettenis, and Reed 2016).

The argument that a diagnosis provides a focus for research is deeply flawed. In the early 1990s, around the time that the "Homosexuality" diagnosis was taken out of the ICD, fewer than 1,000 journal papers on same-sex attraction were published each year. Nowadays, the annual figure is nearly 3,500. As for the development of services, today around 200–250 of those papers annually focus on training and support for professionals. The consequence is that health care providers can now support same-sex-attracted people far better than they could in the early 1990s. We didn't need a homosexuality diagnosis to achieve this. It is unlikely we need a GIC diagnosis either. As for development of health care services, it seems likely to me that this is actually about health care providers wanting to get paid for their services.

At this point, it is worth considering what health care prepubertal gender-diverse children might need. They don't need surgery, hormones, or puberty blockers. They just need space (and the love) to allow them to meet the developmental challenges they face: to explore who they are, to embrace their eventual identity, to become comfortable expressing it, and perhaps to manage any hostile reactions from others. They may also benefit from services providing counseling support and information along the way. So may their parents and teachers. Key clinicians have been telling us for years that these children thrive when allowed to be who they are. And now research is beginning to confirm it.

None of this justifies the inclusion of a GIC diagnosis in the ICD-11. Consider other young people facing similar developmental challenges. Same-sex-attracted youngsters, for example, go through a process of exploring their sexual preferences, embracing them as part of themselves, learning to become comfortable expressing them, and learning to manage the reactions of others. They may benefit from counseling and other services. Their parents or teachers may too. Youngsters thrive when people around them affirm their diversity. And we no longer believe we should target same-sex attraction with a diagnosis. WHO got rid of the homosexuality diagnosis decades ago and was right to do so. The diagnosis turned diversity into a mental disorder and was responsible for great harm to same-sex-attracted individuals so labeled.

Consider youngsters from minority or mixed-ethnic backgrounds. Once again, these individuals often need to explore their sense of identity, learn to embrace it and become comfortable expressing it, and learn to manage hostility from others. They may need support in doing so. Here, too, we understand that the best form of support is affirmative. We understand also that these individuals are not in any way sick or disordered. Medicine does not employ an "ethnic incongruence" diagnosis with these young people, and no one is proposing one.

So when you look at the ICD-11 on the Web, check to see if "Gender Incongruence of Childhood" is there. If it is, it is because WHO was not ready to approach gender diversity in childhood the way it approaches other youth diversities.

References

American Psychiatric Association. 2013. *Diagnostic and Statistical Manual of Mental Disorders,* 5th ed. Washington, DC: American Psychiatric Association.

Drescher, J., P. Cohen-Kettenis, and G. Reed. 2016. "Gender Incongruence of Childhood in the ICD-11: Controversies, Proposal, and Rationale." *Lancet Psychiatry* 3, no. 3: 297–304.

Winter, S. 2017. "Gender Trouble: WHO, ICD-11 and the Trans Kids." *Sexual Health* 14, no. 5: 423–430.

World Health Organization. 1990. *International Classification of Diseases and Related Health Problems*, 10th ed. Geneva: World Health Organization. Note: On June 18, 2018, WHO released an advance preview of ICD-11. At the time of writing it is available at https://icd.who.int/browse11 /l-m/en. The version incorporates all the recommendations made by the Working Group on Sexual Disorders and Sexual Health, including the recommendation for the Gender Incongruence of Childhood diagnosis. ICD-11 is currently slated for approval at the World Health Assembly of May 2019, with a rollout on January 1, 2022.

Sam Winter is a member of the Sexology Team at the School of Public Health, Curtin University, Perth, Australia. He researches in and advocates for the health and rights of trans people worldwide. He was a WHO Working Group member recommending ICD-11's reclassification of trans diagnoses. He authored Lost in Transition, *the first UN report on trans health, and was a lead author for the groundbreaking transgender health series in* Lancet.

Birth, Death, and Things in Between: Challenges of Aging for Gender Non-Conforming Persons
Tarynn M. Witten

I came to the field of aging studies over forty years ago as a mathematician who was trying to make a mathematical model of how genetic recombination could lead to an increased likelihood of cancerous traits. I was also a medical student interested in working with elders (geriatrics). While I was still in school, I attended a presentation on cellular aging that I found fascinating. A year later, I attended a presentation on metastasis, cancer, and aging. My career path was set. I would work on the problem of age-related cancer and its treatment.

Twenty years into my professional career, I was asked to carry out a research survey to examine the subject of violence and abuse against transgender-identified individuals. The study results truly scared me on many levels and set me off on a new path of aging research. I was deeply concerned with how elders of the transgender community were going to live out their lives in a world that often did not seem to care about them. Most health care professionals are not trained to work with trans elders, and many of them refused to work with the trans population. At that time, I was forty years old and trans, and I was deeply worried about what would happen to me as I got older. I would dedicate the next twenty years to research in the field of transgender aging.

The current generation of transgender-identified persons is the first truly out, older age group that is demanding care as they age. In the early days (1950s–1980s), there was a miniscule amount of information on health care challenges faced by the transgender/transsexual community, and there was absolutely no research on the needs of elders. Slowly (in the 1980s–1990s), research began addressing the needs of the elder trans-identified population. We began to understand the general challenges around issues like medical treatment, mental health, violence and abuse, and HIV. My work focused on understanding the general demographics and needs of individuals who were fifty and older. The more I carried out my research, the more I realized how naïve we were and how much work was needed. But research costs money, and in those days there was no funding available for the needed research, so I used my personal resources to fund the work that I was doing.

Much remains to be understood about the challenges of aging in gender non-conforming (GNC) communities across all cultures and nations. While there is a growing information base in medical treatment for members of the GNC population, focus on the elders of this community is slow to increase. Little is known about topics like resilience, religiosity, end-of-life care, HIV and aging, in-home care, and more. Few caregivers are trained to look after GNC-identified persons. Many of today's elders have little savings and are forced to make difficult choices between transitioning and surviving on what little income they have.

When I started my research, there was only one generation of GNC people that we knew about. We now have multiple different age groups in the GNC population, each with its own biomedical and psychosocial needs, about which we know very little. For example, we know little about the effects of very long-term hormone use. We know little about how to develop community outreach programs that will meet the needs of each of the age groups in the GNC population. In addition, we need to understand how being a GNC person intersects with race, class, ability, immigration status, and other realities that influence the aging processes.

As one of my survey respondents so elegantly said, "No one ever chooses to be transgendered and punished for it by being cut off from what society has to offer." This is true for all gender non-conforming persons.

Tarynn M. Witten, PhD, is a full professor of Biological Complexity and adjunct faculty in Physics and in Gender and Women's Studies at Virginia Commonwealth University. She has written over forty books and other publications, and presented over fifty talks, about aging in the GNC population. Dr Witten identifies as a gender non-conforming female. Her website is http://www .people.vcu.edu/~tmwitten.

Introduction

This chapter focuses on the profiles of individuals and organizations that are important to the advancement and acceptance of trans, non-binary, and Two-Spirit people in culture, health care, history, and society. Many of the individuals profiled here have been pioneers for the rights of trans, non-binary, and Two-Spirit people. The organizations and institutions profiled have also been groundbreaking in providing care and resources for trans, non-binary, and Two-Spirit people.

Historical Researchers in Sexology

The following people are important to the field of sexology, which arose in the nineteenth century and is still considered a crucial field of study in the medical, behavioral, and social sciences today. Early sexology was a way to create taxonomies for a broad spectrum of sexual diversity. Although "gender" was not really a term used by the earliest sexologists, many of their ideas about sexuality would later evolve into ideas about what is today understood to be gender.

Mara Keisling, executive director for the National Center for Transgender Equality (NCTE), speaks during a rally for transgender equality on Capitol Hill, June 9, 2017 in Washington, D.C. The NCTE has published very important research about trans people in the United States. (Drew Angerer/ Getty Images)

Richard von Krafft-Ebing (1840–1902)

Richard von Krafft-Ebing, who is also known as the grandfather of sexology, was an Austrian scientist who, over decades, wrote what is, to this day, one of the largest studies in the science of sexology. *Psychopathia Sexualis: With Especial Reference to Antipathic Sexual Instinct: A Medico-Forensic Study* was first published German in 1886 and then translated into English in 1892. Although much of Krafft-Ebing's work has been displaced by more current thought, it still has deep cultural influence in that many of his ideas about sexual behavior and gender identity can still be found in common stereotypes about LGBTQ2+ people.

Krafft-Ebing wrote *Psychopathia Sexualis*, in large part, to look at sexual differences and move them out of the realm of religion and sin and into the realm of science and medicine. Overall, he helped to move authoritative discussions of sexual and gender differences out of the hands of Christian clerics and toward more scientific theories. In considering everything as *sexual difference,* and not differentiating between sexual orientation and gender identity, Krafft-Ebing continued a precedent of conflating sexual orientation and gender identity. Krafft-Ebing considered what is today called trans, non-binary, or Two-Spirit identity as the most degenerate level of homosexuality.

One of the distinguishing features of *Psychopathia Sexualis* is that Krafft-Ebing interviewed hundreds of people who did not fall within what were then the commonly held parameters of normal. They were willing to give him their stories, in many cases, because they did not want to feel alone, and he made it clear that he was interviewing hundreds of people with similar sexual differences. Many of his interviewees also noted that they wanted to be studied so that the medical field and the general public could better understand diversity in nature. Krafft-Ebing provided detailed descriptions of several people whose stories might be understood as trans. In one example, Case 122, who was assigned male at birth, tells Krafft-Ebing, "At an early age I took a dislike to the manly sports practised by

my companions; liked to play with little girls, who suited my
character better than boys; was shy, and easily blushed," and
that when he meets men he finds attractive, their charms affect
him, "as if I were a real woman" (Krafft-Ebing 2012, 375).
Krafft-Ebing referred to this case as an example of "effemina-
tion." If they were alive today, Case 122 might identify as a gay
or bisexual man, or perhaps as a trans person. At the time,
though, Krafft-Ebing did not make a distinction between sexual orientation and gender identity.

Magnus Hirschfeld (1868–1935)

Sexologist Magnus Hirschfeld opened the Institute for Sexual
Science in Germany in 1919. Some of the first known gender
affirmation surgeries took place at the institute. Hirschfeld
made it clear that he wanted to use the science of sexology to
bring about a greater understanding of people's differences. He
wrote, "I believe in Science, and I am convinced that Science,
and above all the Natural Sciences, must bring mankind, not
only truth, but with truth, Justice, Liberty and Peace for all
men" (Mancini 2010, 31). Hirschfeld spent his entire adult life
using the science of sexology to help eliminate prejudice against
people who were not heterosexual and heteronormative, and
people who were not cisgender and cisnormative.

Hirschfeld's Institut für Sexualwissenschaft (Institute for Sex
Research or Institute for Sexology) was in Berlin, which at that
time, under the Weimar Republic, was one of the most open-
minded cities in the world where matters of gender diversity
and sexual orientation were concerned. The institute was the
first of its kind in the world and proved to be a safe place for
anyone wanting counseling and/or treatment for issues around
sex, sexual orientation, and gender identity. People visiting the
clinic ranged from heterosexual couples who were having trouble conceiving, to homosexual and bisexual women and men
who wanted to find community and a medical team who would
respect them, to people who felt that their sex and gender
assigned at birth were not right for them. Hirschfeld welcomed

all people to his clinic with what, today, we would call a "patient-centered" approach to their well-being. Part of the basis for Hirschfeld's empathy and kindness were his own identities as a Jew and a homosexual. One of his biographers notes the following about his approach to the patients coming to the institute:

> He listened attentively and without judgment to his patients' accounts. . . . The emphasis of his treatment was placed on how the patients felt about and experienced their own conditions that society deemed pathological. . . . He encouraged his patients to understand and accept their natures and express them without remorse. (Mancini 2010, 81)

As a part of the thriving homosexual community in Berlin, Hirschfeld began to notice that there were differences between homosexual men who enjoyed dressing in drag as part of a performance, and people who were presumed to be homosexual but who cross-dressed because they felt like women. Although there is a lot of controversy around when the actual term *transvestite* came into use (there are forms of the word dating back over 500 years in Italian, French, and Spanish), what is clear is that Hirschfeld utilized the term to denote people who did not identify with their sex assigned at birth, but rather with the gender identity they expressed by way of cross-dressing.

Many police and medical authorities were still using Krafft-Ebing's idea that cross-dressing meant someone was homosexual, and Paragraph 175 of the German Penal Code made male homosexuality illegal in Germany. Hirschfeld worked with local police in Berlin to get special identity cards for people who were transvestites so that they would not be arrested for being homosexual. By doing so, Hirschfeld was successful in making sure that people whom we would understand to be trans had legitimate identification to prevent them from being arrested.

In 1930, Hirschfeld served as the anatomical authority for the gender affirmation procedures for Lili Elbe, one of the first gender affirmation surgeries in the West. Initially, the procedures seemed to be successful; however, after a year of battling infections and complications, Elbe died. Two years after Lili Elbe's death, while Hirschfeld was out of the country on a speaking tour, the new Nazi Party burned down the institute, including Hirschfeld's extensive library, which may have been the largest in the world chronicling sexuality and gender. As a homosexual Jewish man, Hirschfeld was unable to return to Berlin for fear that he would be transported to a concentration camp. He died in 1935 in exile in Nice, France.

Harry Benjamin (1885–1986)

Harry Benjamin was one of Magnus Hirschfeld's students at the institute in Berlin. His book, *The Transsexual Phenomenon*, which was published in 1966, after he had immigrated to the United States, was the most important book on transsexualism, and one of the most important books in the entire field of sexology, in the twentieth century. Benjamin's book was groundbreaking because it was the first to recommend full treatment for transsexual people. Unlike the works of many sexologists before him, Harry Benjamin's work was published in English and was accessible to anyone who could go into a public library and sit down and read it. Most other sexological writings from people like Krafft-Ebing and Hirschfeld, even if they were translated into English, were not accessible to lay people, but were aimed toward scientists and doctors.

Benjamin's book was accessible in terms of being available for people to read; however, the gender affirmation procedures that he discussed in the book were not necessarily truly accessible to all people interested in undergoing them. For example, if someone who identified as a trans woman did not look or act "feminine enough," they were often denied gender affirmation procedures. Certainly, at the time, trans people who identified themselves as trans *and* gay, lesbian, or bisexual were denied access to hormones and surgical procedures.

In 1979, the Harry Benjamin International Gender Dysphoria Association (HBIGDA) was formed and named in honor of Benjamin's pioneering work. With an entire field of medicine opening up to gender affirmation procedures, there needed to be a set of guidelines and a common code of ethics for medical professionals and medical clinics. The *Standards of Care* (SOC) are a set of health care standards for trans people originally issued by HBIGDA and later by the successor organization, the World Professional Association for Transgender Health (WPATH). There have been seven editions of the SOC because the issues have changed and treatment approaches have evolved over time.

Important Historical Gender-Diverse Individuals

The people explored in this section all present complex examples of gender diversity in historical contexts. Whether all of these individuals would identify today on the trans, non-binary, or Two-Spirit spectrum is not known. Certainly, an argument can be made that some of these historical figures, even before medical gender affirmation was a possibility, would have identified as gender diverse; for example, Catalina/Don Antonio de Erauso, born in sixteenth-century Spain, and We'Wha of the Zuni Nation, born in nineteenth-century New Mexico. Their stories exemplify the ways that the gender binary has always been transgressed. Other people in this section, like Michael Dillon and Roberta Cowell, were some of the earliest people known to go through medically supervised gender affirmation processes.

Pharaoh Hatshepsut (1508?–1458 BCE)

For two decades between 1478 and 1458 BCE Pharaoh Hatshepsut ruled over Egypt during a time of exceptional peace and prosperity. Hatshepsut first came to power when Thutmose II died at a young age. Thutmose II and Hatshepsut had a daughter together; however, Thutmose II's son, Thutmose III, had been born to a secondary wife. Because Hatshepsut was Thutmose II's primary wife and the aunt of Thutmose III, the boy was crowned, but Hatshepsut, in fact, ruled as his regent.

During the second year of Thutmose III's reign, while Hatshepsut was acting as regent, she began to transition to becoming a king herself. Over the course of her twenty years in power, Hatshepsut gradually moved from having artists and temple builders depict her as a queen—a ruler standing in long skirts with her feet close together—to depicting her as a king with a beard, standing in masculine hunting clothing with legs apart.

The following is a modern historian's account of the change in Hatshepsut's presentation on statues: "Early on in her kingship, Hatshepsut attempted to add a layer of masculinity to her feminine forms. . . . [A] life-size limestone statue from her Temple of Millions of Years . . . shows [her] without a shirt, wearing only a king's kilt, but she retains . . . delicate facial features, and even the generous hint of feminine breasts. Eventually, Hatshepsut opted for a fully masculinized image in her statuary, showing herself with wide and strong shoulders, firm pectoral muscles, and no sign of breasts" (Cooney 2014, 101).

On the facade of her Temple of Millions of Years, where she depicted herself as a mummified version of the god Osiris, "the first skin color she chose for these statues was yellow ocher, the traditional color of a woman. As time went on, she opted for orange, an androgynous blend. Finally, she decided to fully masculinize her imagery . . . the latest statues [were in] the red ocher of masculinity" (Cooney 2014, 102). Over the course of twenty years, the changing colors in the statues of Hatshepsut show a full transition across the gender binary.

Elagabalus (204–222 CE)

Elagabalus briefly ruled as a Roman emperor during the years 218–222 CE. Possibly partially due to his gender variance, he is often cited as an example of a failed emperor. Due to the passage of time, the brevity of his rule and his life, and because those who came after him considered him to be such a bad emperor, we know very little about him. However, he was known at the time for his sensuous beauty, enhanced by the use of cosmetics, feminine clothing, and feminine mannerisms.

Ancient historians reported that he wanted to be known as "Empress" and that he offered half of the Roman Empire to any surgeon who could give him female genitalia (Wasson 2013; Mijatovic n.d.).

Jeanne d'Arc (1412–1431)

Jeanne d'Arc (also known as Joan of Arc) was born in 1412 in the hamlet of Domrémy on what was, at the time, the outskirts of France. Her parents were farmers who worked in communal village pastures. In 1429 at the age of seventeen, Jeanne had a vision from God that she was to dress in men's clothing and help lead France in battle against England, their centuries-old enemy. She went to Prince Charles, who was the heir to the French throne, and proposed to him that she should lead an army of peasants. The prince sent the teenager off with an army of 10,000 peasants. During her time as a military leader, Jeanne remained devoutly religious and demanded the same of her soldiers.

D'Arc's success against the English helped France transform into a free nation-state. However, just after she led the army to victory, she was abducted by sympathizers to England's cause. The new French king had become jealous and fearful of d'Arc's power, so rather than pay the king's ransom for her safe return, he did nothing. In the English-controlled prison at Rouen, d'Arc was chained and assaulted, particularly because she refused to wear women's clothing. She continued to tell everyone that her directive to wear men's clothing and to fight for France came from God.

Initially, when her trial began in 1431, d'Arc was charged with witchcraft. The court had to drop the witchcraft charges, though, because d'Arc was clearly a devout Catholic. Ultimately, the judges sentenced her to death because of her refusal to dress in women's clothes and act in the ways they thought women should act. Jeanne d'Arc never wavered in her claim that her masculine gender expression came as a directive from God. Until the moment of her execution, she refused women's clothing and refused to act in any way that was deemed proper for a woman. Jeanne d'Arc was burned at the stake on May 30, 1431. In 1456 the church completely recanted the original sentence, and Jeanne d'Arc, who had been put to death for heresy because of gender nonconformity, was later canonized as a saint.

Catalina/Don Antonio de Erauso (1585–1650)

Catalina/Don Antonio de Erauso, also known as the Lieutenant Nun, was born in 1585 into a large Basque family in the north of Spain. At the age of four, de Erauso was placed in a Dominican convent where some of the nuns were abusive. At the age of fifteen, de Erauso got into an argument with an older nun who became violent. At that point, de Erauso escaped from the convent and fled to a nearby forest:

There, I holed up for three days, planning and re-planning and cutting myself out a suit of clothes. With the blue woolen bodice I had made a pair of breeches, and with the green petticoat I wore underneath, a doublet and hose— my nun's habit was useless and I threw it away, I cut my hair and threw it away. (de Erauso 1996, 4)

Shortly after beginning to live as a young man, de Erauso joined the crew of a ship and sailed to Peru where, for several years, he had numerous adventures working on the ship, fighting in battles, and spending time going from town to town drinking and gambling.

In Guamanga, Peru, de Erauso encountered bad luck at a gambling house, got into a sword fight, and killed a sheriff attempting to arrest him. A senior bishop on his way to church intervened just as the sheriff's men were about to arrest or kill de Erauso. The bishop took the wounded de Erauso into the safety of the church. When the bishop asked de Erauso to recount his story, he revealed that he had been assigned female at birth. At first, the bishop did not believe de Erauso, but de Erauso agreed to a full physical examination by two elderly women who found that de Erauso's virginity was still intact. De Erauso was then sent back into a convent in the year 1620.

Six years later, in 1626, de Erauso's story had become legendary, and Pope Urban VIII gave de Erauso a choice between continuing to be a woman in a convent or to be a man who would leave the convent and go back out into the world. De Erauso chose to embrace manhood. One of the last accounts we have of de Erauso was of him living in Mexico in 1630 as Don Antonio de Erauso, a merchant and mule driver. Accounts of him from the 1640s present him as a person of courage who everyone knew had been assigned female at birth, but who dressed as a man and wore a sword and dagger.

Chevalier/Chevalière d'Éon (1728–1810)

Charles-Geneviève-Louise-Auguste-André-Thimothée d'Éon de Beaumont—known more popularly as the Chevalier/Chevalière d'Éon—is one of the most famous of gender-diverse historical figures. (D'Éon was truly gender fluid, so throughout, d'Éon will be referred to as Chevalier/Chevalière and with neutral pronouns as has commonly been done with their history.) The Chevalier/Chevalière d'Éon was born on October 5, 1728, in Tonnerre, France, into a family with a moderate amount of money and connections to the French court. D'Éon died on May 21, 1810, in exile and in poverty in London, England.

For the first forty-nine years of life, d'Éon lived as a man and held several important positions in the French government including as a captain of the dragoons and as a French spy in England. While d'Éon lived as a man in both England and France, people who knew d'Éon frequently thought that the Chevalier was really a woman who dressed like a man in order to prove that women could do anything that men could do. The rumors that d'Éon was a woman disguised as a man got to the point that in 1777, King Louis XVI ordered d'Éon to wear women's clothing and to cease masquerading as a man.

In 1785, d'Éon decided to return to England; however, the French government refused to grant the Chevalier/Chevalière d'Éon a monthly allowance, which was highly unusual since d'Éon had won the highest military honor as captain of the dragoons. One explanation was that women could not collect pensions from the state. Therefore, d'Éon was unable to collect any veteran's pay for all the years of service in the dragoons and as one of the king's spies. Queen Charlotte of England did provide a small allowance to d'Éon each month, although it was barely enough to pay for food and lodging. D'Éon attempted to make a living through sensationalized public sword duels featuring d'Éon as a woman French military veteran, until an injury at one of the duels caused d'Éon to retire. Upon death in 1810 in London, d'Éon's body was examined by several doctors who reported that, clearly, d'Éon had male genitalia.

During the thirty years that d'Éon lived as a woman, one of their big projects was writing their memoirs and chronicling the lives of numerous people who had been assigned female at birth and who had become men and lived pious lives within the Catholic Church. Between the writings of their own life and the connection that they made between themselves as a person assigned male at birth who was living as a woman and the people assigned female at birth who lived as men to become priests, d'Éon left an amazing legacy that articulates an idea of gender-diverse experience well before the term trans had come into use.

There are numerous ways that Chevalier/Chevalière d'Éon has influenced transgender culture. The British sexologist Havelock Ellis, for example, uses the term "Eonism" to describe what today would be called a transgender identity. And one of the earliest underground trans periodicals and support groups, the Beaumont Society in London, was named after d'Éon.

We'Wha (1849–1896)

We'Wha was a famous Two-Spirit person from the Zuni Nation in what is now called New Mexico. Born in 1849, We'Wha became a member of their mother's clan, which was traditional in Zuni culture. As a teenager, We'Wha was a kachina dancer, which was an honored and sacred tradition within Zuni culture. While We'Wha was being trained in the religious traditions that all of the boys learned, they were also being trained in the more typically women's traditions of cooking and weaving. It is clear that within the Zuni community, all of the elders understood that We'Wha was Two-Spirit, and so the young person was educated accordingly.

Over time, We'Wha's skills in weaving and pottery became famous beyond the Zuni Nation and beyond New Mexico. They received several commissions to create pottery for white missionaries who thought We'Wha was a woman and who were ignorant about Two-Spirit identity. These missionaries would often pay We'Wha with beautiful dresses. The Smithsonian Institution in Washington, D.C. commissioned several pieces of pottery from We'Wha as well.

In 1886, We'Wha was asked to be a special guest at the White House where they met with President Grover Cleveland, who referred to them as a Zuni princess.

James Miranda Barry (1789?–1865)

Although there is still a bit of a mystery around the date of birth for James Miranda Barry, who was assigned female at birth, the first official records show that, in December 1809, a youth named James Miranda Barry, claiming to be the age of twelve, signed the matriculation roster at the University of Edinburgh as a literary and medical student. During his time in medical school, Barry took courses that were above and beyond the basic requirements, and from all accounts he succeeded in all of them. His thesis on groin hernias, written in Latin, earned him honors, and he graduated to an apprenticeship with Sir Astley Cooper, one of London's top surgeons.

While in London, the young Dr. Barry did not tend to socialize with the other young men who were apprenticing because they often spent their evenings drinking, gambling, and fighting in the streets. The two hospitals in London where Cooper operated were on the South Bank of the Thames River, which in the early nineteenth century was a poor and rough part of the city: Guy's Hospital, a "voluntary hospital" that specialized in treating people who were seen as incurable, insane, or both; and St. Thomas's Royal Hospital, which treated people with fevers and sexually transmitted infections (STIs). Many hospitals at the time refused to treat STIs because they viewed patients who had them as morally tainted, but St. Thomas's did not turn anyone away.

After his apprenticeship in London, Barry became a surgeon with the British Army and was sent to South Africa. From the moment he arrived in South Africa in 1816, Barry fought social injustices against black South Africans and other marginalized communities. In one instance, he encountered a slave owner who said that one of his slaves had died from overeating; however, when Barry examined the body, he made it public knowledge that the man had been beaten to death. Throughout his time in South Africa, Barry requested to be stationed at both the prison and the leper colony—places where other white British medical practitioners refused to go. Dr. Barry showed compassion by helping to clean the sickest and weakest people himself, and to make sure that everyone had clean water, fresh air, a fresh and clean place to sleep, and a mainly vegetarian diet. Barry himself was a vegetarian his entire adult life.

After his post in South Africa, where he had upset the British Army authorities by his constant complaints about the ways that they treated the black population, he was sent off to Canada where he worked with foot soldiers who were mistreated by their army leaders. While he was in Canada, he became sick and had to retire from the military and move back to London. He died in the summer of 1865 during a heat wave. The charwoman, Sophia Bishop, ignored his request not to be stripped and washed in preparation for burial. When she washed the doctor's body, she found that he had been assigned female at birth. Aside from Sophia Bishop, nobody came to claim the body of Dr. Barry. He was buried at Kensal Green Cemetery in London.

Frances Thompson (1836?–1876)

The only real information that we have about the life of Frances Thompson comes from her appearances at two moments in U.S. history. As she was an African American person who was born into slavery, her birth was most likely not recorded, but in a congressional committee hearing in Memphis, Tennessee, in 1866, she gave her age as thirty, which would make her birth year 1836.

Frances Thompson was a freed slave from Maryland who had made her way to Memphis, Tennessee, where she lived with an entire community of African American freed slaves in South Memphis. Although Tennessee was part of the Confederacy during the Civil War, the Union Army overtook Memphis in 1862, which made the city a safe zone for African American people. By 1866, South Memphis was a booming village with African American schools, African American businesses, and African American Union soldiers living there. During the first week of May 1866, a large group of white men led by police and businessmen crossed over into South Memphis and began burning down all of the buildings, schoolhouses, and churches. They did not stop with the destruction of property, but then began killing African American men and raping African American women. The week-long reign of violence and terror would become known as the Memphis Massacre.

Frances Thompson and her roommate were two of the women raped and brutalized during the violence. One month after the massacre had ended, a group of four white congressmen from Washington, D.C. came to South Memphis to hear the stories of a group of five African American women who wanted to testify about the violence done to them and to their community. Frances Thompson was one of the five brave women who stood up and let her voice be heard. It is one of the first times in the United States when African American women were allowed to legally testify.

Ten years after the congressional committee heard from the survivors of the Memphis Massacre, Frances Thompson was arrested on masquerading charges. In other words, she was arrested for cross-dressing. Thompson had been assigned male at birth, but in depositions after her arrest, she told the authorities that she had always been a girl and that she had always dressed in feminine clothes. Thompson was stripped of her women's clothing, forced into a male prison suit, and then the guards put her on display in the prison yard and charged a fee for people to come look at her. She died shortly after she was released from prison.

What is amazing about Thompson's story is her courage as an African American woman to testify in front of a congressional committee, and her courage, in the face of ridicule and violence from the prison guards and police authorities, to maintain her gender identity as a woman.

Michael Dillon (1915–1962)

Michael Dillon was the first trans man to undergo a medical transition including hormonal treatments and genital surgeries. Dillon was born into Irish aristocracy on May 1, 1915, and raised on a country estate by three unmarried aunts because Dillon's mother had died in childbirth and Dillon's father was elderly, soon to die, and unwilling to care for his children (Hodgkinson 1989). Expressing strong masculinity from a young age, Dillon recalled that he had always felt like a boy growing up. However, in the earliest years of the twentieth century Dillon knew no words to describe either his gender or sexual feelings. Typical of many transsexual men, he was distressed by the arrival of puberty and used a leather belt as a breast binder.

Dillon attended Oxford University as a young adult, where he expressed his masculinity by wearing short hair and dressing in trousers, which was tolerated as a youthful eccentricity. On occasion, during these years, Dillon also dressed and passed as a man. After leaving university, Dillon's appearance generated many rude and aggressive comments whenever Dillon went out in public. In the 1930s, dress codes for women and men were strictly binary and Dillon's appearance confused and angered people.

In 1939, at age twenty-four, Dillon secretly consulted a doctor who was known as an expert in sexuality issues. He was unwilling to become Dillon's doctor, but he had some testosterone pills that had just recently been created for the first time, and gave some to Dillon to try. Dillon's periods stopped, his voice deepened, and he started to grow facial hair, but he still wore a skirt when out in public. With so many changes and a strange appearance, Dillon felt unable to return home. Instead he found men's work while most men were away fighting World War II and changed his name to Michael. Over time, the effects of the testosterone pills became more pronounced and Dillon lived as fully as a man as possible without the benefit of surgical interventions.

By chance, Dillon met a surgeon who agreed to remove his breasts and then introduced him to another surgeon, Sir Harold Gillies, who had some experience rebuilding penises for soldiers whose penises had been damaged in war. Two years later, in 1944, Dillon convinced the registrar of births that a mistake had been made and had his name on his birth certificate official changed. Meanwhile, Dillon went to medical school, became a doctor, and wrote what was probably the first book to consider gender incongruence: *Self: A Study in Endocrinology and Ethics*. Dillon underwent a four-year-long series of genital surgeries with Gillies during every break in medical school and graduated with completed genitals.

In the early 1950s, Dillon met and fell in love with another famous Briton who underwent gender confirmation surgery, Roberta Cowell. Although they grew close for a while, Cowell did not share Dillon's feelings of love and refused his proposal of marriage. This would prove to be the only love affair that Dillon would ever permit himself. Following this rejection, Dillon became a ship's doctor and spent the next six years happily at sea.

In 1958, Dillon's peace was shattered when a journalist discovered and published that there was a discrepancy between two official listings of members of the aristocracy: Debrett's listed him as male but Burke's listed him as female. Dillon then went to India and took up residence at a Buddhist monastery to wait for the media storm to pass. Eventually, he fully embraced Buddhism, renounced all worldly possessions, and became a Rizong monk. He went on to write five more books, including an autobiography and several about Buddhism. Dillon died in 1962, at age forty-seven, of an unknown illness.

Roberta Cowell (1918–2011)

Roberta Cowell, known as Betty to her friends, underwent hormonal and surgical transition from male to female between 1948 and 1951, and had her ID changed in 1951 (Bell 2013; Cowell 1954). She was the first to do so in Britain and her transition predated that of the more renowned Christine Jorgensen. However, her transition did not hit the newspapers until she published her autobiography in 1954, when it became big news. Prior to her transition, Cowell was told by her doctors that some of her physical characteristics, such as her wide hips, narrow shoulders, hair patterns, and some minor breast development, suggested the possibility that she might be intersex.

Cowell was born in 1918 to a very strict upper-middle-class British white Christian family. As a child, Cowell was nicknamed "circumference" and "bottom" because she was then a chubby boy with big hips. According to Cowell, she was insecure about her masculinity while living as a man and overcompensated by being aggressive and hypermasculine. This was expressed in her very conservative attitudes about gender differences, her disgust and aversion for homosexual men, and in her successes as a competitive race car driver and as a fighter pilot in World War II. In 1941, Cowell married a woman who shared a love of racing and together they had two daughters. During the war, Cowell flew many dangerous missions where she did not expect to survive. She was shot down over Germany in 1944 and spent the last six months of the war as a prisoner under very harsh conditions. Cowell separated from her wife in

1948 and they divorced in 1951 when Cowell legally transitioned to female. Cowell never again saw her daughters.

After the war, Cowell returned to race car driving, and entered psychoanalysis where she realized that she needed to be a woman. Although a doctor who examined her at that time saw some possible evidence of an intersex condition, it was not enough to justify gender affirmation surgery on its own. However, Cowell had a friendship with Dr. Michael Dillon, himself a transsexual man and a physician, who removed Cowell's testicles so that she could present herself to authorities as sufficiently intersex to justify a full medical transition. Her full genital surgery was performed by Sir Harold Gillies, the same surgeon who had performed genital surgery on Michael Dillon.

In the 1950s, after her divorce, Roberta Cowell continued to race cars and fly her own airplanes. She took up living with another woman with whom she forged a deep and lasting friendship. By the 1970s her businesses were not doing well; she attempted to write another book, which in the end was never published. She thereafter remained out of public view. After her friend died in 1990, Cowell remained reclusive and suffered a physically difficult old age. She died alone in 2011 at age ninety-three. In contrast to her fame in the 1950s, her death did not make the news until two years later, probably because she had asked for no publicity. Only her immediate neighbors attended her funeral, her wife having predeceased her and her daughters only learning of her death from the newspaper report two years later.

Christine Jorgensen (1926–1989)

Christine Jorgensen was the first transsexual person to achieve international fame when the story of her transition made front-page headlines in the *New York Daily News* on December 1, 1952. In the month following her outing, mainstream news services wrote the equivalent of a 200-page essay about her, much of it doubting her authenticity. Four months later, the *Los Angeles Times* declared her the "most talked about" person in the world. In 1967 she published her own story in *Christine Jorgensen: A Personal Autobiography*, and a sensationalistic movie, *The Christine Jorgensen Story*, was made about her in 1970 (Docter 2008).

Christine Jorgensen was born May 30, 1926, into a Danish American family in New York City and raised in the Bronx. While growing up, as a young boy, Jorgensen was often traumatized by neighborhood children's unkind reactions to her femininity, friendships with girls, and romantic attractions to males. Although Jorgensen never saw herself as homosexual and tried to act the part of a young man in the 1930s, she was not terribly successful at it. In private, she often dressed as the woman she felt herself to be.

After graduating high school and twice failing the medical exam for compulsory military service in World War II, Jorgensen started to work helping to prepare newsreels as World War II was ending. She was surprised to be called back for another military exam and even more surprised to find that this time she passed. At age nineteen, Jorgensen was in the army. Her job, for the fourteen months that she served, was as a clerk helping to process soldiers who were coming home from war and being discharged.

Due to having been given veteran's benefits for her brief and noncombat army service, Jorgensen had enough money to survive even though she rarely worked a steady job during her early twenties. Largely she was consumed with thoughts of being a woman and the depression that she felt about her inability to remedy her gender incongruence. Whenever she could, she scoured public libraries and the popular press for information that might lead to a solution. Gradually, she came to think of herself as a person who suffered from hormonal imbalances and had underdeveloped genitals. Sometime in 1949, Jorgensen found a doctor who gave her a prescription for estrogen pills and she started to feel much better, and more determined to find a doctor who could physically change her into a woman.

In her library research, Jorgensen had read about experiments in Sweden where sex changes had been accomplished on lab animals. In May 1950, Jorgensen sailed for Denmark, where she had family, on a quest to find the Swedish doctors who she hoped could do the same for her.

In Demark, one of her relatives sent Jorgensen to Dr. Christian Hamburger, who she thought could help. After Jorgensen explained her feelings, the doctor examined her body and declared it that of a healthy male. However, in Denmark, there was an option for the administration of estrogens, and even castration, for homosexual males who were extremely distressed by their feelings. Although Jorgensen did not identify as homosexual, she agreed to be a research subject for Dr. Hamburger so that she could get the treatments she desired. By the end of 1952, Jorgensen was living as a woman on hormones, had been castrated, and her penis had been removed. Only ten days after the last operation, the story (full of inaccuracies) broke in the *New York Daily News*.

In many ways, Christine Jorgensen enjoyed her celebrity. She only once publicly acknowledged that she had been the one who had tipped the story to the *New York Daily News*. Afterward, she cooperated with many news outlets to get her story told, and largely made her living off her notoriety for many years. The tremendous worldwide coverage that her story enjoyed also did a great service to trans people wherever her story was told. At that time, in the early 1950s, there was no public information about trans people. If you were trans, you had no words to describe how you felt and you thought that you were the only person in the world like you. Hearing about Christine Jorgensen gave trans people solace. They knew that they were not the only ones, and they could hope that maybe something could be done for them too.

However, Jorgensen's celebrity also left her no room to live any other kind of life. She was unable ever again to get any kind of work that was not connected to her being a transsexual woman. Out of necessity, and reflecting her passions, she became a professional spokesperson for transsexual people. For thirty years, she performed a nightclub act in which she sang and told stories about her life. She spoke at colleges, universities, churches, and service clubs. She gave innumerable media interviews. Her method was edutainment. Her message was that trans people are people like everyone else who deserve the same respect and dignity as cisgender people.

Christine Jorgensen died of bladder cancer shortly before her sixty-third birthday on May 3, 1989. Two hundred people attended her funeral.

Reed Erickson (1917–1992)

Reed Erickson was a transsexual man who quietly used his personal wealth and influence to improve the lives of countless others, most of whom never even knew his name. Despite being relatively unknown in his lifetime, he was one of the most influential transsexual people in the twentieth century. Reed Erickson launched the Erickson Educational Foundation (EEF) in 1964, a philanthropic and educational organization funded entirely by Erickson. The EEF was active in 1964–1977, during which time it had offices open to the public in Baton Rouge and New York City and again in 1981–1984 in Ojai, California.

The EEF's goals were "to provide assistance and support in areas where human potential was limited by adverse physical, mental or social conditions, or where the scope of research was too new, controversial or imaginative to receive traditionally oriented support." The EEF contributed both active leadership and millions of dollars of behind-the-scenes financial support to three areas of endeavor: homophile organizations (pre–gay pride), mostly through the organization ONE, Inc.; transsexualism; and exploring alternative forms of consciousness such as shamanism, sensory deprivation, dream research, dolphin communication, and *The Course in Miracles*.

Reed Erickson was born in 1917 in El Paso, Texas, and grew up in Philadelphia, Pennsylvania. His mother died while Erickson was still quite young. Shortly after Erickson graduated from high school, Erickson's father moved Erickson, his sister, and the family business to Baton Rouge, Louisiana, where Erickson studied engineering at Louisiana State University, graduating in 1946 as their first female engineering grad. After working briefly as an engineer in Philadelphia, Erickson returned to Baton Rouge to work at his father's company. After his father's death in 1962, Reed Erickson took over the family business and grew it until selling it, at the end of the 1960s, for five million dollars, thereby becoming very wealthy. Subsequent land purchases resulted in Erickson earning even larger amounts of money from oil on his land, eventually amassing a personal fortune estimated at thirty million dollars.

In the years immediately following his second parent's death, and while still living in the conservative southern town of Baton Rouge, Erickson traveled back and forth to New York City to transition as a patient of Dr. Harry Benjamin. By 1965, Erickson had accomplished a legal name change and a legal sex designation change. The following year, Erickson married Aileen Ashton. They remained married for nine years and Erickson became father to two children. He subsequently briefly remarried. Erickson lived for a number of years with his children, his pet leopard, Henry, and his wives in succession, in an opulent home in Mazatlán, Mexico, which he dubbed the Love Joy Palace. Later in life, he moved to Southern California. After many years of good works and philanthropy, he became addicted to illegal drugs and died in Mexico in 1992, at age seventy-four, as a fugitive from U.S. drug indictments.

When Erickson began the Erickson Educational Foundation in 1964, transsexualism was little known to either professionals or the public. The EEF supported, in one way or another, a very large portion of the work done during the 1960s and 1970s by, for, and about transgendered people in the United States.

The EEF published an informative quarterly newsletter and an invaluable set of educational pamphlets, and developed and maintained an extensive referral list of helpful service providers. The importance of EEF's quarterly newsletter (mailing list of 20,000), the pamphlet series, and the referral service would be hard to overemphasize. They were lifelines for trans people for decades. During the 1970s and early 1980s the only literature available was a handful of pathologizing and very hard to access professional publications. Most mental health professionals and physicians considered transsexualism a sick perversion. Television talk show appearances and documentaries were virtually nonexistent. There was no Internet or social media. The few organizations that did exist were mostly small, local, and clandestine. The EEF served as the national clearinghouse and information source for transgendered people who wrote postal mail to the EEF from all over the United States asking for information about their feelings, and for the names of doctors to whom they could turn for help.

The EEF also gave hundreds of thousands of dollars in research grants to fund many important early research efforts in the United States. The roster of the people who benefited from research grants from the EEF reads like a Who's Who of early transgender research. They include, among others, Harry Benjamin, Harold Christensen, Milton Edgerton, Anke Ehrhardt, Deborah Feinbloom, Norman Fisk, Roger Gorski, Richard Green, Donald Laub, Jon K. Meyer, John Money, Ira Pauly, Richard Pillard, June Reinisch, and Paul Walker. EEF funding made possible the second book ever published on transsexualism, Money and Green's (1969) *Transsexualism and Sex Reassignment*. It was also EEF grant money that helped to start the first gender clinic in the United States, at Johns Hopkins University. The EEF was instrumental in organizing the international conferences on transsexualism in 1969, 1971, and 1973 that later became the source of the World Professional Association for Transgender Health, as well as in bringing discussions about transsexualism to conferences of broader interest.

Virginia Prince (1912–2009)

Virginia Prince was one of the early trans activists in twentieth-century America. She had an extensive career as a public speaker, publisher, editor, and author. In 1960, she founded a very influential magazine, *Transvestia,* and was its editor for twenty years. Many people also attribute the source of the word transgender to her. She chose to call herself a transgenderist because she identified neither as a transsexual, nor as a transvestite, nor as a drag queen.

Virginia Prince was born into a middle-class white family in Los Angeles near the end of 1912. She grew up as an active boy and young man. She did well in school and was notable as a track athlete in college. She earned a bachelor's degree in chemistry in 1935, followed by a master's degree in 1937 and a doctorate in 1939, both in pharmacology.

While still only twelve years old, Prince became erotically aroused by dressing in her mother's clothing. By the age of sixteen, in 1929, Prince had become completely committed to cross-dressing for erotic purposes. At this time, she had never heard a word for what she did, nor ever heard of anyone else like her. In 1940, Prince attended a medical presentation given by Louise Lawrence, a transvestite, at the University of California, Berkeley. Prince's interest in Lawrence and the topic led to their friendship. Louise Lawrence (1913–2002) was the center of a small clandestine group of male heterosexual cross-dressers in California at a time when cross-dressing was illegal and extremely stigmatized. Lawrence later began to live full-time as a woman and served as a role model for Prince.

Prince married for the first time in 1941. The marriage produced one son and lasted for ten years, during which time Prince secretly wore her wife's clothing and sometime went out in public dressed as a woman. Her wife's discovery of her cross-dressing contributed to the breakup of the relationship. When Prince sued to gain more visiting time with their son, her sexual pleasure derived from cross-dressing became an issue in court and was reported in at least four newspapers. Surprisingly for 1953, the judge ruled in Prince's favor.

Prince married again in 1956, this time to a woman who already knew that Prince was a cross-dresser. It was also around this time that Prince began to take enough hormones to cause her to grow breasts, but not enough to interfere with her sexual responses. Prince's second wife went out in public with Virginia dressed as a woman, cooperated with Virginia's sexual fantasies, and assisted with presentations about cross-dressing in college classes. However, the marriage was stressful and ended in divorce in 1966.

While still in her second marriage, Prince made contact with a small informal group of local heterosexual male cross-dressers. Prince decided to start a more formal group, which she called "The Hose and Heels Club." This small club later evolved into the much larger Foundation for Full Personality Expression (FPE), and then into the even larger Society for the Second Self (Tri-Ess), which still exists today with chapters all across the United States. Prince also provided advice and guidance to similar groups as they started up in a variety of other countries.

In 1960, Prince started *Transvestia* magazine, which ran for 111 issues and was under her editorship until 1980. The magazine was usually about 90 pages long, had many black and white photographs, and had a personal ads section at the back. At its peak, it had about 1,000 subscribers. During its day, it was one of the most important publications in the trans community.

Around the same time that Prince started her magazine, she was arrested for writing sexually explicit letters to another heterosexual male cross-dresser. The charge was sending obscene material through the U.S. postal system. She was not jailed, but her probationary period included requirements that she not improperly use the postal system, and that she not cross-dress. Her lawyer negotiated permission for her to cross-dress if she did it for educational purposes. So started Virginia Prince's very successful public speaking career advocating for acceptance of heterosexual male cross-dressers.

By 1968, Prince's son was grown, she was no longer married, and she had sold her successful business. At age fifty-five, Virginia Prince began to live full-time as a woman, which she continued to do until her death at age ninety-six.

Virginia Prince was a strong and courageous leader, and a controversial one. Two of her stances about which she has been strongly criticized had to do with who she allowed to join FPE. In Prince's view, only heterosexual men who cross-dressed should be included. No gay men or lesbian women were allowed because Prince felt that homosexual people would never gain acceptance and that their presence would taint the respectability of her organization. She also felt that surgical transitions were unnecessary and did not permit transsexual women or men to join FPE lest wives of cross-dressers, fearing that their husbands would become transsexual, would oppose their membership in FPE if they saw that as a possible outcome of cross-dressing. Nonetheless, there can be no disputing that Virginia Prince was a powerful and effective advocate for heterosexual male cross-dressers at a time when few others would take the risk.

Doctors and Medical Facilities Focusing on Gender Affirmation Procedures

Given the numerous instances of trans, non-binary, and Two-Spirit people feeling alienated and being underserved at medical care facilities, there are many places where trans, non-binary, and Two-Spirit people have increasingly taken leadership in ensuring that health care is provided in sensitive and respectful ways. This has been done through advocacy efforts both from outside and within health care agencies, and by establishing health care organizations under the control of trans, non-binary, or Two-Spirit people.

Stanley H. Biber (1923–2006) and Marci Bowers

Dr. Stanley Biber was a cisgender ally and pioneering surgeon for gender affirmation procedures. In 1969, Dr. Biber, a former army surgeon, started performing gender affirmation (at the time called sex reassignment [SRS]) surgeries at a hospital in Trinidad, Colorado. This small town, at the border between Colorado and New Mexico, became known as "the sex change capital of the world" (Fox 2006). In 2000, Dr. Marci Bowers, a trans woman who was also an obstetrics and gynecology surgeon, joined the medical staff in Trinidad to be mentored on gender affirmation surgical procedures by the world-renowned Dr. Biber. Upon Biber's retirement three years later, he left the clinic in her hands. Bowers is the first known trans woman to carry out gender affirmation surgeries (Nutt 2016). In 2007, Bowers moved to the San Francisco Bay Area to work at the Mills-Peninsula Medical Center south of San Francisco, where she has a multiyear waitlist for people seeking gender affirmation surgery with her. Bowers is also on the faculty at Mount Sinai Hospital in New York City, where she has helped establish the first transgender medical education program in the United States. Dr. Marci Bowers is also one of a few surgeons throughout the world who performs surgical reversals for African women who have suffered genital mutilation and who seek corrective surgery. Bowers does these corrective surgeries for free (Nutt 2016).

Preecha Tiewtranon

Dr. Preecha Tiewtranon, who specializes in plastic and reconstructive surgery, started performing gender affirmation surgeries in Thailand in 1980. His world-renowned clinic, the Preecha Aesthetic Institute (PAI), was the first multidisciplinary clinic for aesthetic and reconstructive surgery in the world. The team of doctors, nurses, and other care providers at the clinic take a holistic approach to all of their gender-affirmation surgery patients. Outside of the clinic, Dr. Tiewtranon's work and educational outreach has extended to local hotels, restaurants, and other services in Bangkok near the PAI so that people who come from all over the world for their gender affirmation procedures feel safe outside of the medical setting. In nearly forty years of his career, Dr. Preecha Tiewtranon has trained numerous other doctors who have come to him from around the world to learn his techniques as well as a "best practices" model of caring for the whole person when working with trans, non-binary, and gender-diverse individuals seeking gender affirmation surgery. For many, too, a trip to Thailand is less expensive than seeking gender affirmation surgery in their home countries. The low cost and high-quality care are both major components of the success of the Preecha Aesthetic Institute.

Sava Perovic (1947–2010)

Dr. Sava Perovic became a global advocate and ally for trans people. He specialized in genital surgery for trans men, which is seen as more difficult than genital surgery for trans women. Born in 1947 in Yugoslavia, Perovic started his medical career at University Children's Hospital in Belgrade, where he became an expert on Peyronie's disease, which is a painful and abnormal bend to the penis caused by scar tissue. With his outstanding surgical skills, he quickly became the chief of the urology department (Barbagli, Sansalone, and Lazzeri 2010). Perovic was always open and approachable, which is partly why he quickly became known as one of the most outstanding surgeons for gender affirmation surgery for trans men. When he was dying of cancer, Perovic knew that his legacy for gender affirmation surgeries and care for trans men needed to continue, so he established the Sava Perovic Foundation and worked with his colleague and mentee Dr. Rados Djinovic and an entire surgical team dedicated to gender affirmation procedures for trans men. Perhaps one of the lasting legacies of Dr. Perovic is that he believed trans health care should be accessible and affordable; he often spoke out against a "business model" of medicine.

Christine McGinn

Dr. Christine McGinn is a retired naval surgeon, a transgender woman, and a lesbian. She and her wife have three children and they run the Papillon Gender Wellness Center in New Hope, Pennsylvania. Moving away from a model of sickness and disease, the center focuses on a holistic approach to gender wellness. After her own transition in 2000, in which Dr. McGinn felt trauma from the transphobia that the medical staff displayed, she decided to retrain specifically in the field of gender affirmation surgical procedures and opened her own clinic so that trans, non-binary, and Two-Spirit people could have their surgery done by a trans person who understands their unique issues and the ways that transphobia often works within Western medical contexts (Arnold 2012). The Papillon Center is a complete care facility in that there is an entire team of doctors, nurses, and counselors who work together with one goal: complete care for trans, non-binary, and Two-Spirit people during their gender affirmation process. In 2017, after U.S. president Donald Trump's reinstatement of a ban against trans, non-binary, and Two-Spirit people serving in the U.S. military, Dr. Christine McGinn began offering free gender affirmation for trans, non-binary, and Two-Spirit people in the U.S. military (Perez 2017). McGinn has been featured on numerous television shows and in films, and is an activist for the rights of trans, non-binary, and Two-Spirit people.

Callen-Lorde

Callen-Lorde is a trans-focused and trans-affirmative clinic located in New York City. The clinic focuses on a full spectrum of health and wellness needs. From the moment a person enters the clinic, they are met with intake forms that offer several gender identities, as well as a place for the new patient to write in an identity if theirs does not appear on the list. The clinic is comprised of nurses, doctors, counselors, and other health care professionals, and a governing board of directors, many of whom are also trans. In recognizing the ways that trans and non-binary people are often mistreated within the majority of medical environments, Callen-Lorde strives to make each patient welcome and to continue an ongoing and holistic health partnership with each patient.

Catherine White Holman Wellness Centre

The Catherine White Holman Wellness Centre, located in Vancouver, British Columbia, Canada, opened in 2011. It is guided by a dedication to providing low-barrier and respectful primary care wellness services to trans, non-binary, and Two-Spirit people using an informed consent model. All services are provided by volunteers who are mostly trans, non-binary, or Two-Spirit, and services are always free for those who do not have insurance or cannot afford to pay. The clinic, open for drop-ins at specified times, offers nursing care, a nutritionist and community kitchen, counseling, massage, and a legal clinic.

Native Youth Sexual Health Network

The Native Youth Sexual Health Network (NYSHN) was created by and for Indigenous youth and works with issues of sexual health and reproductive health. The organization is located in Toronto, Ontario, Canada, but they do outreach and advocacy throughout Canada and the United States. Although they are a broad-range outreach network, they have several programs that focus on Two-Spirit people such as their Two-Spirit Mentors Support Circle, outreach concerning healthy sexuality and fighting transphobia, and a Two-Spirit resource directory.

Sherbourne Clinic

The Sherbourne Clinic in Toronto, Ontario, Canada, was founded in 2002 with a mission to improve the health of underserved populations. One of their main client groups is LGBTQ2+ people, and they provide a range of services for trans, non-binary, and Two-Spirit people including transition-related surgery referrals; respite care after transition-related surgeries; a variety of support groups for trans, non-binary, and Two-Spirit people; training and related guidelines and protocols for health-care providers; and parenting groups for trans, non-binary, and Two-Spirit parents and prospective parents.

Tangerine Community Health Center

In November 2015, Tangerine Community Health Center, the first trans-focused general health care clinic in Southeast Asia, opened its doors in Bangkok, Thailand. The doctors, nurses, counselors, and trans-community advocates who worked there knew that many trans people were not comfortable going to mainstream clinics for basic health care needs like blood tests or for treatment of viral or bacterial infections. The clinic offers a holistic approach to each patient. One of the growing populations of patients coming to the clinic is trans men.

Tom Waddell Urban Health Clinic

The Tom Waddell Urban Health Clinic, which is located in the Civic Center/Tenderloin area of San Francisco, offers health care to some of the city's most marginalized communities and does not turn patients away if they are unable to pay. The clinic honors the late Dr. Tom Waddell, founder of the Gay Games and community-based physician, who died in 1987 from AIDS. The doctors and nurses at the clinic noticed that people who identified as trans, non-binary, intersex, and Two-Spirit were much less likely to seek medical care until their condition was dire. In 1993, a grassroots group of health care providers and members of the trans community decided to start a "Transgender Tuesdays" program at the health clinic. For twenty-five years, the clinic has been "committed to providing quality, integrated healthcare in an atmosphere of trust and respect."

Activists

The following are activists who have done groundbreaking work for trans, non-binary, and Two-Spirit people. Each one of them has devoted their life to making the world a more accessible and positive place for people who are gender diverse.

Leslie Feinberg (1949–2014)

Leslie Feinberg was an American writer, historian, activist, and communist who worked tirelessly to advocate for workers' rights around the world, and for the rights of people of all genders to have full access to health care, education, and fair working conditions. Feinberg was assigned female at birth, but never identified as a girl; Feinberg did not identify as a boy, either. At the time that Feinberg was struggling with a gender identity that did not fit within the restrictions of the gender binary, the terms non-binary or genderqueer were not in use, and neither was the use of the neutral "they" pronoun for people like Feinberg. Instead, Feinberg invented the neutral pronouns *ze* and *hir*, which are often still used in non-binary and genderqueer communities. These are the pronouns that will be used throughout this profile in memory of, and in honor of, hir life and work.

The first work Feinberg published was hir 1980 short autobiographical booklet, *Journal of a Transsexual*; and then twelve years later, ze published hir 1992 Marxist pamphlet, *Transgender Liberation: A Movement Whose Time Has Come*. In length, this publication may be small; but in this pamphlet, one can find the seeds of Feinberg's other groundbreaking texts that have forever changed the face and direction of trans history, helped guide future trans historians, and illuminated the ways that trans history is inherently tied to movements fighting against colonialism, racism, sexism, heterosexism, cissexism, classism, and nationalism. In hir first words of this pamphlet, Feinberg wrote, "This pamphlet is an attempt to trace the historic rise of an oppression that, as yet, has no commonly agreed name. We are talking here about people who defy the 'man'-made boundaries of gender" (Feinberg 1992, 5).

The following year, Feinberg published the book that ze will most likely forever be known best for—*Stone Butch Blues*, which is a semiautobiographical novel about a person assigned as female at birth but who never identifies as a woman. This book bridges the gap between lesbian identity and trans identity, a gap that, sadly, resonated throughout Feinberg's life. In a June 2018 *New York Times* article, author Kaitlyn Greenidge wrote about the ways that Feinberg's novel still resonated twenty-five years later:

> [A]s we all are trapped in a political discourse that emptily refers to empathy and knows enough to speak about

trauma, but only in the abstract, and in which there appear to be "sides" on the question of what is the most ethical way to imprison children, "Stone Butch Blues" is exactly the book all of us should be reading. (Greenidge 2018)

Although Feinberg's book does not discuss controversies around immigration, or other specific matters in current global politics, the core ideals found in the book are relevant to today's controversies and issues. Feinberg's ability, in all of hir works, to illuminate core human rights issues is part of what makes hir writing classic and enduring.

While *Stone Butch Blues* continues to be a classic for readers from all walks of life, hir other enduring and important text is the 1996 *Transgender Warriors: Making History from Joan of Arc to Dennis Rodman.* This book has served as a road map for people wanting to learn about transgender history. As with all of hir writings, Feinberg's look at gender diversity from the ancient world to the twentieth century is very enjoyable and accessible; Feinberg believed that education should be free and available to everyone and ze wrote accordingly. In the United States, it is one of the most used books for high school and college classes with an LGBTQ2+ focus. Feinberg's other books include *Trans Liberation: Beyond Pink or Blue,* published in 1999, which includes many of Feinberg's speeches as well as interviews with other trans, non-binary, and gender-diverse leaders like Sylvia Rivera; *Drag King Dreams,* published in 2006, which is a novel about Max, who bartends at a club where butch lesbians perform as drag kings; and, hir final book before ze died, *Rainbow Solidarity: In Defense of Cuba,* which was published in 2009 and brings together Feinberg's commitment to communism, trans rights, and human rights.

Outside of hir work as an author, Feinberg worked tirelessly as a political and social advocate for human rights with a special focus on intersecting oppressions and the need for workers' rights. Feinberg not only spoke out against oppressions, but also acted on hir political convictions. On a speaking tour in

San Francisco in 2007 on May 1, which is International Workers Day, Feinberg asked the LGBT bookstore A Different Light, in San Francisco's Castro neighborhood, the LGBTQ2+ center of the city, to show support to the workers' movement by closing the shop for a day. Feinberg even said that ze would gladly come to the financially struggling bookstore, give a reading, and talk to anyone and everyone who came in as long as the store did not begin selling hir new book until after 12:01 a.m. on May 2. The bookstore refused Feinberg's request, and Feinberg did not give a talk there. In this conflict, Feinberg was able to discuss with hir audiences the need for all oppressed people to work together—something that Feinberg wrote about in hir very first publication when ze said, "Genuine bonds of solidarity can be forged between people who respect each other's differences and are willing to fight their enemy together" (Feinberg 1992, 22).

Feinberg was also a staunch advocate for the complete acceptance of trans, non-binary, and Two-Spirit people within the larger LGBTQ2+ community because trans people are often left behind by more mainstream gay and lesbian rights movements. One of hir biggest stands against transphobia within the lesbian and feminist community was hir stand with Camp Trans, which was created to protest transphobia at the Michigan Womyn's Festival held every summer for forty years in Hart, Michigan. This was defined as a women-only space; however, trans women were not welcome and some trans men, who still wanted to connect with the women's community, were allowed to participate to some extent as long as they were not too vocal about being men. Camp Trans was a protest site located across from the festival entrance as a way to bring awareness to how trans women were not seen as women by the group that *should* be the first to embrace them—radical feminists. Feinberg is featured with Camp Trans in a short documentary film by trans film director Rhys Ernst in the series *We've Been Around.*

When Leslie Feinberg died in November 2014 of complications from Lyme disease, hir last words, as reported by hir partner, Minnie Bruce Pratt, for an article in *The Advocate,* were "Remember me as a revolutionary communist" (Pratt 2014). The pronouns used in Pratt's obituary referred to Feinberg as "she" and "her." According to a note from *The Advocate,* Pratt claimed that Feinberg chose these pronouns for the obituary. This controversy over Feinberg's pronouns actually underscores the ways that trans, non-binary, and Two-Spirit people—and perhaps especially non-binary people—are often forced, linguistically, back into a gender binary. Feinberg's life illuminates some of the ways that all people need to be respected. Ze and hir are still pronouns used within trans and non-binary communities, thanks to Leslie Feinberg.

Georgina Beyer

Georgina Beyer, born in Wellington, New Zealand, is a political pioneer. She is Maori. She is a trans woman. She is a former sex worker. And, in 1999, she was the first known transgender person in the world to be elected to a parliament. Prior to her election to Parliament, in 1995, she was elected mayor of the city of Carterton, making her the first trans person ever elected to a mayoral position. For her run for Parliament, Beyer was the Labour Party candidate for her conservative Wairarapa electoral area, and most people at the time thought she had no chance of beating Paul Henry, an older white conservative cisgender man who did not take Beyer seriously as an opponent. She beat him by over 3,000 votes (Casey 2018). Part of the reason Beyer was so successful, even in a conservative district, was her openness to being approachable, available, and out and about at numerous local events, such as judging local sheep races. In her office on the main street of Carterton, Beyer had an open door policy, which meant that anyone and everyone could come in and talk to her about their community concerns. In hindsight, Beyer says, "I think I was just a breath of fresh air. What people responded to was honesty, being straight up, being approachable" (Casey 2018).

In her first speech on the floor of the New Zealand parliament in 2000, she said the following:

> I am the first transsexual in New Zealand to be standing in this House of Parliament. This is a first not only in New Zealand, ladies and gentlemen, but also in the world. This is an historic moment. We need to acknowledge that this country of ours leads the way in so many aspects. We have led the way for women getting the vote. We have led the way in the past, and I hope we will do so again in the future in social policy and certainly in human rights. (Goldson and Wells 2001)

Beyer, who had also been elected to school boards prior to her run for the mayoral position, was perfectly happy sitting as the mayor for Carterton, and she had no further political ambitions. In 1998, however, she was approached by Sonja Davies, an iconic Labour Party leader in Parliament. Beyer admits to originally not liking the idea of running for Parliament, but with more persuasion from the Labour Party, she decided to move forward with her campaign (Beyer 2007).

During her eight-year tenure in New Zealand's parliament, Beyer used her position as a powerful leader within the governmental system to introduce and advocate for some of the most radical social justice laws, not only in New Zealand, but in the world. She was one of the biggest supporters of New Zealand's Civil Unions Bill. As a former sex worker, Beyer also knew from experience that sex workers need legal rights and legal protections, an idea that is still seen as too radical in many parts of the world. She worked tirelessly to pass the Prostitution Reform Act, which, once again, made New Zealand one of the "firsts" in the world. As a member of Parliament, Beyer always had a sense of humor. She would often joke with other MPs that politics and prostitution were the same sort of work, in that both groups had to sell themselves (Casey 2018).

Beyer had very personal reasons for wanting to make sure that the Prostitution Reform Bill made it successfully through Parliament. In 1979, she was attacked and sexually assaulted by a group of men. As a trans woman of color who was also a sex worker, Beyer knew that if she went to the police, not only would the men who molested her not face any consequences, but she would also be setting herself up to be revictimized by the police. In her final speech to parliament, Beyer stated:

I have been proud to be a staunch supporter of some of the most controversial conscience issues in this Parliament in the last few years, particularly prostitution reform and, of course, the Civil Union Bill. . . . I will never resile from having been a staunch supporter of both of those. In regard to the Prostitution Reform Act . . . I think it is legislation that will work. It may need some review—and, of course, that is under way—in the future. But, again, the world has not fallen in, in my opinion, because of the passing of that legislation. If anything, we are all far more aware of a situation that, frankly, we were quite ignorant about beforehand. (Beyer 2007)

After leaving Parliament in 2007, Beyer fell upon hard times and was unable to find work. Regardless of the fact that she had been a successful member of the New Zealand parliament for eight years, when she was ready to go out into the workforce again, she still faced racism and transphobia. She also became very ill and had to undergo a kidney transplant, but she is back on the road to health. The LGBTQ2+ community in New Zealand has looked after her and honored her and her lifetime of work. When interviewed in February 2018 before her appearance as part of Wellington's Pride festival, Beyer talked about the younger LGBTQ2+ generation serving as her inspiration: "My faith now lies with this younger generation to stand on my shoulders, just as I stood on the shoulders of those who went before me. I've done my bit to move the needle, now it's your turn" (Casey 2018).

Louis Graydon Sullivan (1951–1991)

In his all too short life, Lou Sullivan made gigantic steps forward for trans, non-binary, and gender-diverse people around the world, and in particular, for trans men. Sullivan grew up in a Wisconsin Catholic family. From a very early age, he knew that everyone had "got it wrong" when they assigned him female at birth. Beyond the fact that Lou knew he was a boy and not a girl, he also knew he was attracted to other boys. Given that he was growing up in Wisconsin in the 1950s and 1960s, there was not much information about transgender people at all—and if there was, references to Christine Jorgensen's gender affirmation procedures, which began in the same year Sullivan was born, were the basis for most people's information about transsexual people. At that time, being transsexual and proceeding with gender affirmation also carried with it the requirement that the person was going to be heterosexual after the transition. Sullivan kept extensive diaries about being transsexual and gay throughout his life. In 1973, when he was twenty-two years old, Sullivan wrote the following as he was trying to understand his feelings as a gay trans man: "I don't know if there was anyone that's ever felt as I do. . . . how they coped, what they did. . . . how do I find out what someone like me does?" (Sullivan 1973).

In 1975, at the age of twenty-four, Lou Sullivan left Wisconsin for the San Francisco Bay Area because he realized that he would be more accepted there, socially and culturally, as a gay trans man. Lou's family was incredibly supportive of him; before he left town, his mother had a tailor make a nice men's suit for him. His grandmother was the first person in his family to consistently say his correct name and use his correct pronouns. His siblings and father were also very supportive—his father later offered to help him financially with his gender affirmation surgery (Strauss 2018).

Once in San Francisco, Sullivan started working immediately to make life better for other trans men—especially bisexual and gay trans men. At the Janus Information Facility, a trans outreach and resource center in the community, he was one of the first peer counselors who was a trans man. Beyond the local level, Lou fought to convince the American Psychiatric Association and the Harry Benjamin International Gender Dysphoria Association (HBIGDA) to recognize that trans men could be gay or bisexual. While Lou sought doctors and clinics who would work with him toward gender affirmation, and was rejected, his community in San Francisco accepted him. Lou had queer male lovers and a large community of support. Rhys Ernst says the following in his short documentary on Sullivan: "Lou knew who he was. His friends and partners did, too. It was the gender professionals who stood in the way" (Ernst 2016).

After he had been living in San Francisco as a fully out gay trans man for over six years, Sullivan was finally able to get a doctor to prescribe testosterone for him, and he was also eventually able to have top surgery; however, he continued to be rejected by numerous gender clinics for bottom surgery. Their main argument was that they had never heard of this type of surgery for a trans man who wanted to be gay, and they did not want to be the ones to set the precedent. In a scathing letter to Stanford University's gender clinic, Sullivan wrote the following:

It is unfortunate that your Program cannot see the merit of each individual, regardless of their sexual orientation. The general human populace is made up of many sexual persuasions—it is incredible that your Program requires all transsexuals to be of one fabric. I had even considered lying to you about my sexual preference of men, as I knew this would surely keep me out of your Program, but I felt it important to be straightforward, possibly paving the way for other female-to-males with homosexual orientations—and we do exist. (Strauss 2018)

One of the most important points in Lou Sullivan's letter to Stanford is that he felt he needed to be honest with them not only for himself, but for future gay and bisexual trans men who may be seeking gender affirmation. It was precisely this sort of advocacy on Sullivan's part that finally helped to pave the way for gay and bisexual trans men to be able to successfully seek gender affirmation procedures if they chose to do so, and if they were financially able to do so.

In 1986, Lou Sullivan was finally able to undergo bottom surgery. That same year, he also found out that he was HIV+ in a time when having HIV was a death sentence. In one of his final interviews before he died in 1991, Sullivan commented that he took a certain pleasure in informing some of the gender clinics that had rejected him because they thought that he could not live as a gay man because "it looks like I'm gonna die like one" (Strauss 2018).

Louis Graydon Sullivan left the world having made a plethora of contributions, considering he only lived to be forty years old. Through his advocacy for himself and for his community, he forced various Western medical gatekeepers to reassess their rules around caring for trans men who were gay or bisexual. He also founded FTM International, the longest running global outreach, information, and advocacy group for trans men. Sullivan was also one of the founders of the GLBT Historical Society in San Francisco, where his extensive diaries are part of the GLBT Historical Society's archive, which is available to the general public for free. In 2010, the Sean Dorsey Dance queer and trans dance group utilized Sullivan's diaries to create an award-winning dance performance entitled *Uncovered: The Diary Project*, which, through readings from Sullivan's diaries and Dorsey's choreography, became a beautiful tribute to the life and continuing legacy of this trans pioneer.

Lydia Foy

Dr. Lydia Foy, a retired Irish dentist and trans woman, began a two-decades-long battle in 1993 when she "applied to the office of the Registrar General for a new birth certificate to reflect her gender" and was refused (Transgender Equality Network

Ireland n.d.). Foy refused to take no for an answer and, in 1997, initiated High Court proceedings to change her birth certificate to reflect her gender identity. Three years later, in 2000, a justice heard her case and took two more years to make a decision, at which time he rejected her claim. However, Justice McKechnie's rejection was very strategic, because he was trying to force the Irish and U.K. governments to come up with a way to recognize trans people's genders; he urged the governments to look to other European countries for examples. Over the course of several years, many more appearances in front of the court, the formation of an Irish Gender Recognition Advisory Group, and countless hours of advocacy, "the Gender Recognition Act was passed on July 15th 2015 and Dr Foy became the first person to be legally recognised by this Act" (Transgender Equality Network Ireland n.d.). It took Dr. Foy twenty-two years to get her birth certificate changed, but her work made a new law for all people seeking a birth certificate change in Ireland. For her work, Dr. Lydia Foy was honored with the European Citizens Prize (Free Legal Advice Center 2018).

Mauro Cabral Grinspan

Mauro Cabral Grinspan (often referred to as Mauro Cabral) is an intersex, trans, and queer activist and academic from Córdoba, Argentina. He is the executive director of Global Action for Trans* Equality (GATE), an international advocacy organization. In 2006, Grinspan was one of the human rights experts who elaborated the Yogyakarta Principles at Gadjah Mada University in Yogyakarta, Indonesia. These principles were developed to establish principles to guide the application of international human rights laws to questions of gender identity and sexual orientation. In a 2016 interview, Grinspan explained, "The idea was to create a tool supporting LGBT activism in the UN. The seminar took place in 2006 after several failed attempts in the UN to introduce sexual orientation and gender identity in resolutions" (Ausserer 2016). However, Grinspan also noted that this 2006 resolution was not nearly progressive enough:

I do not necessarily agree with the language. For example, the principles do not talk explicitly about bodily issues or about gender expression.

Bodies are policed in multiple ways. In their proposed universalism the Yogyakarta Principles ignore most of them, and racism, classism, ageism, sexism and cissexism, and ableism are not related to human rights violations based on sexual orientation and gender identity. Intersex issues are implicitly linked to medical abuses, and those abuses are related to gender identity. This framework has been historically criticized by the intersex movement. (Ausserer 2016)

As a Latinx, queer, intersex, trans man, Grinspan certainly understands the need for people to be protected in *all* of their diversity. In 2017, he was a signatory to the Yogyakarta Principles +10, which were an attempt to address some of the concerns that he articulated in relation to the original Yogyakarta Principles.

From 2005 to 2007, Grinspan coordinated Trans and Intersex outreach in the International Gay and Lesbian Human Rights Commission's (IGLHRC) South American office. IGLHRC was originally created as a global watchdog and advocacy organization that documented human rights abuses against people based on sexual orientation, gender identity and gender expression, and HIV/AIDS status because Amnesty International did not originally consider these oppressions on their list of human rights violations. It is in large part through the work of organizations like IGLHRC and GATE that Amnesty International now does consider these types of violations.

Grinspan and GATE advocated for the World Health Organization (WHO) to revise the section on gender diversity in the *International Classification of Diseases* (ICD) as part of their revisions culminating in ICD-11. The ICD and the *Diagnostic and Statistical Manual of Mental Disorders* (DSM), which is used by the American Psychiatric Association, have a had a long track

record of pathologizing people with differences of sex development (intersex) and/or people who are trans, non-binary, and
gender diverse. As Grinspan noted in an article he wrote for *The
Guardian*, "For us, the ICD process represents a historic opportunity to achieve trans depathologisation while ensuring full
access to fundamental rights: legal gender recognition, access to
gender affirming healthcare, and coverage under public and private healthcare systems" (Cabral 2017).

In June 2018, the WHO announced that transsexualism
and related categories would be removed from the classifications of mental and behavioral disorders. This is a positive step
forward; however, GATE and other advocacy groups like Trans
Equality Network Ireland (TENI) were "dismayed" to see the
ways that WHO and the ICD, in their language revision, still
stigmatize people with mental health issues, and that they do
not recognize the ways that transphobia and cissexism perpetu-
ate mental health issues for trans, non-binary, and gender-
diverse people (GATE 2018).

Michelle Suárez Bértora

Michelle Suárez Bértora has a long list of firsts in her home country of Uruguay, population 3.4 million, and one of the most progressive countries in South America concerning LGBTQ+ rights.
In 2010, she became the first trans person in Uruguay to complete a university degree. She is the first trans person practicing
law in Uruguay. In 2014, she became the first trans person elected
to the Uruguayan legislature. She is also the first trans person
to be elected as an alternate senator for the Communist Party of
Uruguay.

Suárez Bértora, who was assigned male at birth, knew from
early childhood that she was female. She was very fortunate
because both of her parents, her mother in particular, were very
supportive of their trans daughter. At the young age of fifteen,
Suárez Bértora became Michelle and started the gender affirmation process. She was always a very intellectual and philo-
sophical child and knew that she wanted to become a lawyer to

advocate for the rights of marginalized people in Uruguay. Her mother's death in 2009 was devastating for her, but she also used her grief to throw herself into her work as the legal adviser for Obejas Negras (Black Sheep), an LGBTQ+ rights organization that has helped change the shape of LGBTQ+ rights in Uruguay, making it one of the most progressive and safe countries in South America for LGBTQ+ people. In an interview, she discussed the ways that laws that she advocated for at a national level can also help to shape changes in social and cultural attitudes and prejudices:

> When these legal changes are accompanied by real social debates, that is, triggers that make us discuss the issue in the internal and family sphere and discuss it with our children, neighbors, friends, co-workers, there are real social debates and true cultural changes. (Formoso 2015)

Michelle Suárez Bértora has advocated successfully for many social and legal changes in Uruguay for marginalized communities, including, as a large woman herself, advocating against fat phobia and discussing the ways that all women—cisgender and transgender—are expected to fit into a specific physical type.

Jamison Green

Jamison (James) Green) is an American trans man who is an educator, author, and advocate. In an interview for GLSEN, an LGBTQ2+ K–12 educator's project, "Unheard Voices: Stories of LGBT History," he recalls the first day of kindergarten: "I always hated wearing dresses, but my parents dressed me up and we walked in. . . . The Kindergarten teacher welcomed me and she said, 'The little girls are over there.' But as soon as I saw the guys with the trucks I went right over there in my little dress and started playing" (Green 2011). Green never truly identified with the female sex designation that was assigned to him at birth, and at the age of fifteen (in 1963), he quit using the name given to him at birth and embraced the name "Jamie."

Although Green struggled to be himself in early adulthood, it was not until he was in his thirties in 1976 that he saw Steve Dain, a teacher in California who had transitioned from female to male, on television. Green recalls, "He was handsome, articulate, self-confident, poised." Dain's being out openly as a successful trans man helped give Green the courage to move forward with gender-affirmation procedures in 1988 (Green 2011).

Green began working for FTM International at the behest of his friend Lou Sullivan, a gay trans man, when Sullivan was dying of AIDS. Once Green took over FTM International, it grew to become the largest group in the world working on issues focused specifically on trans men.

Beyond his work for FTM International, Green became a leading advocate for trans rights when he worked on the passage of San Francisco's Transgender Protection Ordinance in the early 1990s—San Francisco was the second place in the United States to pass such a law; the state of Minnesota was the first. From the 1990s to the current time, Green has continued to work tirelessly with numerous trans, non-binary, and Two-Spirit rights organizations, including as the founder and director of the Transgender Law and Policy Institute. From 2014 to 2016, Green held the position of president of the World Professional Association for Transgender Health, the second trans person to hold that position. In an interview with Andrea Jenkins for the Transgender Oral History Project, Green discusses the importance of the work of WPATH and the ways that medicine and the law can still be the most difficult institutions for trans, non-binary, and Two-Spirit people to navigate:

The intersection of law and medicine is where we are most oppressed and it's also where we're most vulnerable. It's also where we need the most support in order to find our place in society and to be healthy. Without health care you're not a human being. (Green 2016)

As an author, Jamison Green has written or co-authored several articles on problems of invisibility that trans men often face. His groundbreaking book *Becoming a Visible Man* was published in 2004. In 2005 it won "Best Book in Transgender Studies" from the Center for Lesbian & Gay Studies (CLAGS) in New York and was also a finalist for a Lambda Literary Award.

As an educator, Green works with corporations and educational institutions in creating inclusive trans, non-binary, and Two-Spirit policies and in making safe spaces for trans, non-binary, and Two-Spirit people. He works with mental health professionals, people in law enforcement, and policymakers. His belief that education will bring about positive change at various institutions is borne out of his decades of struggle and activism. His outlook on the future for trans, non-binary, and Two-Spirit people is a positive one:

> I have to be optimistic—I have to be optimistic, otherwise I wouldn't do what I do. I believe that the world can change in a positive way, I believe that there is room for all of us, I believe that we don't have to compete with each other. (Green 2016)

Rupert Raj

Rupert Raj, born in 1952, is a retired Canadian trans activist of Indian and Polish parentage. Raj reports that, growing up in Ottawa, Ontario, he remembered knowing that he was really a boy by the age of three. After the tragic death of both of his parents when he was sixteen, Raj began cross-dressing as often as possible. At his own request, Raj began to see a psychiatrist from whom he first heard the word transsexual, and immediately knew that it was right for him. Toward the end of his high school years, Raj chanced upon a news release about a new clinic in Portland, Oregon, that was performing gender-affirming surgeries for trans men. This both provided hope that something could be done and pushed Raj to despair at how inaccessible it was for him. At age eighteen, he committed himself to a psychiatric hospital to prevent himself from committing suicide. After his release, Raj attempted a relationship with a lesbian woman, which only confirmed for him that he was actually a man.

Raj started living as a man when he entered Ottawa's Carleton University in 1971. He informed the registrar that he was a "female-to-male transsexual" and the registrar obligingly registered him under his then-chosen name of Nicholas Christopher Ghosh, without requiring any legal or medical documentation. Early in the school year, Raj traveled to New York City where he met with a doctor who agreed to prescribe male hormones to initiate his physical transition.

In the summer of 1972, Raj had his chest surgery done and made contact with three trans women who had started the first trans rights organization in Canada, the Association of Canadian Transsexuals (ACT) in Toronto, Ontario. Around the same time, he published his first article, "On Transsexualism," in a small Ottawa newsletter for gays and lesbians and made his first attempt to speak to the media about transsexualism (he cancelled the appearance because the interviewer was too interested in his urinary habits). Over the next several years, Raj was able to get a hysterectomy, had his identification papers changed to male, and graduated from university. He achieved his final genital surgery at age sixty in 2012.

In 1975 Raj moved to Vancouver, British Columbia, and began a short-lived campaign to get the province of Ontario to pay for gender-affirming surgeries. By 1978, Raj had moved to Calgary, Alberta, having heard that good phalloplasties were being done at a hospital there. While there, he and his partner, "Eugene," began the Foundation for the Advancement of Transsexuals (FACT) and started the first national trans newsletter in Canada, *Gender Review: A FACTual Journal*, which Raj edited from 1978 to 1982. Largely written by Raj, it was distributed to trans activists, professionals who worked with trans people, and publishers of other trans newsletters in the United States.

After Raj moved to Toronto, Ontario, in 1979, he invited trans woman Susan Huxford-Westfall to join him in FACT. Together, they established FACT chapters in Toronto, Hamilton, Kitchner, and Ottawa, Ontario, and in Montreal, Quebec, and Winnipeg, Manitoba. The Toronto chapter met every two weeks as a support group, and Raj and Huxford-Westfall spoke on behalf of FACT to newspaper reporters, on radio and television broadcasts, to university classes, to medical professionals in hospitals, and with service agencies. Raj also appeared on a Sally Jesse Raphael television talk show in 1986 along with his sister and several others. Raj left the leadership of FACT in 1982, although he continued as a volunteer peer counselor until 1986.

Redirecting their energies in 1982, Raj and Huxford-Westfall started the first counseling and educational service for trans men, Metamorphosis Medical Research Foundation (MMRF); a newsletter, *Metamorphosis: The Newsletter Exclusively for F-M Men*; and a confidential directory of contact information for trans men. MMRF ran until 1988, at which time Raj launched a new set of ventures, a private consulting firm called Gender Worker (later adding another person to become Gender Consultants) and the *Gender NetWorker* newsletter for counselors working with trans people. This endeavor enjoyed some success but was short-lived, concluding in mid-1990 when Raj removed himself from activism due to his feeling depleted from his efforts.

Approached by a trans woman friend at the end of the century, Raj was enticed back into activism. In addition to leading some training sessions for professionals, Raj and another trans man initiated a weekly Trans Men/FTM Peer-Support Group at the Toronto gay center. Raj left the leadership after only one year due to once again feeling overwhelmed by the intensity of the work, but the group continued under other leaders for at least another fifteen years. Around the same time as the FTM group was starting, Raj became the subject of a video documentary about his activism, *Rupert Raj Remembers*, which showed at alternative film festivals.

As the twenty-first century began, Raj joined forces with Toronto trans activist Susan Gapka for several years, leading support groups and training workshops; writing about trans, non-binary, and Two-Spirit health; consulting with lawyers and politicians; and speaking with the media on trans, non-binary, and Two-Spirit issues. Also around this time, Raj was recognized for his decades of work on behalf of trans people with a Lifetime Community Achievement Award from a 2001 trans-focused conference at Ryerson University in Toronto and another from a group that works with trans youth.

After earning a master's degree in counseling psychology in 2001, Raj was qualified to work as a professional counselor and got a job on a six-month contract with the Children's Aid Society of Toronto doing specifically LGBT youth work. Afterward, unable to find another job in his chosen field, Raj started his own RR Consulting business specializing in LGBTQ2+ clients. Out of this work, Raj authored a well-received professional publication about counseling gender-diverse people using a transpositive therapeutic model that he had developed. Finally, in 2002, Raj found employment that truly suited him. He began working as a mental health counselor at the progressive and trans-affirming Sherbourne Health Centre in Toronto. While there, he provided counseling for individuals, couples, and families; ran various groups for trans, non-binary, and Two-Spirit people; spearheaded trans, non-binary, and Two-Spirit Pride activities; and advocated for trans, non-binary, and Two-Spirit health more generally.

Over the next decade, Raj continued his work at the Sherbourne Health Centre and also his educational and more political activist work. He made many presentations to professional, corporate, government, and educational groups based on his therapeutic model for working with trans, non-binary, and Two-Spirit people. His work was honored with a City of Toronto Access, Equity and Human Rights Pride Award in 2007, and again in 2010 with a Steinert and Ferreiro Award presented by the Community One Foundation of Toronto. Raj also teamed up with a number of other activists to form a group dedicated to convincing the province of Ontario to pay for gender-affirming procedures for citizens of Ontario, which became official policy in 2008. Also in 2008, Raj joined forces with Dan Irving to produce the anthology *Trans Activism in Canada: A Reader*, published in 2014.

While in his sixties, Raj was again honored for his decades of work on behalf of trans, non-binary, and Two-Spirit people. In 2013 his papers were inducted into the Canadian Lesbian and Gay Archives (CLGA) and his portrait was included in the CLGA's National Portrait Collection. Raj also spoke on a panel of founders of trans activism at the 2016 Moving Trans History Forward conference put on by the Chair in Transgender Studies at the University of Victoria, Canada. In 2017, at his retirement party just before his sixty-fifth birthday, he received a Youth Role Model of the Year Award from his friends and admirers. His final gift to trans, non-binary, and Two-Spirit people was his 2017 self-published book of his memoirs chronicling his many years of struggle and service (Raj 2017).

Jin Xing

Jin Xing, born in 1967 to privileged Korean Chinese parents, knew from at least the age of six that she was supposed to be a girl. At age twenty-nine, she became one of the first people to have her gender change accomplished and officially recognized in China. Since then, she has probably done more to raise public awareness and improve public opinion about trans people in the People's Republic of China than any other single individual. Jin is among the most well-known celebrities in China. She is a celebrated choreographer and dancer, she has been a hugely popular talk show host, and she has served as a judge on a widely watched Chinese television talent show.

Jin Xing started her dancing career at age nine when she joined the People's Liberation Army dance troupe. Subjected to extreme discipline and regular beatings that she said would be deemed child abuse in many parts of the world, the young boy who she then was rose through the ranks to become a colonel while still a teenager. Her training included Chinese opera, Russian ballet, dancing, acrobatics, the use of machine guns, and how to place bombs to blow up bridges. In 1987, with the permission of the Communist Party of China and the People's Liberation Army, Jin spent four years in New York City studying dance with some of the best dancers in America: José Limón, Merce Cunningham, and Martha Graham. After achieving success in New York, Jin traveled to Europe where she danced in Rome and Brussels. But it was while in New York that Jin Xing first learned about transsexuality and the possibility that she could live as the woman that she knew herself to be.

Jin Xing started to become a celebrity in China in 2013 when she served as a judge on the inaugural season of China's *So You Think You Can Dance* television show. Her acerbic opinions about the judging and the contestants were wildly popular on Weibo, China's version of Twitter, earning her the nickname "poison tongue" and catapulting her to fame. She followed this notoriety with her own television chat show and later hosted a popular dating show as well. The influence of the Jin Xing talk show, which had an estimated 100 million viewers, has caused her to be likened to Oprah Winfrey and to be seen as a force for social change. In 2017, the British Broadcasting Company (BBC) went so far as to include her on their annual list of 100 "inspirational and innovative women," citing her as a leader in breaking through "the glass ceiling" holding back many women (BBC 2017).

While enjoying huge popularity, Jin Xing has had to overcome tremendous obstacles and withstand pervasive prejudice against trans people in order to reach the heights that she has obtained. After her gender-affirming surgery in 1995, surgeons told her that a nerve in her leg was so badly damaged that she would no longer be able to dance, and would always walk with a limp. As a professional dancer, this was enough to make her consider suicide. Instead, Jin Xing refused this prognosis, underwent grueling and intensely painful treatments to reverse the problem, and went on to start her own highly successful dance troupe in Shanghai in 2000. However, when she first returned to the stage after her gender change, although she was already a star as a dancer prior to undergoing gender-affirming surgery, the headlines greeted her with "What is a sick trans-sexual doing on our stages?" (Davidson 2015). From another perspective, Jin Xing has also been criticized by feminists for her conservative views, especially about gender relations as displayed on her very popular *Chinese Dating* television show that features parents attempting to find spouses for their children. She is reported to have said that she endorsed the idea that men are superior to women and that "women should not be too outspoken" and "must not try to compete with men" (Beibei 2017).

Jin Xing is married and the mother of three children, whom she adopted as a single parent prior to her marriage. She met her husband, German businessman Heinz-Gerd Oidtmann, when traveling back from Paris in first class on an Air France flight. As she tells the story, she was not initially interested in him but he pursued her even after she told him that she was a transsexual woman with three children—thinking that this would scare off most men. Undeterred, he continued to court her and they were married within a year (Rahman 2016).

Attorneys and Judges

As a historically marginalized group, transgender people have had, and continue to have, major battles for recognition as human beings. Perhaps the two most fraught places for trans people are in the areas of health care/medicine and the law. This section explores individuals who work within legal systems to help give trans people access to the law and to enshrine trans people's rights and dignity within the law.

Kylar William Broadus

Kylar William Broadus is the CEO of the Trans People of Color Coalition and works at the Transgender Legal Defense & Education Fund (TLDEF), founded in 2003. TLDEF is a nonprofit organization that works on numerous legal cases involving trans, non-binary, and Two-Spirit rights in the areas of health care, public accommodation, and employment, to name a few. As a Black trans man, Broadus states the following:

> [M]y Black identity precedes all identities. People see me as Black before anything else. . . . I get the structural and institutional racism that this country has been built upon. . . . We must not let the "conquer and divide" mentality or the isolation that sometimes exist in our Black/SGL/LGBTQ communities at large interfere with our efforts to empower each other and build our communities. (Maglott 2017)

It was in the face of this sort of "divide and conquer" mentality that Broadus became even more vocal with his advocacy work. In the United States, an ENDA (Employment Non-Discrimination Act) bill was being debated in Congress; however, some cisgender gay and lesbian people argued that trans, non-binary, and Two-Spirit people should not be included in the bill in order for it to pass. This split that occurred in the LGBTQ2+ community is what motivated Broadus to become even more outspoken about the intersections of racism and transphobia in the law. As of fall 2018, there still is not an all-inclusive ENDA bill in the United States.

Dean Spade

Dean Spade is a white trans man and law professor at Seattle University School of Law, where he teaches courses such as Gender and the Law, Poverty and the Law, and the Law and Social Movements. Spade believes in full accessibility to the law for all people and has been an outspoken legal and activist voice for some of society's most marginalized communities, who often deal with intersecting oppressions. For example, in a series of informational legal videos, he focuses on trans people of color with disabilities. He is the author of numerous articles that focus on issues surrounding legal access for trans, non-binary, and Two-Spirit people, and his 2011 book, entitled *Normal Life: Administrative Violence, Critical Trans Politics and the Limits of the Law,* is now in a second edition as well as in a Spanish translation. One of Spade's most important contributions to trans, non-binary, and Two-Spirit law was his founding of the Sylvia Rivera Law Project in 2002—a program named after trans pioneer and Stonewall veteran Sylvia Rivera that focuses predominantly on issues facing trans people living in poverty who do not have access to legal representation.

Shannon Price Minter

Shannon Price Minter is a white trans man who has served as an outstanding lawyer for over two decades in the forefront of the LGBTQ2+ rights movements. Minter is the legal director of the National Center for Lesbian Rights (NCLR), a leading legal advocacy organization for LGBT people. The Transgender Law Center also formed out of NCLR. Most famously, Minter was the lead counsel for California's landmark marriage equality case that eventually made its way to the United States Supreme Court, although Minter himself was not the counsel at the U.S. Supreme Court. He has won numerous awards including the Ford Foundation's Leadership for a Changing World award. He also serves on the board of the Transgender Law & Policy Institute.

Phyllis Randolph Frye

Since 2010, the world has seen a steady stream of trans judges appointed to the bench. In the United States, Judge Phyllis Randolph Frye was appointed as the associate judge for the City of Houston Municipal Courts in 2010, becoming the first openly out trans judge in the country. The fact that she is a sitting judge in the historically conservative state of Texas makes her appointment all the more historic. Frye has worked for over sixty years as an LGBTQ2+ rights advocate, and identifies as a lesbian. She is lovingly known as "The Grandmother of Transgender Law." Although she is a judge, she also continues to practice law and focuses solely on trans, non-binary, and Two-Spirit clients (adults and children) who face many areas of discrimination within the state of Texas. One case at a time, she tries to change the legal landscape of the Lone Star State. In 2015, she won an award from the National Center for Transgender Equality.

Kael McKenzie

Kael McKenzie became the first open and out trans, non-binary, or Two-Spirit judge in Canada in 2017. McKenzie is a member of the Manitoba Métis Nation, and in his first words after having been sworn in, he began by acknowledging that the ceremony was taking place on Indigenous land that has been colonized for over a century. His wife and two sons attended his historic swearing-in ceremony (CBC News 2016). McKenzie is a military veteran of the Canadian Forces where, when he was eighteen years old, he was assumed to be a lesbian; however, he already knew he identified as a man. He says the following about his experience there:

When I was in the Canadian Forces, I was in during a time that was before sexual orientation had been added as a [form of] discrimination, and it was around that time that I really started to understand what some of the issues involving the LGBT community were. (Beaumont 2015)

While in the Canadian military, he worked on a committee there for LGBTQ2+ rights in the armed services; afterward, when he went to college, he helped create LGBTQ2+ safe spaces there; as a lawyer, he co-chaired a conference focused on LGBTQ2+ issues (Beaumont 2015).

Joyita Mondal

In 2017, Joyita Mondal was sworn in as the first out trans judge in India. Mondal is a young trans woman (twenty-nine at the time she was sworn in) who has faced numerous hardships in her life. She was born into a traditional Hindu family in West Bengal; at an early age, Mondal had to leave school because she was bullied for her gender nonconformity. She slept at bus stations and begged for money on the streets. After she moved away from her home district, she began to work for the rights of *hijras* and other gender-diverse people. Mondal also took correspondence courses and eventually earned a law degree. She sees her appointment as a judge in a very complex light:

> All governments want to appoint one person from a weaker community to a top post so that voices of others of the community are muffled. I would not let that happen. Even if two–three percent of transgenders [*sic*] in Islampur get dignified jobs, I would consider my appointment beneficial for my community. They would not have to work as sex workers for Rs 150–200 and can have a good sleep at night. Even now, as I move around in air-conditioned cars, my people beg during the day and work as sex workers at night. (*Think Change India* 2017)

Instead of seeing her appointment as a complete victory, Mondal has a keen understanding of the areas in which she needs to continue to work even harder for her community.

Celebrities

For any marginalized community, it is important to have public role models. Sports figures and television, music, and film celebrities are often the most visible people to the eye of the general public. For trans, non-binary, and Two-Spirit people, in particular, such public personas are crucial to overcoming a sense of isolation. This is especially so for trans, non-binary, and Two-Spirit people who may live in more remote locations and who may not have access to the same information as people in urban centers. Trans, non-binary, and Two-Spirit celebrities also contribute to building empathy among cisgender people who are not in direct personal contact with trans, non-binary, and Two-Spirit people. Regardless of where one lives, the media bring the world into one's home.

Chaz Bono

Chaz Bono grew up in the spotlight as the daughter of the late singer Sonny Bono and singer/actress Cher. Since coming out as a trans man, Bono has advocated for trans, non-binary, and Two-Spirit rights and is featured in the documentary film *Becoming Chaz* (2011). Also in 2011, he was a featured dancer on the American reality show *Dancing with the Stars*, where he received a lot of media attention as a trans man visible on mainstream American television. By being himself in such a public way, Chaz Bono has made the existence of trans men, and trans people in general, more visible to millions of viewers.

Laverne Cox

Actress Laverne Cox's character, Sophia Burset, in the award-winning television show *Orange Is the New Black*, could be based on the lives of many African American trans women held within the prison-industrial complex. Cox was the first openly trans, non-binary, or Two-Spirit person to receive an Emmy Award nomination. Outside of Hollywood, though, Cox has used her star power to become a trans rights advocate. She has her own column in *The Huffington Post* and has used her clout to produce the 2014 documentary series about trans youth entitled *The T Word* and the 2016 documentary *Free CeCe*, which focused on the young African American trans woman CeCe McDonald who, in self-defense, killed a man who brutally raped and beat her.

Lana and Lilly Wachowski

In June 2015, the Wachowski siblings (along with J. Michael Straczynski) released their television show, *Sense8*, on Netflix. Before their transitions, the Wachowskis, now both trans women, Lana and Lilly, were the directors for the film sensation *The Matrix* and *V Is For Vendetta*. In *Sense8*, the Wachowskis had a vision of the world they would like to see—one where people of all nations, gender identities, socioeconomic situations, and sexual orientations could work together for the betterment of humanity. One reviewer of the show notes that the Wachowskis have created relationships that "form an ideal utopia within an otherwise chaotic world. Most of the sensates represent the 'other,' the ones who threaten preconceived notions of 'normalcy' even though they do not pose a threat" (Gerber 2017). For many viewers, the Wachowskis have provided an antidote to still "far-too-prevalent" transphobic representations in popular culture. In particular, the Wachowskis chose trans woman Jamie Clayton to play the character of Nomi Marks, who is a trans woman in a positive transracial relationship with her lesbian partner, Amanita.

Jamie Clayton

Trans actress Jamie Clayton, who plays lesbian trans woman Nomi Marks on *Sense8*, was thrilled to be able to play a trans person on screen and to work with the Wachowskis. Clayton said, "Playing a trans-character on a show being shepherded by Lana Wachowski, I knew I would be protected and represented in a way that trans people have never been represented before on TV" (Ge 2015). The moment Clayton found out that she had been selected for the role, she understood how important this was going to be for her, for the Wachowskis, and also for viewers tuning in:

> [I]t gave Lana an opportunity to write her first trans character, and therefore just bathe her in authenticity and her wanting to make sure that an actor, who happens to

be trans . . . make sure that they get the part. Then it brought the other layer of authenticity to the character. And that's resonating so deeply with the audience at home. (Huddleston 2017)

Ian Alexander

Following their positive trans representation with *Sense8*, Netflix wanted to include another trans person as a main character in their new show, *The OA*. Teenage Asian American trans man Ian Alexander had been struggling with coming out as trans when he found the casting call on a trans support website that asked specifically for a young Asian American trans man. Alexander said, "It's just so rare to see Hollywood casting an Asian-American trans boy, let alone any trans boy, that I felt like I had no other choice but to audition" (Weik 2017). Not only did Alexander get the role, but the director often deferred to him when it came to trans issues. The show's writers wanted to make sure to "get it right," so they often asked Ian Alexander to come up with his own writing and work for the show. On one hand, that put a lot of pressure on the teenager; however, it also ensured the role's authenticity, which is why his character and the show have gained a lot of accolades.

Artists

In the twenty-first century, the art world has seen an explosion of work by trans, non-binary, and Two-Spirit artists as well as trans, non-binary, and Two-Spirit themed pieces created by allies. Often, art that is focused on trans, non-binary, and Two-Spirit themes focuses on intersecting identities, politics, and culture. Art is an outstanding medium with which to reach larger audiences, and art can give a voice to those who are usually silenced.

Robin Hammond

Robin Hammond was born in New Zealand and has lived in Africa, France, and Japan. He is an ally to gender-diverse people around the world and strives to help make their lives visible through his photography. Hammond is an international humanitarian and photojournalist who has won four Amnesty International awards for human rights journalism as well as Pictures of the Year International World Understanding Award. Through his work, Hammond strives to look at the ways that trans, non-binary, and gender-diverse people are often over-looked in terms of global human rights issues.

Hammond is most famous for his photography in the January 2017 *National Geographic* special issue, which focused on trans, non-binary, and Two-Spirit children. In June 2018, Hammond, in collaboration with the famous British singer Elton John, released a series of photographs exploring the lives of LGBTQ+ people in Africa. Many of the portraits are of gen-der-diverse people in numerous African countries where it is illegal to be gender diverse. Hammond's captions explain the trauma and human rights violations that they face on a daily basis. In one color photo, a trans man sits on a bed looking away from the camera. The caption reads:

> This transgender man, who declined to give his real name, was nearly burned alive in 2009. His assailants poured gasoline and were dragging him to a bonfire when his father intervened. In an attempt to "cure" him, his father sent him to a prayer camp in Benin where he was physically abused and raped. (John 2018)

Marilyn Roxie

Marilyn Roxie is an American artist and curator who splits their time between the United States and the United Kingdom. They work in the media of music video, experimental film, photomontage, and generative art. In 2010, they designed the genderqueer flag, which is now displayed internationally as the genderqueer and non-binary flag. The colors of the flag are lav-ender, white, and dark chartreuse.

Annually in June, Roxie curates the *Just Experimenting* film screening at the Center for Sex and Culture in San Francisco, which is "a selection of experimental films dealing with liminal and marginalized identity and behavior in gender and sexuality" (personal communication). Roxie's own experimental films have been shown in Berlin, San Francisco, and Manchester and are available online. In their film *HE*, Roxie explores trans, non-binary, and gender-diverse and queer romance and desire through a lens of dreams and fantasies, and in their film *Nature Twink* they explore cultural assumptions around the word "twink," a term used for skinny young white gay men.

Throughout Roxie's work, they explore "androgyny, the relationship between submission and masculinity, and the relationship of found images to creative authorship" (personal communication).

Zackary Drucker and Rhys Ernst

Drucker and Ernst are most famously known as the producers of the American award-winning television program *Transparent*. Drucker, who is a trans woman, and Ernst, who is a trans man, also chronicled their full gender transitions as a couple over a six-year period, and in 2014 they were honored by being part of the Whitney Biennial for their photographic art project entitled *Relationship*. As a trans couple, they felt it was important to have their work displayed to the large numbers of people who visit the Whitney Museum in New York.

While Drucker and Ernst work on making trans lives visible at art museums and within American popular culture by way of their work on *Transparent*, they each also work on other, less mainstream art projects. One of Drucker's recent works is an experimental film on the evolution of identity, *They Answered Us in Unison*. Drucker is also working on the *Flawless Sabrina Archive*, a nonprofit organization that houses the archives of iconic queer gender outlaw, drag performer, and activist Flawless Sabrina/Jack Doroshow. Drucker continues to focus on cross-generational projects to ensure that future generations know their history.

Ernst also wants to make sure that the stories of trans, non-binary, and Two-Spirit people are told, and that trans, non-binary, and Two-Spirit history becomes more visible and accessible for all. His award-winning short documentary film series, *We've Been Around,* does just that. These short films that can be viewed for free online include the stories of the early gay trans activist Lou Sullivan (1951–1991), the historic African American trans woman Lucy Hicks Anderson (1886–1954), and gospel-singing trans man Wilmer "Little Axe" Broadnax (1916–1992), to name a few.

Yishay Garbasz

Yishay Garbasz is a British/Israeli trans woman artist who lives and works in Berlin. Her various art pieces, which include large-scale installations and photography, tend to focus on trauma across generations. One of Garbasz's projects, entitled *In My Mother's Footsteps,* is a photographic exhibit of her mother, who was a Jewish survivor of the Holocaust. Garbasz explains her motivation for photographing the concentration camps where her mother was held:

> My mother lost parts of her soul in those places and I had to go back to collect them. . . . As I am a photographer, the camera was going to be my tool to help me see. (Shandler and Garbasz 2009)

Garbasz's photo exhibits often focus on intersectionality and have included projects on the Fukushima Nuclear Exclusion Zone and the Peace Lines of Northern Ireland. In each case, she remains very physically and mentally present when she explores various social and cultural traumas in her photography. She says, "People think that their voice as an artist is somewhere far away, over some obstacle: for me it is right where you stand. What you're facing right now, is your voice" (Hugill

2016). In 2010, she was recognized as the woman filmmaker of the year in Berlin.

Sean Dorsey and Shawna Virago

Sean Dorsey and Shawna Virago are partners in life and partners in art. Virago notes that they are "avowed enemies of the gender binary and heterosexism" (Anderson-Minshall 2017). Together, they have made the San Francisco Bay Area (already known to be a mecca for LGBTQ2+ people and organizations) an internationally known focal point for trans art and culture.

Dorsey and Virago created the Fresh Meat Festival of queer and trans performance, which is a three-day show every year in June featuring numerous trans and queer artists. In addition to work on Fresh Meat, Dorsey runs free dance classes for people who identify across the trans spectrum and who have been told that their bodies are not "right" for dance: people with disabilities, people who are large, and people who do not conform to expressing themselves within the gender binary. Virago is also a musician and the artistic director of the Transgender Film Festival, which is the oldest and largest in the world and takes place every November to commemorate the Transgender Day of Remembrance. Both Dorsey and Virago have won numerous awards for their various art endeavors.

Dorsey is a dance choreographer and dancer and head of the Sean Dorsey Dance company, which is comprised of cisgender and transgender gay, bisexual, and heterosexual men of different ethnicities.

In the 2018 world premiere of the show *Boys in Trouble,* Sean Dorsey Dance's unique combination of modern dance, music, and spoken word explored the ways that trans and queer masculinities often are misrepresented in the broader culture. Other award-winning shows choreographed by Dorsey include *The Missing Generation,* which combines memoirs and diary entries of queer and trans people during the AIDS epidemic in the United States, and *Uncovered: The Diary Project,* which explores the diaries of the late gay trans man Lou Sullivan. On

June 20, 2018, *The Missing Generation* became the first production by a U.S. trans artist presented by the prestigious Joyce Theater in New York City.

Virago's music is a combination of punk, rockabilly, folk, and blues. In her 2018 song, "Tranimal," Virago sings about the ways that non-binary trans people, in particular, are viewed as less than human. Her 2017 album, *Heaven Sent Delinquent*, won several indie music awards.

Oral History Projects

Knowing one's history is essential to one's identity and to the struggle for recognition, acceptance, and full human rights. This is even more so for trans, non-binary, Two-Spirit, and other gender-diverse people whose presence the larger society has often attempted to systematically repress and erase. Learning the history of one's people can be done in many ways, not the least of which is through hearing others tell the stories of their lives. Trans, non-binary, Two-Spirit, and other gender-diverse people need to know how we got to where we are today, and people in the future will want to hear the stories of today for the same reasons. Oral histories, retained in archives, are an indispensable way for people to learn their heritage. As expressed in the Universal Declaration on Archives, issued in 2010 by the International Council on Archives and adopted in 2011 by the United Nations Educational, Scientific and Cultural Organization (UNESCO):

> Archives record decisions, actions and memories. Archives are a unique and irreplaceable heritage passed from one generation to another. . . . They are authoritative sources of information . . . [that] play an essential role in the development of societies by safeguarding and contributing to individual and community memory. Open access to archives enriches our knowledge of human society, promotes democracy, protects citizens' rights and

enhances the quality of life. (International Council on Archives 2010)

Very little of the history of trans, non-binary, and Two-Spirit people has yet been written. We are now at a crucial time when the people who initiated the second wave of self-conscious activism that began in the 1960s are reaching the ends of their lifetimes. Now is the time to record their living memories before it is too late to do so. Three projects that are engaged in that work are the Canadian-led international LGBTQ History Digital Collaboratory, the Transgender Oral History Project at the Jean-Nickolaus Tretter Collection in LGBT Studies at the University of Minnesota Libraries, and the "To Survive on This Shore" project by Jess T. Dugan and Vanessa Fabbre.

LGBTQ History Digital Collaboratory

LGBTQ History Digital Collaboratory is a project involving partners in Canada, the United States, and the United Kingdom. Several components of the project focus on retrieving and preserving the stories of trans, non-binary, and Two-Spirit people. The TransPartners Project records oral history interviews with the romantic partners of trans men who were with their trans partners for at least six month before or during their transitions. Another project is developing an archival collection based on the papers and an oral history of Mirha-Soleil Ross, a trans woman media artist, activist, and sex worker who lived in Toronto from the early 1990s to 2008. A third oral history element of the collaboratory traces the fight to get the province of Ontario, Canada, to pay for gender affirmation treatments by recording the voices of the people who worked for the policy change and those who were affected by it. Finally, an oral history project under the auspices of the Transgender Archives at the University of Victoria, Canada, records life histories of veteran trans, non-binary, and Two-Spirit activists in Canada and the United States whose work stretches back to the 1970s. A series of books are planned chronicling the lives of these pioneering trans, non-binary, and Two-Spirit activists to help others to understand the forces that shaped them in an era when there was almost no social acceptance for trans, non-binary, and Two-Spirit people.

Transgender Oral History Project

The Transgender Oral History Project at the Jean-Nickolaus Tretter Collection in LGBT Studies at the University of Minnesota Libraries consists of two waves of oral histories. In the first iteration, the project focused on video recording oral histories of trans, non-binary, and Two-Spirit people in the upper Midwest of the United States. Two hundred video interviews were recorded by Andrea Jenkins. Interviewees represent a wide swath of ages, races, classes, life experiences, gender identities, and expressions. Some of the people interviewed were activists and many were simply trans, non-binary, and Two-Spirit people talking about their lives. Many of the videos and transcripts have been posted, along with an online exhibit, on the website of the Tretter Collection. The second phase looks at trans, non-binary, and Two-Spirit community activism and policy work throughout the United States.

To Survive on This Shore

Professional photographer artist Jess T. Dugan and social work professor Vanessa Fabbre recognized that there were very few images or stories in public circulation depicting the lives of trans, non-binary, and Two-Spirit elders. Starting in 2013, they set out to remedy this by photographing and interviewing a wide range of trans, non-binary, and Two-Spirit people over the age of fifty in the United States. They worked to represent the broadest possible group of people across race, socioeconomic class, geographic location, gender identity, and also in terms of the age at which they transitioned. They interviewed and photographed eighty-eight people from ages fifty to ninety who had transitioned as early as 1970 and as recently as 2016. Their 2018 book, *To Survive on This Shore*, tells the stories of sixty-five of the people they photographed and interviewed. Oral histories of all eighty-eight are to be held in the archival collections of the Transgender Archives at the University of Victoria, Canada; the Kinsey Institute at the University of Indiana, Bloomington; and the Sexual Minorities Archives in Holyoke, Massachusetts.

Advocacy and Professional Organizations

The following organizations, which range from academic institutions and historic archives to human rights advocacy groups, all focus on empowering trans, non-binary, and Two-Spirit communities. They are all focused on giving voice and agency to trans, non-binary, and Two-Spirit people.

Chair in Transgender Studies

The Chair in Transgender Studies was established in January 2016. Located at the University of Victoria, Canada, it is the only such chair in the world. The chair is a research and community outreach office. Professor Aaron Devor, who conceived of the chair and secured initial funding for it from the philanthropic Tawani Foundation of Chicago, is the inaugural chair. While Devor offers courses in transgender studies, the office of the chair does not offer a program of study leading to certification or a degree. The scholars and staff affiliated with the Chair in Transgender Studies are committed to generating and communicating solid reliable information about the real world that can be used to drive social change and improve the well-being of trans, non-binary, and Two-Spirit people; and supporting and building healthy communities by facilitating activities of interest to trans, non-binary, and Two-Spirit people and their allies.

The programs of the Chair in Transgender Studies support both existing and new scholars to pursue careers in Transgender Studies; build local, national and international linkages with others working in Transgender Studies; conduct and publish research; provide scholarships and fellowships; sponsor biennial Moving Trans History Forward conferences; sponsor colloquia, lectures, and arts events year round; advise government and nonprofit agencies on policies and practices; educate students and the public; and operate the Transgender Archives at the University of Victoria.

Among the most significant activities of the Chair in Transgender Studies are the biennial series of international Moving Trans History Forward conferences, led by the Chair in Transgender Studies. These conferences were also conceived by Devor and began in 2014. The conferences draw together people from teens to octogenarians, from all around the world. These gatherings are not just for scholars or just for community people. They create opportunities for cross-fertilization among people who contribute as community activists, students, researchers, educators, artists, service providers, family members, and allies. Conferences, which span several days, consider the history of trans activism and research, the crucial issues that impact trans, non-binary, and Two-Spirit people today and in the future, locally, nationally and globally. These highly successful conferences draw many hundreds of people from countries in the Americas, Europe, Asia, and the Middle East.

Another of the most significant contributions of the Chair in Transgender Studies is the operation of the Transgender Archives at the University of Victoria. The Transgender Archives were also founded by Professor Aaron Devor, with collecting starting in 2007 and an official launch in 2011. The Transgender Archives preserve original documents recording the contributions of pioneering activists, community leaders, and researchers who have contributed to the betterment of trans, non-binary, and Two-Spirit people. These items include thousands of books (many of them rare or hard to find), pamphlets, newsletters, organizational records, court cases, news clippings, conference proceedings, scrapbooks, letters, diaries, photos, videos, audio recordings, paintings and drawings, erotica, and ephemera and realia such as trophies, T-shirts, posters, matchbook covers, playing cards, and buttons. Records of research related to trans, non-binary, and Two-Spirit people go back to the nineteenth century, while records in the Transgender Archives of activism by trans, non-binary, and Two-Spirit people are in fifteen languages from twenty-three countries on all continents except Antarctica and span more than half a century. If everything in the Transgender Archives were placed on one long shelf, it would be over 530 feet long (equal to 1.5 football fields long). The Transgender Archives collections comprise the largest trans-focused archives in the world. Collections are open to all members of the public for free.

Other programs of the Chair in Transgender Studies include a scholarships and fellowships program for undergraduate and graduate students; hosting university-based scholars in residence and community-based researchers from around the world; a distinguished visiting speakers series; lectures by graduate students and local academic and community-based scholars; social events, some specifically for trans, non-binary, and Two-Spirit people, and others open to the general public; arts and cultural events featuring trans, non-binary, and Two-Spirit people; and an active social media presence.

Aaron Devor, as chair in Transgender Studies, also makes meaningful contributions to advancing Transgender Studies in other ways. These include having been active in the World Professional Association for Transgender Health (WPATH) since 1992, during which time he has been an author of Versions 6 and 7 of *Standards of Care for the Health of Transsexual, Transgender and Gender Nonconforming People*, is guiding their translation into world languages, and is a member of the committee working toward Version 8, as well as serving as the historian for WPATH. He frequently speaks to the media and is often called upon to provide advice and education to policy makers. He has published widely in Transgender Studies, delivered more than twenty keynote addresses to audiences around the world, and has received a number of awards for his work in Transgender Studies.

Transgender Europe (TGEU)

Transgender Europe (TGEU), a charitable advocacy organization for trans, non-binary, and gender-diverse people in Europe, was started in November 2005 in Vienna, Austria, at the first meeting of the European Transgender Council. It began as a volunteer organization and has since grown to have a paid staff of ten guided by an international volunteer steering committee headquartered in Berlin, Germany. The 2018 steering committee included representatives from France, Croatia, Norway, Sweden, the Netherlands, Italy, and Ireland.

TGEU is made up of member organizations and is devoted to working for equality for all trans, non-binary, and gender-diverse people in Europe. They work by raising awareness and advocating on behalf of trans, non-binary, and gender-diverse people both directly as TGEU and by supporting and participating in national and international initiatives and organizations. At last count, TGEU had 105 participating member organizations located in 42 different European countries ranging from Iceland, Norway, Finland, and Sweden in the north; to Turkey, Croatia, Malta, and Israel in the south; and from Ireland, the United Kingdom, Spain, and Portugal in Western Europe; to Russia, Kazakhstan, Tajikistan, and Kyrgyzstan in the east.

One of the central ways that TGEU supports advocacy on behalf of trans, non-binary, and gender-diverse people is by conducting detailed research into the conditions they face. TGEU publishes comprehensive reports that are made available to member organizations and the public. The information in these reports has proven to be extremely valuable in providing reliable data that has been effective in motivating policy makers to action. TGEU has been provided funding for their work by the European Union, the U.S. State Department, the Government of the Netherlands, Open Society Foundations, the Arcus Foundation, and the Heinrich Böll Stiftung Foundation. They report an annual income of over one million euros.

One of TGEU's larger undertakings is the Transrespect versus Transphobia Worldwide (TvT) research project. TGEU works on this project with twenty partner organizations, more than eighty activists, and more than twenty-five researchers and experts from around the world. Together, they gather both quantitative data in the form of facts and figures, and qualitative data in the form of real-life stories, to build pictures of global circumstances for trans, non-binary, and gender-diverse people. The TvT project draws from three main ongoing research projects.

One source of information for TvT is the Trans Murder Monitoring project. This project systematically collates information from worldwide reports of murders of trans, non-binary, and gender-diverse people in sixty-two countries. This data forms the basis of the annual lists read out every year at Transgender Day of Remembrance (TDOR) ceremonies enacted around the world on November 20. TDOR is done to ensure that the many trans, non-binary, gender-diverse, and Two-Spirit people (largely trans women of color) murdered each year are not forgotten. The Trans Murder Monitoring project is the backbone of this commemoration.

Another source of information for the TvT project is a Legal and Social Mapping project, which records laws and health care practices related to trans, non-binary, and gender-diverse people in 118 countries. A third component that contributes to the TvT project comes from a survey on the Social Experiences of Trans and Gender Variant People conducted by TGEU in coordination with organizations in India, the Philippines, Serbia, Tonga, Turkey, Venezuela, and Thailand.

The results of these collaborative research projects are displayed on an extremely informative website that includes graphics of color-coded interactive world maps backed by detailed data about many aspects of life for trans, non-binary, and gender-diverse people in each country. A similar set of maps specific to Europe are regularly updated by TGEU.

In order to increase accessibility and to enable the greatest advocacy effectiveness, another project of TGEU is the translation of TvT reports into a variety of world languages. In the service of increasing capacity for sustained research and advocacy, TGEU has also undertaken training sessions in different regions of the world. In the past several years, they have provided capacity-building workshops in Hungary, Australia, Mexico, Italy, Thailand, and other parts of Asia.

Another ongoing project of TGEU is the ProTrans project that monitors and reports on violence and human rights violations against trans, non-binary, and gender-diverse people in the Eastern European and Central Asian countries of Armenia, Georgia, Hungary, Kyrgyzstan, Moldova, Russia, Serbia, Turkey, and Ukraine. The information gathered in the research component is used for advocacy in order to improve the human rights situation of trans, non-binary, and gender-diverse people in the region, and to guide efforts in building community-based support services for survivors of violence.

A recent project of TGEU was the report *Mapping Digital Landscape of Trans Activism in Central Asia and Eastern Europe.* This report provides an overview of how trans, non-binary, and gender-diverse activists in twenty-six countries of Central Asia and Eastern Europe powerfully use the Internet as an organizing tool at the same time that they feel extremely vulnerable to surveillance and violence from governments and transphobic individuals and groups. The report includes clear-headed advice from those in the region about how they have coped with the difficulties that they have faced.

One of the main reasons that the research done by TGEU is valuable is because it can be used in advocacy work to improve the lives of trans, non-binary, and gender-diverse people. TGEU itself also engages in human rights advocacy work in European contexts. They have been involved in such work before the European Commission, the European Parliament, the Council of Europe, and the Organization for Security and Co-operation in Europe. Working as TGEU and in conjunction with other human rights organizations, TGEU also presents *amicus curiae* (third-party) legal briefs and participates in class-action law suits. To strengthen these actions, TGEU created a formal network of legal professionals working on cases for trans, non-binary, and gender-diverse people in courts of Europe.

The magnitude of the research, public education, advocacy, and capacity-building that is coordinated and communicated through the offices of TGEU is monumental. It makes an unparalleled contribution to the ability of trans, non-binary, and gender-diverse individuals and groups to more effectively advance human rights and equality for all trans, non-binary, and gender-diverse people.

World Professional Association for Transgender Health (WPATH)

The World Professional Association for Transgender Health (WPATH) is the largest organization in the world serving the health needs of trans, non-binary, Two-Spirit, and gender-diverse people. It was originally incorporated in the United States in 1979 and, until 2007, was called the Harry Benjamin International Gender Dysphoria Association (HBIGDA) in honor of Dr. Harry Benjamin (1885–1986), who wrote the first book about transsexualism and was a longtime advocate for supportive medical treatments for trans people (then called transvestites and transsexuals) at a time when few people were. The WPATH is governed by an executive committee consisting of a president, past-president, president elect, secretary, and treasurer and a board of ten directors who serve in staggered terms of four years. Annual General Meetings are held at WPATH biennial conferences.

There are four categories of membership. Full membership is open to professionals working in "academic and applied disciplines that contribute, or have the potential to contribute, to the wellbeing of transgender individuals and to the field of transgender health." Since 2017, there have been two levels of dues for full members. Professionals from "least developed countries" pay one-third of the regular memberships dues. Supporting membership is available to people who wish to be involved in WPATH but are not working in related professions. Emeritus members are retired full members. Student memberships are for graduate students whose studies would qualify them for full membership upon graduation. In 2018 there were 2,220 members of WPATH in forty-eight countries. While most members of WPATH are cisgender, a significant minority of members are trans, non-binary, Two-Spirit, or gender diverse, a number of whom have held senior leadership positions in recent years.

Throughout the organization's early years, trans, non-binary, and Two-Spirit people were primarily seen as patients and were rarely involved in any kind of leadership capacity with the exception of the founding board of directors, which included Jude Patton, who was then the co-director of Renaissance, a transsexual service organization. Trans, non-binary, and Two-Spirit people did not again appear in WPATH's leadership until the dawning of the twenty-first century. Jude Patton again served on the board of directors from 1997 to 2001 along with trans physician Dr. Sheila Kirk, who also served as secretary-treasurer from 2001 to 2005. By 2003, trans activist and author Jamison Green had joined the board, and in 2005 trans activist and legal expert Stephen Whittle had become president-elect, serving as president from 2007 to 2009 and past-president from 2009 to 2011. Jamison Green remained on the board and served as president from 2013 to 2015 and past-president until 2018. Over the intervening years, more and more trans, non-binary, and Two-Spirit people have become members who have added their voices and votes to influence the direction of the organization.

The WPATH does most of its work through three main avenues: conferences, publication of standards of care (SOC), and professional training.

Every two years since 1969 there has been an international symposium or conference that brings together professionals who work in the area of gender dysphoria. The earliest conferences were sponsored by a now-defunct organization, the Erickson Educational Foundation (EEF). When the EEF stopped sponsoring conferences, a group founded the precursor to WPATH, HBIGDA, in 1979 to carry on that work. In 2018, the twenty-fifth biennial WPATH conference was held in Buenos Aires, Argentina, and brought together over 900 professionals from around the world to share information and to learn from one another.

Around the same time as HBIGDA was first formed, a committee of HBIGDA created the first version of a set of standards of care intended to provide some basic expectations for what constituted ethical and competent care of transsexual people. This step was motivated by the fact that unscrupulous and incompetent people were known to be exploiting, maiming, and disfiguring trans people who were desperate for medical care. Subsequent revisions were issued in 1980, 1981, 1990, 1998, 2001, and 2011. Despite its well-intentioned origins, the document quickly came to be seen by trans people as being more about protecting physicians from lawsuits than about making sure that trans, non-binary, Two-Spirit, and gender-diverse people got the care that they needed.

As the organization evolved, the focus shifted to being more concerned about the health of trans people and both the name change in 2007 to the World Professional Association for Transgender Health and the approach of the standards of care reflected this. Version 7, published in 2011, was titled *Standards of Care (SOC) for the Health of Transsexual, Transgender, and Gender Nonconforming People* and was generally well received both by professionals and members of trans, non-binary, Two-Spirit, and gender-diverse communities. It has been translated into eighteen world languages and is widely used by governments, health insurance providers, and individuals.

Since November 2015, WPATH has been delivering a Global Education Initiative (GEI) that consists of a series of live interactive and interdisciplinary training sessions that can lead to becoming a WPATH Certified Provider. In order to become certified, a professional must be a member of WPATH; complete a two-day foundations course, ten hours of advanced training, and ten hours of GEI electives; be mentored by an approved WPATH mentor for ten hours; spend five hours listening at an approved meeting of trans, non-binary, Two-Spirit, or other gender-diverse people; have documented experience as a service provider or researcher; know and agree to comply with the latest version of the *Standards of Care*; commit to twenty hours of continuing education every two years; and pass an exam. This initiative is the first ever attempt to certify that particular individuals are well trained to deliver services to trans, non-binary, Two-Spirit, and other gender-diverse people. As of 2018, 2,500 people have received training under this program.

In keeping with its mission and vision, the WPATH has also taken an active role in urging social action in some regards. It has issued public statements calling for the depsychopathologization of gender variance; in support of the rights of trans, non-binary, Two-Spirit, and other gender-diverse people to serve openly in the military, and to receive treatment paid for by the military; and in support of the rights of trans, non-binary, Two-Spirit, and other gender-diverse people to freely express their genders. WPATH has also publicly urged governments to permit legal gender changes without any requirement of medical or psychological interventions, to allow more than two gender options on official records and documents, and to respect the privacy rights of trans, non-binary, Two-Spirit, and other gender-diverse people.

Gender Odyssey and Philadelphia Trans Wellness Conferences

During the last decade of the twentieth century and the first decades of the twenty-first century, trans, non-binary, and Two-Spirit people have increasingly built large and impactful organizations to serve their communities and to improve public perceptions. Conferences by and for trans, non-binary, and Two-Spirit people have become an essential part of this process.

Two very successful examples of this work are the Gender Odyssey conferences and the Philadelphia Trans Wellness conferences, both of which held their first events in 2001.

Gender Odyssey conferences were the brainchild of Aidan Key, a trans man living in Seattle, Washington. He and a group of volunteers first conceived of the Seattle conferences as being focused on the needs of transmasculine people. By 2007, Key's vision had expanded and Gender Odyssey became two conferences, one for trans adults in general and one for families. By 2012, Gender Odyssey increased its reach still further by adding another conference for professionals who work with trans, non-binary, and Two-Spirit people. The year 2017 saw Gender Odyssey branch out again into a second conference for professionals held in Los Angeles. In 2018 they added a second family conference in Los Angeles and dropped their general adults' programming stream. In 2019, they are expanding to San Diego as well. Each year, thousands of people benefit greatly from attending the Gender Odyssey conferences.

The Philadelphia Trans Wellness conferences also started in 2001 and have grown steadily in size each year. The conferences, funded by the Philadelphia Foundation, are a project of the Mazzoni Center, a service provider devoted to health and well-being for LGBTQ people. Like Gender Odyssey, the Philadelphia Trans Wellness conferences provide special conference programming tracks for families and professionals working with trans, non-binary, and Two-Spirit people and a broad range of more general programming. In part due to the fact that there is no fee for general admission, these Philadelphia Trans Wellness conferences served more than 10,000 people from 32 countries in 2018.

National Center for Transgender Equality (NCTE)

The first decades of the twenty-first century have also seen the rise of significantly impactful advocacy organizations working for the welfare of trans, non-binary, and Two-Spirit people. In the United States, the National Center for Transgender Equality was established in 2003, with Mara Keisling at the head. They center their work in Washington, DC and provide support to local organizations across the United States. Their focus is on using national-level advocacy to end violence and improve policies that affect the lives of trans, non-binary, and Two-Spirit people in the United States. They have been involved in campaigns concerning access to health care; changing gender markers on identification documents; improving conditions for trans, non-binary, and Two-Spirit prison inmates; and strengthening non-discrimination laws in employment, housing, and education.

Among the many important projects of the National Center for Transgender Equality are two large-scale surveys. *Injustice at Every Turn*, released in 2011, was a joint project with the National Gay and Lesbian Task Force and involved 6,450 trans, non-binary, and Two-Spirit respondents (Grant et al. 2011). At the time, it was the largest and most comprehensive survey of trans, non-binary, and Two-Spirit people ever accomplished and proved to be highly influential among decision-makers. Four years later, the National Center for Transgender Equality released the 2015 U.S. Transgender Survey. This time, the number of trans, non-binary, and Two-Spirit people surveyed more than quadrupled to 27,715, once again making it the largest and most comprehensive study of trans, non-binary, and Two-Spirit people ever done (James et al. 2016). The immense power of having this kind of data at hand for use in advocacy efforts is hard to overstate and enables trans, non-binary, and Two-Spirit people to effectively shift public thinking and policies toward improvements in the lives of trans, non-binary, and Two-Spirit people.

Trans and Intersex Organizing in Africa

Neo S. Musangi from Nairobi, Kenya wrote the following:

To be so often harassed in these streets is to signal the danger of your being. It is to take a risk with yourself. To continue walking these streets is to understand that your body presents itself as available for insults, advances, rape, for jokes. (Musangi 2014)

Throughout much of the African continent, it is extremely dangerous to be a trans, intersex, and/or lesbian, gay, or bisexual person. Numerous African countries have laws that still criminalize LGBTQ+ people. South Africa remains one of the few African countries that has laws in place meant to fully protect LGBTQ+ people; although that does not mean that South Africa is completely safe for LGBTQ+ people. In many non-Eurocentric and Western places, there is no differentiation made between sexual orientation, sex, and gender. In other words, someone who is cisgender and gay can be seen in the same light as a person who is born with differences of sex development (also known as someone who is intersex) or someone who is trans. The organizations in this section are all located in Africa, and they strive to make the entire continent a safer place for LGBTQ+ Africans.

Gender DynamiX

Founded in 2005 in South Africa, Gender DynamiX is a grassroots organization that works to advance trans human rights. Gender DynamiX was co-founded by a cisgender ally, Liesl Theron, and Lex Kirsten, a trans man who was her partner at that time. Gener DynamiX works with media, legal advocacy, health care education, and community outreach in order to educate the larger community about the lives of trans, non-binary, and gender-diverse people.

Since South Africa has a complex legacy of apartheid rule, one of the main focuses for Gender DynamiX was to make sure that *all* trans, non-binary, and gender-diverse South Africans were able to have a voice. In South Africa, many LGBTQ+ groups were still racially segregated. In the course of Gender DynamiX's work, the organization has made sure to include South Africans from all of the diverse racial and ethnic communities in the country. As of 2018, the executive director is Sibusiso Kheswa, a black South African trans man who does advocacy and media outreach. Advocates are working against a law in South Africa that says that anyone seeking gender affirmation has to be diagnosed with a disease, and are working to shorten the twenty-five-year waiting period for gender affirmation treatments.

Transgender Intersex Africa (TIA)

Transgender Intersex Africa (TIA) is a group founded by African transgender people in 2010. TIA was created specifically to do outreach to trans, non-binary, gender-diverse, and intersex communities in disadvantaged areas of South Africa. Many of the people with whom they work live in rural areas or in smaller towns.

In their specific focus on intersecting identities—the fact that their constituency often suffers from racial oppression as well as gender and/or sex oppression—TIA works to make safe spaces for trans, intersex, non-binary, gender-diverse black South Africans. Often, health care systems may not treat a white trans person very well, but a trans, non-binary, or gender-diverse person of color is often treated even worse. TIA strives to hold the health care system, the legal system, and other governmental systems accountable and to make them accessible for *all* trans, non-binary, gender-diverse, and intersex people. Part of what can help TIA in their endeavors is the fact that, at least officially, South Africa has among the world's most progressive human rights laws, and TIA aims to make sure that the systems of power in that country abide by the laws.

Sexual Minorities Uganda (SMUG)

In 2004, Victor Mukasa, a trans person, became the founding director of Sexual Minorities Uganda (SMUG) and served in that capacity until 2007, when Mukasa asked Pepe Julian Onziema to take his place. By 2012, Mukasa had fled Uganda in fear for his life and was granted asylum in the United States.

He continues to work supporting refugees and is the director of a human rights organization. Onziema remains in Uganda for the time being working on LGBTQ+ human rights, which is a constant struggle against the police and Ugandan laws. In 2018, two different events that were organized by SMUG had to be either cancelled or postponed. On May 17, 2018, SMUG was to host an International Day Against Homophobia and Transphobia; however, the police and the minister of Ethics and Integrity forced the event to stop. Onziema stated, "We are deeply saddened and concerned with this trend that continues to undermine Uganda's human rights obligations under its Constitution and International Human Rights law" (Sexual Minorities Uganda 2018). Only three weeks earlier, another event that was to focus on LGBTQ+ issues, a special conference on the needs of key underrepresented populations, was also closed down. Although the people working with SMUG face daily harassment from police and other authorities, the group has an outstanding support system throughout the world, and the information on their website is available to anyone in Uganda who can access the Internet.

References

Anderson-Minshall, Jacob. 2017. "How One Trans Couple Keep Their Fire." *The Advocate*, July 10, 2017. https://www.advocate.com/current-issue/2017/7/10/how-one-trans-couple-keep-their-fire.

Arnold, Chris. 2012. *Trans* (film). RoseWorks.

Ausserer, Caroline. 2016. "Mauro Cabral: We Need an Intersex Version of the Principles." Heinrich Böll Stiftung: The Green Political Foundation, May 13, 2016. https://www.boell.de/en/2016/05/13/we-need-intersex-version-principles.

Barbagli, Guido, Salvatore Sansalone, and Massimo Lazzeri. 2010. "Obituary for Sava Perovic: Pioneer of

Reconstructive Surgery of the Male Genitalia, Born in Yugoslavia on February 21, 1947, He Died in Belgrade on April 4, 2010, at the Age of 63." *European Urology* 58: 324.

BBC. 2017. "100 Women 2017: Who Is on the List?" November 1, 2017. http://www.bbc.com/news/world -41380265

Beaumont, Hilary. 2015. "Kael McKenzie Didn't Set Out to Be a Trailblazer—Now He's Canada's First Transgender Judge." *Vice News*, December 22, 2015. https://news .vice.com/article/kael-mckenzie-didnt-set-out-to-be-a -trailblazer-now-hes-canadas-first-transgender-judge.

Beibei, Luo. 2017. "How China's Trans Icon Just Fuels More Patriarchy." *Sixth Tone*. November 7, 2017. http://www .sixthtone.com/news/1001139/how-chinas-trans-icon-just -fuels-more-patriarchy.

Bell, Matthew. 2013. "'It's Easier to Change a Body Than to Change a Mind': The Extraordinary Life and Lonely Death of Roberta Cowell." *Independent*, October 17, 2013. https://www.independent.co.uk/news/people/profiles /its-easier-to-change-a-body-than-to-change-a-mind-the -extraordinary-life-and-lonely-death-of-roberta-8899823 .html.

Beyer, Georgina. 2007. Speech transcript, New Zealand Parliament. February 14, 2007. https://www.parliament .nz/en/pb/hansard-debates/rhr/document/48HansS _20070214_00001114/ beyer-georgina-debate-on-prime-minister-s-statement.

Cabral, Mauro. 2017. "I Am Transgender and Being Myself Is Not a Disorder." *The Guardian*, February 24, 2017. https:// www.theguardian.com/global-development-professionals -network/2017/feb/24/im-transgender-why-does-the-who -say-i-have-a-mental-disorder.

Canadian Lesbian and Gay Archives. N.d. "Rupert Raj and Trans Activism, 1973–1988." http://digitalcollections

.clga.ca/exhibits/show/rupert-raj-and-trans-activism-/rupert
-raj-and-trans-activism-.

Casey, Alex. 2018. "Georgina Beyer Still Has a Fire in Her
Belly." *The Spinoff*, February 14, 2018. https://thespinoff
.co.nz/society/14-02-2018/georgina-beyer-still-has-a-fire
-in-her-belly/.

CBC News. 2016. "Kael McKenzie Sworn In as 1st
Transgender Judge in Canada." February 12, 2016. http://
www.cbc.ca/news/canada/manitoba/transgender-judge-kael
-mckenzie-manitoba-appointment-1.3446720.

Cooney, Kara. 2014. *The Woman Who Would Be King*. New
York: Crown, 2014.

Cowell, Roberta. 1954. *Roberta Cowell's Story*. New York:
British Book Centre.

Davidson, Nicola. 2015. "The Former Chinese Army Colonel
Turned Sex-Change Dance Star." *Financial Times*, July 20,
2015. https://www.ft.com/content/fd458128-306a-11e5
-91ac-a5e17d9b4cff.

De Erauso, Catalina. 1996. *Lieutenant Nun: Memoir of a
Basque Transvestite in the New World*, trans. Michele Stepto
and Gabriel Stepto. Boston: Beacon Press, 1996.

Docter, Richard F. 2008. *Becoming a Woman: A Biography of
Christine Jorgensen*. New York: Haworth Press.

Ernst, Rhys. 2016. "Lou Sullivan." *We've Been Around*,
documentary film. http://www.wevebeenaround.com/lou/.

Feinberg, Leslie. 1992. *Transgender Liberation: A Movement
Whose Time Has Come*. New York: World View Forum.

Formoso, Sofi. 2015. "Michelle Suárez: The First Trans
Lawyer in Uruguay." *Sin Etiquetas*, February 9, 2015.
http://sinetiquetas.org/2015/02/09/michelle-suarez-la
-primera-abogada-trans-de-uruguay/. Author translation.

Fox, Margalit. 2006. "Stanley H. Biber, 82, Surgeon
Among First to Do Sex Changes, Dies." *New York Times*,

January 21, 2006. https://www.nytimes.com/2006/01/21
/us/stanley-h-biber-82-surgeon-among-first-to-do-sex
-changes-dies.html.

Free Legal Advice Centre (FLAC). 2018. "Lydia Foy: The
Woman at the Heart of Securing Transgender Rights
in Ireland." *thejournal.ie,* June 9, 2018. http://www
.thejournal.ie/lydia-foy-flac-report-4060076-Jun2018/.

GATE. 2018. Press Release, "On Trans Depathologization,
Mental Health and Stigma: ICD-11 Is Released." June 27,
2018. https://transactivists.org/trans-depathologization
-mental-health-stigma/.

Ge, Linda. 2015. "Sense8 Star Jamie Clayton on Playing a
Trans Character Well Past Transition: 'Nomi Is the First'."
The Wrap, July 28, 2015. https://www.thewrap.com
/sense8s-jamie-clayton-on-playing-a-trans-character-not
-going-through-transition-nomi-is-the-first/.

Gerber, Justin. 2017. "The Wachowskis' Sense8 Paints a
Unified Utopia." May 2, 2017. https://consequenceof
sound.net/2017/05/the-wachowskis-sense8-paints-a
-unified-utopia/.

Goldson, Annie, and Peter Wells. 2001. *Georgie Girl* (film).
Women Make Movies.

Grant, Jaime M., Lisa A. Mottet, Justin Tanis, Jack Harrison,
Jody L. Herman, and Mara Keisling. 2011. *Injustice
at Every Turn: A Report of the National Transgender
Discrimination Survey.* Washington: National Center for
Transgender Equality and National Gay and Lesbian Task
Force.

Green, Jamison. 2011. Interview for GLSEN's "Unheard
Voices: Stories and Lessons for Grades 6–12." https://www
.glsen.org/unheardvoices.html.

Green, Jamison. 2016. Interview with Andrea Jenkins for the
Transgender Oral History Project at the Jean-Nickolaus
Tretter Collection in GLBT Studies at the University

of Minnesota Libraries, p. 14. March 20, 2016. https://
umedia.lib.umn.edu/sites/default/files/archive/60
/application/pdf/1553607.pdf.

Greenidge, Kaitlyn. 2018. "The Best Book for 2018 is 25
Years Old." *New York Times*, June 23, 2018. https://www
.nytimes.com/2018/06/23/opinion/sunday/the-best-book
-for-2018-is-25-years-old.html.

Hodgkinson, Liz. 1989. *Michael, Nee Laura*. London:
Columbus Books.

Huddleston, Kathie. 2017. "Exclusive: Jamie Clayton
Prepares Us for an Action Packed, Racy Season 2 of
Netflix's *Sense8*." *SyFy Wire*, May 5, 2017. http://www
.syfy.com/syfywire/netflix-sense8-jamie-clayton
-interview.

Hugill, Alison. 2016. "Body//Trauma and Identity: An
interview with Yishay Garbasz." *Berlin Art Link*, April 19,
2016. http://www.berlinartlink.com/2016/04/19/body
-trauma-and-identity-an-interview-with-yishay-garbasz/.

International Council on Archives. 2010. *Universal
Declaration on Archives*. http://www.ica.org/6573
/reference-documents/universal-declaration-on-archives
.html.

James, Sandy E., Jody L. Herman, Susan Rankin, Mara
Keisling, Lisa Mottet, and Ma'ayan Anafi. 2016. *The Report
of the 2015 U.S. Transgender Survey*. Washington, DC:
National Center for Transgender Equality.

John, Elton. 2018. "'God Knows Us. God Loves Us': Life on
the Margins in L.G.B.T. Africa." *New York Times*, June 22,
2018. https://www.nytimes.com/interactive/2018/06/22
/opinion/sunday/LGBT-Africa.html.

Krafft-Ebing, Richard von. 2012. *Psychopathia Sexualis: With
Especial Reference to Antipathic Sexual Instinct; A Medico-
Forensic Study* (original first edition in German 1877),
10th ed. reprint. London: Forgotten Books.

Maglott, Stephen A. 2017. "Kylar William Broadus." *The Ubuntu Biography Project.* https://ubuntubiographyproject .com/category/broadus-kylar-william/.

Mancini, Elena. 2010. *Magnus Hirschfeld and the Quest for Sexual Freedom: A History of the First International Sexual Freedom Movement.* New York: Palgrave Macmillan.

Mijatovic, Alexis. N.d. "A Brief Biography of Elagabalus: The Transgender Ruler of Rome." http://outhistory.org /exhibits/show/tgi-bios/Elagabalus.

Musangi, Neo S. 2014. "In Time and Space." In *Reclaiming Afrikan: Queer Perspectives on Sexual and Gender Identities,* curated by Zethu Matebeni, Atholone, South Africa, p. 54.

Nutt, Amy Ellis. 2016. "Meet the Gender-Affirmation Surgeon Whose Waiting List Is Three Years Long." *Washington Post,* April 22, 2016. https://www .washingtonpost.com/national/health-science/meet -the-gender-affirmation-surgeon-whose-waiting-list-is -three-years-long/2016/04/22/a4019f2e-f690-11e5-8b23 -538270a1ca31_story.html.

Perez, Medardo. 2017. "Ex-Navy Surgeon Promises Free Surgery for Transgender Troops." *NBC News,* July 31. 2017. https://www.nbcnews.com/feature/nbc-out/ex -navy-surgeon-promises-free-surgery-transgender-troops -n788126.

Pratt, Minnie Bruce. 2014. "Transgender Pioneer and *Stone Butch Blues* Author Leslie Feinberg Has Died." *The Advocate,* November 17, 2014. https://www.advocate .com/arts-entertainment/books/2014/11/17/transgender -pioneer-leslie-feinberg-stone-butch-blues-has-died.

Rahman, Abid. 2016. "Meet the Oprah of China, Who Happens to Be Transgender." November 1, 2016. *Hollywood Reporter.* https://www.hollywoodreporter .com/features/meet-oprah-china-who-happens-be -transgender-942750.

Raj, Rupert. 2017. *Dancing the Dialectic: True Tales of a Transgender Trailblazer.* North Charleston, SC: CreateSpace Independent Publishing Platform.

Sexual Minorities Uganda. 2018. "Statement on Closure of Event to Mark International Day Against Homophobia, Biphobia and Transphobia." May 22, 2018. http://sexualminoritiesuganda.com/statement-on-closure-of-event-to-mark-international-day-against-homophobia-biphobia-and-transphobia/.

Shandler, Jeffrey, and Yishay Garbasz. 2009. *Yishay Garbasz: In My Mother's Footsteps.* Berlin: Hatje Cantz.

Strauss, Dean. 2018. "Lou Sullivan." *Making Queer History,* May 21, 2018. https://www.makingqueerhistory.com/articles/2018/5/21/lou-sullivan.

Sullivan, Lou. 1973. From Sullivan Journal, February 13, 1973, box 1, folder 10, LGS Papers, as quoted in Brice D. Smith, *Lou Sullivan: Daring to Be a Man Among Men.* Oakland: Transgress Press, 2016, p. 21.

Think Change India. 2017. "From School Dropout to India's First Transgender Judge: Meet Joyita Mondal." *Think Change India,* October 12, 2017. https://yourstory.com/2017/10/first-transgender-judge-india/.

Transgender Equality Network Ireland. N.d. "Dr. Lydia Foy's Case." http://www.teni.ie/page.aspx?contentid=588.

Wasson, Donald. 2013. "Elagabalus." https://www.ancient.eu/Elagabalus/.

Weik, Taylor. 2017. "Meet the OA Actor Who Wants to Help Pave the Way for Trans Representation." *NBC News,* February 2, 2017. https://www.nbcnews.com/news/asian-america/meet-oa-teen-actor-who-wants-help-pave-way-trans-n714406.

Introduction

This chapter covers data and documents regarding trans, non-binary, Two-Spirit, and other gender-diverse people. Here, you will find demographics for trans people in the United States (note that the survey only used the word "transgender" as the umbrella term); issues for trans, non-binary, and Two-Spirit students in the K–12 school system; discussion of the International Transgender Day of Remembrance; and the *Standards of Care* published by the World Professional Association for Transgender Health (WPATH), as well as graphs and charts that illustrate current data.

Data

Demographics

The Williams Institute is a think tank at the University of California at Los Angeles (UCLA) Law School that does high-quality academic research about issues related to sexual orientation and gender identity. They distribute their research results to lawmakers, policymakers, media, and the public. The data that they have produced on how many people in the United

---

An activist in Kiev, Ukraine, on November 20, 2016. The Transgender Day of Remembrance is observed around the world on November 20th as a time to commemorate all of the gender-diverse people murdered due to transphobia in the preceding year. (STR/NurPhoto via Getty Images)

States identify as transgender is based on state-by-state surveys done by the Centers for Disease Control. Overall, they found that 0.6 percent of Americans identify as transgender (1.4 million people). Younger people, ages eighteen to twenty-four, are the most likely to identify as transgender (0.66 percent); 0.58 percent of people ages twenty-five to sixty-four identify as transgender; and 0.5 percent of those over sixty-five years of age identify as transgender. (See Table 5.1.)

Table 5.1.   Number of Adults Identifying as Transgender in the United States (2016)

| State | Age | | | | | |
| | 18–24 | | 25–64 | | 65 and older | |
	Population	Percentage	Population	Percentage	Population	Percentage
United States	205,850	0.66	967,100	0.58	217,050	0.50
Alabama	3,250	0.67	15,450	0.61	3,700	0.53
Alaska	500	0.60	1,950	0.48	250	0.42
Arizona	4,700	0.72	20,800	0.63	4,850	0.50
Arkansas	1,850	0.65	9,150	0.61	2,300	0.52
California	33,450	0.84	154,750	0.77	29,050	0.63
Colorado	3,200	0.63	14,900	0.53	2,750	0.45
Connecticut	1,750	0.52	8,450	0.44	2,100	0.40
Delaware	700	0.73	3,050	0.64	800	0.55
District of Columbia	2,600	3.14	9,900	2.66	1,950	2.72
Florida	13,450	0.75	66,750	0.67	19,350	0.55
Georgia	8,700	0.86	39,500	0.75	7,450	0.66
Hawaii	1,200	0.89	5,700	0.77	1,550	0.72
Idaho	750	0.47	3,250	0.41	750	0.35
Illinois	7,150	0.57	34,500	0.50	7,750	0.46
Indiana	4,700	0.62	18,950	0.56	4,450	0.50
Iowa	1,100	0.35	4,900	0.31	1,350	0.29
Kansas	1,500	0.49	6,300	0.43	1,500	0.38
Kentucky	2,400	0.57	12,200	0.52	3,000	0.49
Louisiana	3,150	0.66	14,550	0.60	3,100	0.52

Maine	650	0.56	3,650	0.50	1,050	0.45
Maryland	3,200	0.57	15,650	0.49	3,300	0.43
Massachusetts	4,550	0.66	20,150	0.56	5,050	0.53
Michigan	4,800	0.48	22,400	0.43	5,600	0.39
Minnesota	3,450	0.69	16,750	0.58	3,950	0.54
Mississippi	2,100	0.66	9,400	0.62	2,150	0.53
Missouri	3,600	0.60	17,000	0.54	4,400	0.50
Montana	400	0.40	1,800	0.34	450	0.30
Nebraska	800	0.44	3,650	0.39	900	0.35
Nevada	1,750	0.70	3,700	0.61	1,750	0.49
New Hampshire	650	0.50	3,100	0.43	750	0.39
New Jersey	3,950	0.51	21,050	0.44	5,050	0.41
New Mexico	1,800	0.85	8,000	0.75	1,850	0.62
New York	11,150	0.56	54,150	0.51	12,850	0.47
North Carolina	6,600	0.68	31,050	0.60	7,150	0.53
North Dakota	300	0.34	1,050	0.30	300	0.29
Ohio	5,550	0.50	27,150	0.45	7,000	0.41
Oklahoma	2,800	0.72	12,600	0.64	2,900	0.55
Oregon	2,800	0.76	13,700	0.65	3,150	0.55
Pennsylvania	6,100	0.48	29,250	0.44	8,250	0.40
Rhode Island	650	0.56	2,800	0.51	750	0.46
South Carolina	3,150	0.64	14,250	0.58	3,450	0.50
South Dakota	350	0.39	1,400	0.34	350	0.30
Tennessee	4,250	0.68	21,550	0.63	5,150	0.56
Texas	19,600	0.73	88,950	0.66	15,700	0.55
Utah	1,350	0.42	4,950	0.36	800	0.30
Vermont	450	0.67	2,000	0.59	550	0.53
Virginia	5,150	62.00	24,000	0.54	5,200	0.49
Washington	4,850	0.73	23,150	0.62	4,700	0.52
West Virginia	750	0.44	4,150	0.42	1,200	0.38
Wisconsin	2,700	0.49	13,150	0.43	3,250	0.39
Wyoming	200	0.37	1,000	0.32	200	0.29

Source: Andrew R. Flores, Jody L. Herman, Gary J. Gates, and Taylor N. T. Brown. 2016. "How Many Adults Identify as Transgender in the United States?" Los Angeles: The Williams Institute. Available online at https://williamsinstitute.law.ucla.edu/wp-content/uploads/How-Many-Adults-Identify-as-Transgender-in-the-United-States.pdf. Used by permission.

Results of the U.S. National Transgender Survey (2015)

The U.S. National Transgender Survey, produced by the U.S. National Center for Transgender Equality, is the largest survey of trans, non-binary, and Two-Spirit people ever done. Conducted in the summer of 2015, it was an anonymous online survey of trans, non-binary, and Two-Spirit people ages eighteen to eighty-seven, living in all parts of the United States, reporting more than 500 different identities and a wide range of sexual orientations. People could take the survey either in English or Spanish, and 27,715 people did so.

Perhaps unsurprisingly, the results of the survey showed that trans, non-binary, and Two-Spirit people suffered from high levels of discrimination and abuse in every area surveyed, including in their homes, in schools, at work, and in public places. One result of these living conditions is that trans, non-binary, and Two-Spirit people live in poverty much more than the general U.S. population, and many can only find work in the underground economy. These experiences were found to have significantly affected the mental and physical health of the people surveyed, with among the most distressing findings being that 40 percent reported that they had attempted suicide in their lifetimes—nearly nine times the national average. Of course, those who were successful in their attempts were no longer alive to reply to the questions, so the actual number is probably even higher. Furthermore, when race, ethnicity, immigration status, and disabilities are taken into account, it is clear that hardships for these groups are multiplied. (See Figures 5.1 through 5.6, and Tables 5.2 through 5.4.)

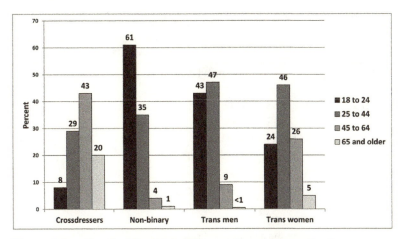

Figure 5.1. Gender Identities of Survey Respondents, by Age

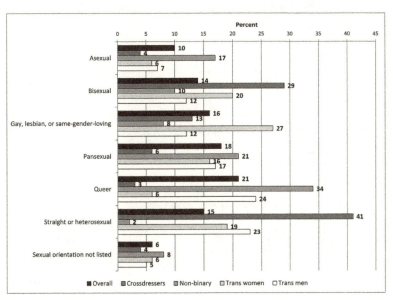

Figure 5.2. Sexual Orientations of Survey Respondents

Experiences of people who were out as transgender in K–12 or believed classmates, teachers, or school staff thought they were transgender.

Table 5.2. School Experience in Grades K–12

Experiences	% of those who were out or perceived as transgender
Verbally harassed because people thought they were transgender	54%
Not allowed to dress in a way that fit their gender identity or expression	52%
Disciplined for fighting back against bullies	36%
Physically attacked because people thought they were transgender	24%
Believe they were disciplined more harshly because teachers or staff thought they were transgender	20%
Left a school because the mistreatment was so bad	17%
Sexually assaulted because people thought they were transgender	13%
Expelled from school	6%
One or more experiences listed	**77%**

Thirteen percent of survey respondents reported having been physically attacked in the past year. The types of attacks were varied, as noted in the table.

Table 5.3. Reports of Being Physically Attacked

Type of Physical Attack	% of those physically attacked
Grabbed, punched, or choked	73%
Something thrown at them (such as a rock or bottle)	29%
Sexually assaulted	29%
With another weapon (like a baseball bat, frying pan, scissors, or stick)	7%
With a knife	5%
With a gun	3%
Not listed above	9%

Almost one-half (47 percent) reported that they had been sexually assaulted during their lifetime.

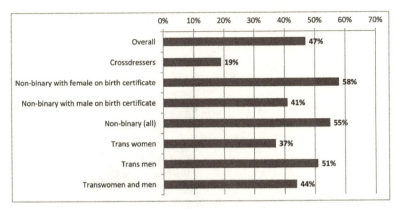

Figure 5.3.   Reports of Being Sexually Assaulted

The unemployment rate among respondents (15 percent) was three times higher than the unemployment rate in the U.S. population (5 percent), with racial and ethnic minorities experiencing higher rates of unemployment. Nearly one-third (29 percent) were living in poverty, more than twice the rate in the U.S. population (14 percent).

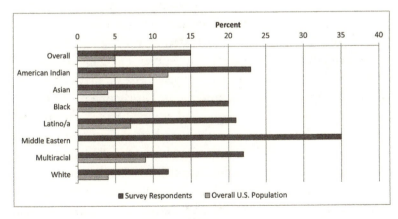

Figure 5.4.   Unemployment and Poverty

One in eight (12 percent) of survey respondents reported that they had ever been sex workers. Half of those who had done this kind of work were trans women and almost one-quarter (23 percent) were non-binary people assigned female at birth.

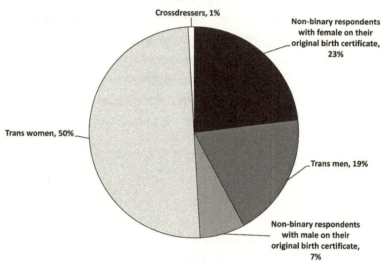

Figure 5.5.   Involvement in Sex Work

One in five (20 percent) survey respondents did not use at least one type of public accommodation in the past year because they feared they would be mistreated as a transgender person.

More than half (59 percent) of survey respondents avoided using a public restroom in the past year because they were afraid of having people harass or abuse them. Nearly one in ten (9 percent) people said that someone had stopped them from using a restroom in the past year. In the year before they answered the survey, 12 percent said that they had been verbally harassed, and 1 percent had been physically attacked or sexually assaulted in a restroom. Almost one-third (32 percent) of survey respondents restricted how much they ate and drank so that they wouldn't have to use a public bathroom when they were away from home.

Table 5.4. Use of Public Accommodations

Location Visited	% of those who said staff knew or thought they were transgender
Public transportation	34%
Retail store, restaurant, hotel, or theater	31%
Drug or alcohol treatment program	22%
Domestic violence shelter or program or rape crisis center	22%
Gym or health club	18%
Public assistance or government benefit office	17%
Department of Motor Vehicles	14%
Nursing home or extended care facility	14%
Court or courthouse	13%
Social Security office	11%
Legal services from an attorney, clinic, or legal professional	6%

As a result of employing these strategies to avoid harassment and abuse, 8 percent had suffered a urinary tract infection, kidney infection, or another kidney-related problem during the past year. The chart shows how many people avoided using public toilets.

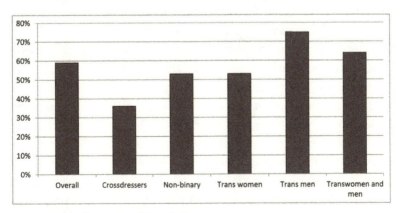

Figure 5.6. Restroom Experiences

Source: S. E. James, J. L. Herman, S. Rankin, M. Keisling, L. Mottet, and M. Anafi. 2016. *The Report of the 2015 U.S. Transgender Survey.* Washington, DC: National Center for Transgender Equality. Available online at https://transequality .org/sites/default/files/docs/usts/USTS-Full-Report-Dec17.pdf.

Transgender Day of Remembrance

Transgender Day of Remembrance (TDOR) takes place on November 20 each year at many locations around the world. TDOR grew out of the "Remembering Our Dead" project started in 1998 by Gwendolyn Ann Smith. The original project was to honor the memory of Rita Hester, a trans woman who was murdered by an unknown assailant for being trans. Each year since then, a list is recorded that includes the names, locations, and causes of death for each person known to have been murdered because someone perceived them as trans, non-binary, or gender variant.

Commemorative ceremonies generally center on a candle-light vigil and a reading of the list of names and particulars of those known to have died during the preceding 365 days due to transphobic violence. Not everyone on the list necessarily identified as trans, non-binary, or Two-Spirit, but their names are added to the list if the circumstances of their murder indicate that enmity toward trans, non-binary, and Two-Spirit people was a motivating factor for the murder.

Between January 2008 and September 2017 a total of 2,609 gender-variant people were recorded as murdered in seventy-one countries worldwide. Where the occupations of the dead were known, 62 percent of them were sex workers. A dispro-portionate number of the victims have been trans women of color. In the year between October 1, 2016, and September 30, 2017, there were 325 murders of trans and gender-diverse people reported worldwide. Table 5.5 shows the total number of people reported murdered in various countries in the period 2008 to June 2016 and a partial listing of names from Trans-gender Europe.

A map or list of where the deaths have been reported reflects not only where transphobic violence has occurred but also reflects which places record where transphobic violence is monitored. The fact that a location does or does not show up on the record may not be a fair representation of the relative safety of that location. Rather, it may only say something about the reporting and monitoring practices in that country. Transphobic violence and murder are known to be underreported, or simplistically reported as being the result of another intersecting factor, thereby erasing the full extent of violent transphobia.

Table 5.5   Total Number of Transphobic Murders 2008–2016 in Countries That Provided Data

1	2–8	9–20	21–50	51–100	101–250	> 250
Afghanistan	Australia	Bolivia	Guatemala	Honduras	Columbia	Brazil
Algeria	Bangladesh	Cambodia	Italy	India	Venezuela	Mexico
Austria	Canada	Chile	Pakistan		United States	
Belize	Cuba	China	Peru			
Hungary	France	Malaysia	Philippines			
Iran	Germany	Thailand	Turkey			
Japan	Guyana	Uruguay				
New Zealand	Nepal					
Poland	Netherlands					
Portugal	Nicaragua					
South Korea	Paraguay					
Tanzania	Russia					
	Serbia					
	South Africa					
	Spain					
	Uganda					
	United Kingdom					

Following is an abbreviated list of some of the 325 people murdered in 2017 due to transphobic violence:

Name: Kitkat Mae Fermin
Age: 18
Date of death: 10/02/2016
Location of death: Davao City (Philippines)
Remarks: The victim was shot in the head.

Name: Brandi Bledsoe
Age: 32
Date of death: 10/08/2016
Location of death: Cleveland (USA)
Remarks: Brandi was found dead with a plastic bag around her head and reports of head trauma. She died of a gunshot wound to the chest.

Name: Itzel Durás Castellanos
Age: 19
Date of death: 10/08/2016
Location of death: Ciudad de Mexico (Mexico)
Remarks: Someone Itzel knew went to her house, they argued, and he killed her by stabbing her eight times. The accused was arrested by the police.

Name: W. Rodrigues Alexandre
Age: not reported
Date of death: 10/08/2016
Location of death: Duque de Caxias (Brazil)
Remarks: The victim was beaten to death.

Name: Yasmin Montoy
Age: 20

Date of death: 10/10/2016

Location of death: Sao Paulo (Brazil)

Remarks: Yasmin's body had marks of the violence she suffered and an injury in her head, "probably done with a stick." However, despite friends' stories, the police report says that she died because of an overdose.

Name: W.

Age: 20

Date of death: 10/24/2016

Location of death: São José dos Campos (Brazil)

Remarks: The body was found in a bush, in the outermost zone of the city.

Name: N. N.

Age: not reported

Date of death: 10/25/2016

Location of death: Santo Domingo (Dominican Republic)

Remarks: The victim was shot dead.

Name: Emily Duque

Age: not reported

Date of death: 10/26/2016

Location of death: Caracas (Venezuela)

Remarks: Emily was killed by a pimp who wanted to charge her to work, a situation Emily refused.

Source: TvT research project. 2017. "Trans Murder Monitoring (TMM) TDoR 2017 Update." Transrespect versus Transphobia Worldwide. Available online at http://transrespect.org /en/trans-murder-monitoring/tmm-resources/. Used by permission from Transgender Europe.

Documents

WPATH *Standards of Care* (2011)

The World Professional Association for Transgender Health (WPATH) is an international body that is recognized worldwide as the most authoritative source of information about transition-related treatments for trans, non-binary, and Two-Spirit people. The organization (then called the Harry Benjamin International Gender Dysphoria Association) published its first version of Standards of Care (SOC) in 1979. Revisions have been published periodically since then (1980, 1981, 1990, 1998, 2001). Version 7, Standards of Care (SOC) for the Health of Transsexual, Transgender, and Gender Nonconforming People, was published in 2011 and consists of 112 pages of guidance. It is available in eighteen languages and is widely used by government health agencies, health insurance companies, therapists, physicians, and consumers. Among others, sections of the SOC address treatment of children and adolescents, mental health issues, hormone therapies, reproductive health, voice and communication therapies, surgeries, primary health care questions, people living in institutions, and people with differences of sex development.
The document states that:

The overall goal of the SOC is to provide clinical guidance for health professionals to assist transsexual, transgender, and gender nonconforming people with safe and effective pathways to achieving lasting personal comfort with their gendered selves, in order to maximize their overall health, psychological well-being, and self-fulfillment. . . . WPATH recognizes that health is dependent upon not only good clinical care but also social and political climates that provide and ensure social tolerance, equality, and the full rights of citizenship. Health is promoted through public policies and legal reforms that promote tolerance and equity for gender and sexual diversity and that eliminate prejudice, discrimination, and stigma. WPATH is committed to advocacy for these changes in public policies and legal reforms.

The following are the criteria for obtaining hormonal and surgical transition services.

Summary of Criteria for Hormone Therapy and Surgeries

As for all previous versions of the *SOC*, the criteria put forth in the *SOC* for hormone therapy and surgical treatments for gender dysphoria are clinical guidelines; individual health professionals and programs may modify them. Clinical departures from the *SOC* may come about because of a patient's unique anatomic, social, or psychological situation; an experienced health professional's evolving method of handling a common situation; a research protocol; lack of resources in various parts of the world; or the need for specific harm reduction strategies. These departures should be recognized as such, explained to the patient, and documented through informed consent for quality patient care and legal protection. This documentation is also valuable to accumulate new data, which can be retrospectively examined to allow for health care—and the *SOC*—to evolve.

Criteria for Feminizing/Masculinizing Hormone Therapy (one referral or chart documentation of psychosocial assessment)

1. Persistent, well-documented gender dysphoria;

2. Capacity to make a fully informed decision and to consent for treatment;

3. Age of majority in a given country (if younger, follow the *SOC* for children and adolescents);

4. If significant medical or mental concerns are present, they must be reasonably well controlled.

Criteria for Breast/Chest Surgery (one referral)

Mastectomy and creation of a male chest in FtM patients:

1. Persistent, well-documented gender dysphoria;

2. Capacity to make a fully informed decision and to consent for treatment;

3. Age of majority in a given country (if younger, follow the *SOC* for children and adolescents);

4. If significant medical or mental health concerns are present, they must be reasonably well controlled.

Hormone therapy is not a pre-requisite.

Breast augmentation (implants/lipofilling) in MtF patients:

1. Persistent, well-documented gender dysphoria;

2. Capacity to make a fully informed decision and to consent for treatment;

3. Age of majority in a given country (if younger, follow the *SOC* for children and adolescents);

4. If significant medical or mental health concerns are present, they must be reasonably well controlled.

Although not an explicit criterion, it is recommended that MtF patients undergo feminizing hormone therapy (minimum 12 months) prior to breast augmentation surgery. The purpose is to maximize breast growth in order to obtain better surgical (aesthetic) results.

Criteria for genital surgery (two referrals)

Hysterectomy and ovariectomy in FtM patients and orchiectomy in MtF patients:

1. Persistent, well documented gender dysphoria;

2. Capacity to make a fully informed decision and to consent for treatment;

3. Age of majority in a given country;

4. If significant medical or mental health concerns are present, they must be well controlled;

5. 12 continuous months of hormone therapy as appropriate to the patient's gender goals (unless the patient has a medical contraindication or is otherwise unable or unwilling to take hormones).

The aim of hormone therapy prior to gonadectomy is primarily to introduce a period of reversible estrogen or testosterone suppression, before a patient undergoes irreversible surgical intervention.

These criteria do not apply to patients who are having these surgical procedures for medical indications other than gender dysphoria.

Metoidioplasty or phalloplasty in FtM patients and vaginoplasty in MtF patients:

1. Persistent, well documented gender dysphoria;

2. Capacity to make a fully informed decision and to consent for treatment;

3. Age of majority in a given country;

4. If significant medical or mental health concerns are present, they must be well controlled;

5. 12 continuous months of hormone therapy as appropriate to the patient's gender goals (unless the patient has a medical contraindication or is otherwise unable or unwilling to take hormones);

6. 12 continuous months of living in a gender role that is congruent with their gender identity.

Although not an explicit criterion, it is recommended that these patients also have regular visits with a mental health or other medical professional.

The criterion noted above for some types of genital surgeries— i.e., that patients engage in 12 continuous months of living in a gender role that is congruent with their gender identity—is based on expert clinical consensus that this experience provides ample opportunity for patients to experience and socially adjust in their desired gender role, before undergoing irreversible surgery.

Source: World Professional Association for Transgender Health. 2011. *Standards of Care for the Health of Transsexual, Transgender, and Gender Nonconforming People, 7th Version.* Available online at https://www.wpath.org/publications/soc. Used by permission.

WPATH Resolutions and Statements on Needed Social Changes (2010–2017)

The World Professional Association for Transgender Health, as a leading influencer of public policy, has issued a number of statements intended to guide policymakers and support movement for social changes that will improve the lives of trans, non-binary, Two-Spirit, and other gender-diverse people. In 2010, WPATH issued a call for gender variance to no longer be considered to be an illness and for steps to be taken to reduce the stigma associated with gender nonconformity. In 2014, WPATH issued a further public statement urging authorities around the world to remove all laws against gender expressions that do not conform to stereotypical expectations. A 2017 WPATH statement took a position that no one should have to go through diagnosis, or any particular psychological or medical treatments, in order to change their identity documents to match their sense of who they are. It further asked governments to provide more than two gender options on identity documents.

May 26, 2010

WPATH De-Psychopathologisation Statement

The WPATH Board of Directors strongly urges the de-psycho-pathologisation of gender variance worldwide. The expression of gender characteristics, including identities that are not ste-reotypically associated with one's assigned sex at birth is a com-mon and culturally-diverse human phenomenon which should not be judged as inherently pathological or negative. The psy-chopathologisation of gender characteristics and identities reinforces or can prompt stigma, making prejudice and dis-crimination more likely, rendering transgender and transsexual people more vulnerable to social and legal marginalisation and exclusion, and increasing risks to mental and physical well-being. WPATH urges governmental and medical professional organizations to review their policies and practices to eliminate stigma toward gender-variant people.

July 15, 2014

WPATH Statement Concerning Cross-dressing, Gender-Nonconformity, and Gender Dysphoria

The World Professional Association for Transgender Health (WPATH) calls for the repeal of laws criminalizing gender non-conformity and expression of transgender identity. . . . Some people experience gender dysphoria at such a level that the distress meets criteria for a formal diagnosis that might be classified as a mental disorder. Such a diagnosis is not a license for stigmatization or for the deprivation of civil and human rights. . . . A disorder is a description of something with which the person might struggle, not a description of the person or the person's identity. . . . Transsexual, transgender, and gender-nonconforming individuals are not inherently disordered. Rather, the distress of gender dysphoria, when present, is the concern that might be diagnosable, and for which various treatment options are available. . . .

Gender-nonconformity exists in every known culture. . . . scientific and medical evidence indicates that gender variance should not be regarded as something wrong or something to be corrected because of beliefs or assumptions about gender or sex. . . . Cross-dressing, for example, is not inherently a manifestation of pathological or criminal behavior. People may cross-dress for a variety of reasons. A transsexual or transgender person wearing the clothing of "the opposite sex" is not cross-dressing, but is dressing in conformity with their core gender identity, a psychological feature common to all persons. . . . WPATH recognizes that health is dependent upon not only good clinical care, but also social and political climates that provide and ensure social tolerance, equality, and the full rights of citizenship for transgender, transsexual, and gender nonconforming people.

November 15, 2017

WPATH Identity Recognition Statement

The World Professional Association for Transgender Health (WPATH) recognizes that, for optimal physical and mental health, persons must be able to freely express their gender identity, whether or not that identity conforms to the expectations of others. WPATH further recognizes the right of all people to identity documents consistent with their gender identity, including those documents which confer legal gender status. . . . WPATH opposes all medical requirements that act as barriers to those wishing to change legal sex or gender markers on documents. These include requirements for diagnosis, counseling or therapy, puberty blockers, hormones, any form of surgery (including that which involves sterilization), or any other requirements for any form of clinical treatment or letters from doctors. WPATH argues that marital and parental status should not be barriers to recognition of gender change, and opposes requirements for persons to undergo periods living in their affirmed gender, or for enforced waiting or 'cooling off' periods after applying for a change in documents. Further, court and judicial hearings can produce psychological, as well as financial and logistical barriers to legal gender change, and may also violate personal privacy rights or needs.

WPATH advocates that appropriate gender recognition should be available to transgender youth, including those who are under the age of majority, as well as to individuals who are incarcerated or institutionalized. WPATH recognizes that there is a spectrum of gender identities, and that choices of identity limited to Male or Female may be inadequate to reflect all gender identities. An option of X, NB (non-binary), or Other (as examples) should be available for individuals who so choose. WPATH urges governments to eliminate barriers to gender recognition, and to institute transparent, affordable and otherwise accessible administrative procedures affirming self-determination, when gender markers on identity documents are considered necessary. These procedures should be based in law and protect privacy.

Source: World Professional Association for Transgender Health. Public Policies. Available online at https://www.wpath .org/policies. Used by permission.

International Classification of Diseases' Gender Incongruence Diagnosis (2018)

In most of the world beyond the United States and Canada, physicians rely on the International Classification of Diseases *(ICD) created by the United Nations' (UN) World Health Organization (WHO). When trans, non-binary, Two-Spirit, and other gender-diverse people request medical assistance with adjusting their bodies to better express their gender identities, physicians must justify their treatments with an appropriate diagnosis. The diagnosis slated to be available in Version 11 of the ICD when it is implemented in January 2022 is "Gender Incongruence," and it is to be found in a chapter called "Conditions Related to Sexual Health."*

Chapter 17 Conditions related to sexual health
Gender incongruence

Description

Gender incongruence is characterized by a marked and persistent incongruence between an individual's experienced gender and the assigned sex. Gender variant behaviour and preferences alone are not a basis for assigning the diagnoses in this group.

HA60 Gender incongruence of adolescence or adulthood

Description

Gender incongruence of adolescence and adulthood is characterized by a marked and persistent incongruence between an individual's experienced gender and the assigned sex, as manifested by at least two of the following: 1) a strong dislike or discomfort with the one's primary or secondary sex characteristics (in adolescents, anticipated secondary sex characteristics) due to their incongruity with the experienced gender; 2) a strong desire to be rid of some or all of one's primary and /or secondary sex characteristics (in adolescents, anticipated secondary sex characteristics) due to their incongruity with the experienced gender; 3) a strong desire to have the primary and/or secondary sex characteristics of the experienced gender. The individual experiences a strong desire to be treated (to live and be accepted) as a person of the experienced gender. The experienced gender incongruence must have been continuously present for at least several months. The diagnosis cannot be assigned prior the onset of puberty. Gender variant behaviour and preferences alone are not a basis for assigning the diagnosis.

HA61 Gender incongruence of childhood

Description

Gender incongruence of childhood is characterized by a marked incongruence between an individual's experienced/expressed gender and the assigned sex in pre-pubertal children. It includes a strong desire to be a different gender than the assigned sex; a strong dislike on the child's part of his or her sexual anatomy or anticipated secondary sex characteristics and/or a strong desire for the primary and/or anticipated secondary sex characteristics that match the experienced gender; and make-believe or fantasy play, toys, games, or activities and playmates that are typical of the experienced gender rather than the assigned sex. The incongruence must have persisted for about 2 years. Gender variant behaviour and preferences alone are not a basis for assigning the diagnosis.

HA6Z Gender incongruence, unspecified

This category is an **'unspecified'** residual category.

Source: ICD-11 is not yet officially approved. An ICD-11 version for preparing implementation in Member States, including translations, was released on June 18, 2018. ICD-11 will be presented at the Seventy-second World Health Assembly for endorsement by Member States in May 2019. http://www .who.int/classifications/icd/revision/en/. Used by permission: *ICD-11 (version for implementation) Geneva: World Health Organization, 2018. ICD-11 codes may be subject to change.*

Laws and Human Rights in Europe (2018)

Transgender Europe (TGEU), started in 2005, is an advocacy organization for trans, non-binary, and gender-variant people in Europe. TGEU is made up of 105 member organizations from

42 different European countries. One of the central ways that TGEU supports advocacy on behalf of trans, non-binary, and Two-Spirit people is by conducting detailed research and publishing comprehensive reports that have proven to be extremely valuable in providing reliable data that has been effective in motivating policy-makers to action.

One of TGEU's larger undertakings is the Transrespect versus Transphobia Worldwide (TvT) research project, which builds pictures of global circumstances for trans, non-binary, and gender-variant people and displays the data on color-coded interactive world maps. A more specific focus of TGEU's research and advocacy work is the situation in European countries. They also produce and periodically update an index, a map, and a summary of the rights of trans, non-binary, and gender-diverse people throughout the countries of Europe. A summary appears below.

Fast Facts Trans Rights Europe Index

Legal Gender Recognition (LGR)

Procedures exist in: 41 countries
Out of these:

- 31 have legal certainty
- 10 have no legal certainty (procedures only, but no law)
- 34 request a diagnosis
- 7 request NO diagnosis
- 5 are based on self-determination
- 14 demand sterility
- 27 demand NO sterility
- 27 require medical interventions
- 21 request a divorce
- 20 request NO divorce

- 33 have age barriers
- 8 have NO age barriers
- 1 offer recognition for non-binary identities

Within the EU:

- 27 countries enable LGR
- 7 demand sterility
- 20 demand a mental health diagnosis
- 11 demand divorce
- 21 have an age barrier

Asylum

- 16 countries offer international protection on grounds of gender identity
- 13 out of these are EU member states
- 15 EU countries offer NO international protection on grounds of GI (and are thus violating EU law)
- 13 countries have positive measures (policies) in place

Non-Discrimination

- 27 countries protect against discrimination in employment
- 10 EU member states do not protect against discrimination in employment (and are thus violating EU law)
- 22 countries protect against discrimination in access to goods & services
- 14 EU member states do not protect against discrimination in goods & services (and are thus violating EU law)
- 22 countries protect against discrimination in other spheres of life

Bias-motivated Crime

Laws exist in: 13 countries

- 5 countries have positive measures (policies) in place combating bias-motivated crime and hate speech

Healthcare

- 18 offer protection against discrimination in healthcare
- 1 have depathologised trans identities
- 2 prohibit conversion therapy

Family

- 4 recognize trans parenthood

Equality Body Mandate
Equality Bodies in 25 countries have an Equality Body mandate inclusive of gender identity

- 11 EU member states have no equality body mandated to work on gender identity

Source: Transgender Europe. 2018. "Trans Rights Europe Map 2018." Available online at https://tgeu.org/trans-rights-map -2018/. Used by permission of Transgender Europe.

Kavanagh v. Canada (Attorney General) (2001)
Many jurisdictions around the world are grappling with how to balance the needs of transgender prisoners with those of other inmates. In particular, the placement of trans women inmates and the responses of correctional services to their health needs have been of major concern. In most places, trans women who have completed genital surgeries and have had their identity documents corrected have been placed in correctional facilities with cisgender

women. Trans men have similarly been placed in men's correctional institutions.

One issue is whether trans women who have not completed vaginoplasty should be placed in prisons that correspond to their gender identities or in prisons that correspond to their genital status. Most places have chosen to use genital configuration as a deciding factor, citing concerns about the safety of cisgender women inmates. As a result, such trans women usually have been held in men's institutions while such trans men have been held in women's prisons.

A further consideration is about whether trans women who have begun hormonal treatments should be permitted to continue them while incarcerated. Many locales have opted to deny inmates their hormone treatments, while some have continued them, and some have continued them at a reduced level.

Finally, there is the question of trans inmates completing transition while in custody. Most jurisdictions have refused to support this level of treatment, citing lack of expertise to ensure good care, or lack of funding.

Synthia Kavanagh was a Canadian trans women who had been taking hormones since the age of thirteen, had begun her transition, and had been conditionally approval for gender affirmation surgery when she was arrested and convicted of second-degree murder in 1989. The trial judge recommended that she be housed in a women's prison but, in accordance with their policies at the time, the Correctional Service of Canada (CSC) placed her in a men's prison and ceased her hormonal treatments. Ms. Kavanagh filed a human rights complaint. In 2001, the Canadian Human Rights Commission found that she should be permitted hormonal and surgical treatments, at the expense of Correctional Services of Canada, and that she should be housed in a women's prison once her gender affirmation surgeries were complete. This decision set an important precedent for the treatment of trans inmates. Selections from the decision are provided below. The numbers in square brackets are the paragraph numbers in the decision.

[35] CSC's current policy . . . was promulgated in 1997. It is this policy, and, in particular, Sections 30 and 31 thereof, that is under consideration in this proceeding. The relevant provisions provide: . . .

> 30. Unless sex reassignment surgery has been completed, male inmates shall be held in male institutions.
>
> 31. Sex reassignment surgery will not be considered during the inmate's incarceration.

. . . [134] Ms. Kavanagh's complaints are brought pursuant to section 5 of the Canadian Human Rights Act. Section 5 makes it a discriminatory practice, in the provision of services customarily available to the general public, to deny access to any such service to any individual, or to differentiate adversely in relation to any individual, on a prohibited ground of discrimination. Section 3 of the Act designates sex and disability as prohibited grounds of discrimination.

[135] There is no dispute that discrimination on the basis of Transsexualism constitutes sex discrimination as well as discrimination on the basis of a disability.

[136] Pursuant to section 15 (g) of the Act, it is not a discriminatory practice to deny access to a service to an individual where there is a bona fide justification for that denial. . . .

[141] CSC's policy requiring that anatomically male prisoners be held in male institutions clearly has an adverse, differential effect on pre-operative male to female transsexual inmates. . . . CSC indeed concedes that the policy is prima facie discriminatory, on the basis of both sex and disability.

[142] Having found a prima facie case of discrimination on the basis of sex and disability, the onus shifts to CSC to establish that it has a bona fide justification for its policy. . . .

[160] . . . We find that, . . . having regard to the unique nature of the carceral setting and the needs of the female inmate population, it is not possible to house pre-operative male to female transsexuals in women's prisons. . . .

[162] We agree with CSC that the creation of a dedicated facility for pre-operative transsexuals in transition is simply not feasible. . . .

[165] Synthia Kavanagh's descriptions of the treatment she encountered in CSC's male institutions . . . is very troubling. [W]e . . . found her to be an articulate and compelling witness. . . . [W]e find that pre-operative transsexuals are a particularly vulnerable group of inmates, who require special consideration concerning their placement within the prison setting.

[166] CSC has not justified its policy with respect to the placement of transsexual inmates in its current form, as the policy fails to recognize the special vulnerability of the pre-operative transsexual inmate population. . . .

[167] . . . [T]here does not appear to be any requirement that CSC staff who come into regular contact with transsexual inmates have any kind of training regarding the special needs of this population. Such a requirement should be part of any CSC policy dealing with the placement of transsexual inmates.

[183] . . . [W]e find that CSC has failed to justify its blanket policy prohibiting inmate access to sex reassignment surgery. . . .

[192] We have found that CSC's policy with respect to the placement of pre-operative transsexual inmates has a discriminatory effect on transsexual inmates. . . .

[193] We have also found that CSC's blanket prohibition on sex reassignment surgery has a discriminatory effect on transsexual inmates because of their sex and their disability, and that CSC has been unable to justify such a blanket policy.

[194] For these reasons, Ms. Kavanagh's complaints are sustained.

[197] . . . It is . . . necessary that CSC take steps, in consultation with the Commission, to formulate a policy that ensures that the needs of transsexual inmates are identified and accommodated.

[198] We have found that Section 31 of CSC's Health Service Policy is discriminatory on the basis of both sex and disability, and that CSC has failed to justify a blanket prohibition on access to sex reassignment surgery. We therefore order that CSC cease applying the provisions of Section 31.

Source: Canadian Human Rights Tribunal. *Kavanagh v. Canada (Attorney General)*. Decided August 31, 2001. 41 CHRR 119. Available online at https://www.canlii.org/en/ca/chrt/doc /2001/2001canlii8496/2001canlii8496.html.

Correctional Services of Canada's Interim Policy Bulletin 584: Bill C-16 (Gender Identity or Expression) (December 27, 2017)

In subsequent years, the CSC continued to revise and update their policies. A notice about their December 2017 update is provided here.

Why were the policies changed?

The above policies are currently under review in light of the coming into force on June 19, 2017, of Bill C-16, which, among other things, amends the Canadian Human Rights Act by adding "gender identity or expression" as prohibited grounds of discrimination.

Pending promulgation of policy amendments, the following principles and changes to operational practice are effective immediately, and override any direction found in Commissioner's Directives or Guidelines.

Principles and Changes to Operational Practice

The Correctional Service of Canada (CSC) is committed to ensuring a safe, inclusive and respectful environment for everyone, including staff, offenders, contractors, volunteers and visitors.

CSC has a duty to accommodate based on gender identity or expression, regardless of the person's anatomy (i.e. sex) or the gender marker on identification documents. This includes placing offenders according to their gender identity in a men's or women's institution, Community Correctional Centre or Community-Based Residential Facility, if that is their preference, unless there are overriding health or safety concerns which cannot be resolved. Offenders may also choose whether strip and frisk searches and urinalysis testing are conducted by a male or a female staff member. As well, CSC staff must use offenders' preferred name and pronoun in oral interaction and written documentation. . . .

Steps must be taken to maximize the privacy and confidentiality of any information related to an offender's gender identity. Information about an offender's gender identity will only be shared with those directly involved with the offender's care, and only when relevant. Any conversations or consultations amongst staff or with the offender, including discussions regarding cell sharing and intake interviews, must occur privately, out of hearing range of anyone else that does not need to know.

Offender requests related to gender identity or expression will be accommodated except where, or to the extent that, following discussions, including with the offender, it has been established and documented by the Service that there would be overriding health or safety concerns which cannot be resolved. . . .

When an offender seeks to be accommodated on the basis of gender identity or expression, an individualized protocol will be developed. This will include, as applicable:

- program participation
- access to and participation in spiritual ceremonies, in consultation with Elders or Spiritual Advisors
- urinalysis
- monitoring under camera surveillance
- frisk searches
- strip searches (including recording thereof)
- decontamination showers
- staff response to voluntary nudity
- access to private and safe showers and/or toilets (as applicable/feasible)
- medical escorts

The protocol will be developed in consultation with the offender and documented in a Memo to File. . . . The Memo to File will also include the offender's preferred name and pronoun. The protocol will be carried out with respect for human dignity and in accordance with CSC Values and the Standards of Professional Conduct.

The Double-Bunking Cell Placement Assessment User Guide vulnerability risk assessment criteria now include the requirement to consider the needs of inmates with gender identity or expression considerations.

Inmates will be permitted to purchase effects from the catalogue for men and/or for women. The only restrictions are for safety, health or security reasons, as determined by the institution's type (men's or women's) and security level. . . . Consultation with a Psychologist or Physician is no longer required in order to grant this permission.

At the discretion of the Institutional Head on a case by case basis, inmates transferred from one institution type (men's or women's) to another may be authorized, within a 30-day window, to retain personal property items received from outside sources as it would be applicable to an admission or readmission. . . . If the decision of a transfer or a placement to a different institution type (men's or women's) does not correspond to the offender's preference, the offender will be advised of the rationale in writing.

The Assistant Commissioner, Human Resource Management, will ensure that training in the area of gender identity or expression continues to be made available to all staff and is kept current.

As new or updated policy documents, communication products and offender programs are implemented, they will reflect gender-inclusive language rather than binary language. . . .

How was this interim policy developed?

This Interim Policy Bulletin was developed by Strategic Policy in consultation with various sectors within National Headquarters, and following input from internal and external stakeholders on the policies under review.

Who will be affected by this policy?

All staff and offenders are affected by the policy changes.

Source: Correctional Service Canada. Interim Policy Bulletin 584, Bill C-16 (Gender Identity or Expression. Available online at http://www.csc-scc.gc.ca/acts-and-regulations/584 -pb-en.shtml. Used by permission.

Transgender People in the Military (2016–2017)

Whether or not trans, non-binary, and Two-Spirit people should serve in the U.S. military has been a topic of much debate in recent years. However, eighteen countries around the world have successfully integrated trans, non-binary, and Two-Spirit troops for some time: Argentina, Australia, Austria, Belgium, Canada, the Czech Republic, Denmark, Estonia, Finland, France, Germany, Israel, the Netherlands, New Zealand, Norway, Spain, Sweden, and the United Kingdom. The Canadian military lifted its ban on trans, non-binary, and Two-Spirit troops serving in 1992 and has continued to develop more inclusive policies ever since. All indications are that it has benefited individual service members and has had no detrimental effect on the Canadian Forces. Similarly, the Israeli Defence Forces also support trans soldiers in recent years.

On June 30, 2016, U.S. secretary of defense Ash Carter, serving under President Barack Obama, announced that transgender troops would be welcome to serve in the U.S. military. This an edited transcript of that announcement:

I am here today to announce some changes in the Defense Department's policies regarding transgender service members. And before I announce what changes we're making, I want to explain why. . . . The first and fundamental reason is that the Defense Department and the military need to avail ourselves of all talent possible in order to remain what we are now, the finest fighting force the world has ever known. . . . We have to have access to 100 percent of America's population for our all-volunteer force to be able to recruit from among them the most highly qualified and to retain them.

. . . Now, while there isn't definitive data on the number of transgender service members, RAND looked at the existing studies out there, and their best estimate was that about 2,500 people out of approximately 1.3 million active-duty service members, and about 1,500 out of 825,000 reserve service members are transgender, with the upper end of their range of estimates of around 7,000 in the active component and 4,000 in the reserves. . . . And I have a responsibility to them and to their commanders to provide them both with clearer and more consistent guidance than is provided by current policies. . . . Americans who want to serve and can meet our standards should be afforded the opportunity to compete to do so. After all, our all-volunteer force is built upon having the most qualified Americans, and the profession of arms is based on honor and trust.

. . . Based on its analysis of allied militaries and the expected rate at which American transgender service members would require medical treatment that would impact their fitness for duty or deployability, RAND's analysis concluded that there would be, quote, "minimal readiness impacts from allowing transgender service members to serve openly," end quote. And in terms of cost, RAND concluded that health care costs would represent, again in their words, "an exceedingly small proportion of DOD's overall health care expenditures."

Now, as a result of this year-long study, I'm announcing today that we're ending the ban on transgender Americans in the United States military. Effective immediately, transgender Americans may serve openly and they can no longer be discharged or otherwise separated from the military just for being transgender. Additionally, I have directed that the gender identity of an otherwise qualified individual will not bar them from military service or from any accession program. . . . Implementation will begin today. Starting today, otherwise qualified service members can no longer be involuntarily separated, discharged or denied reenlistment or continuation of service just for being transgender. . . . I'm also confident that we have reason to be proud today of what this will mean for our military, because it is the right thing to do, and it's another step in

ensuring that we continue to recruit and retain the most qualified people.

Source: U.S. Department of Defense. 2016. "Press Briefing
by Secretary Carter on Transgender Service Policies in the Pen-
tagon Briefing Room" (June 30, 2016). Available at https://
www.defense.gov/News/Transcripts/Transcript-View/Arti-
cle/822347/department-of-defense-press-briefing-by-secre-
tary-carter-on-transgender-service/.

*Just over one year later, on July 26, 2017, President Donald Trump
sent out a series of tweets saying:*

After consultation with my Generals and military experts,
please be advised that the United States Government will not
accept or allow . . . Transgender individuals to serve in any
capacity in the U.S. Military. Our military must be focused on
decisive and overwhelming . . . victory and cannot be burdened
with the tremendous medical costs and disruption that transgender in the military would entail. Thank you.

Source: https://twitter.com/realDonaldTrump/status/890193
981585444864; https://twitter.com/realDonaldTrump/status
/890196164313833472;https://twitter.com/realDonaldTrump
/status/890197095151546369.

*Since that time, repeated court challenges have continued to thwart
any implementation of the proposed ban on trans people serving in
the U.S. military, and fifty-six retired U.S. generals and admirals
have signed a statement opposing President Trump's wish to ban
trans people from military service, saying:*

The Commander in Chief has tweeted a total ban of honorably
serving transgender troops. This proposed ban, if implemented,
would cause significant disruptions, deprive the military of mis-
sion-critical talent, and compromise the integrity of transgender

troops who would be forced to live a lie, as well as non-transgender peers who would be forced to choose between reporting their comrades or disobeying policy. As a result, the proposed ban would degrade readiness even more than the failed "don't ask, don't tell" policy. Patriotic transgender Americans who are serving—and who want to serve—must not be dismissed, deprived of medically necessary health care, or forced to compromise their integrity or hide their identity.

President Trump seeks to ban transgender service members because of the financial cost and disruption associated with transgender military service. We respectfully disagree, and consider these claims to be without merit.

Source: Palm Center. 2017. "Fifty-Six Retired Generals and Admirals Warn That President Trump's Anti-Transgender Tweets, If Implemented, Would Degrade Military Readiness." August 1, 2017. Available at https://www.palmcenter.org/fifty -six-retired-generals-admirals-warn-president-trumps-anti -transgender-tweets-implemented-degrade-military-readiness/. Used by permission of the Palm Center.

ALL-GENDER RESTROOM

Introduction

The following are a list of various resources that will be of interest for further research on the various topics that have been covered in the chapters throughout this book. This list is not exhaustive; however, we have made it as comprehensive as possible. This section is divided into the following sections: Books; Journals; Art, Film, Media, and Television; Websites; and, finally, Organizations and Outreach.

Books

Ames, Jonathan, ed. *Sexual Metamorphosis: An Anthology of Transsexual Memoirs*. New York: Vintage Books, 2005.
　　This anthology includes historic writings from sexologists in the nineteenth and twentieth centuries as well as personal narratives from famous trans people such as Christine Jorgensen and Renée Richards. The personal stories of various trans people are engaging and accessible.

Beam, Chris. *Transparent: Love, Family, and Living the T with Transgender Teenagers*. Orlando: A Harvest Book, 2007.
　　Chris Beam, an investigative reporter, weaves together the stories of Ariel, Christina, Dominique, and FoxxJazzell,

---

There has been much controversy about what bathrooms trans people should use in public places. One easy solution is to have some "all genders" bathrooms in all public places. (Sheila Fitzgerald/Dreamstime.com) all young trans teens in urban settings. The author looks at intersecting identities and the ways that these teens cope in a transphobic world.

Beard, Richard. *Becoming Drusilla: One Life, Two Friends, Three Genders*. London: Vintage Books, 2008.

Richard Beard's memoir explores his friendship with his motorcycling friend, Drew, who worked in an engine room on a passenger ferry that crosses the English Channel. Drew then comes out as Drusilla and undergoes gender affirmation surgery. Beard struggles with his friend's transition, but they venture on a hiking trip to Wales. This is a beautiful, difficult, and honest book.

Beemyn, Jenny, and Susan Rankin. *The Lives of Transgender People*. New York: Columbia University Press, 2011.

Beemyn and Rankin's survey includes nearly 3,500 participants who identify all across the trans and non-binary spectrum. Organized into five chapters that include demographics, experiences, and issues faced by trans and non-binary youth, the book covers a large amount of information in an accessible way. The appendices in the back provide readers with the survey tool the authors used, as well as protocols for interviewing people, and finally an analysis of the information and statistics that were gathered.

Benjamin, Harry. *The Transsexual Phenomenon*. New York: Julian Press, 1966.

Dr. Harry Benjamin's groundbreaking book was first published in 1966 and, to this day, remains a classic for anyone interested in the history of trans people and Western medicine. When the book was published, what set it apart from writings by other sexologists studying transsexual people (the words "transgender" and "trans" were not as widely used at the time) was that Benjamin recommended that transsexual people should receive gen-der-affirming treatments at a time when other experts did not. The book was also entirely accessible to anyone who had a public library card. Benjamin's book also provided a foundation for the *Standards of Care* (SOC) that are still in use.

Bergman, Bear. *Is That for a Boy or a Girl?* Illustrated by Rachel Dougherty. Toronto: Flamingo Rampant, 2015.
Bergman's children's book includes gender nonconform-ing children of color, differently abled children, and their friends. The book explores societal stereotypes about what clothes, toys, and activities are for boys or for girls while it breaks down the gender binary and looks at the ways that we force children into gendered boxes.

Besnier, Niko, and Kalissa Alexeyeff, eds. *Gender on the Edge: Transgender, Gay, and Other Pacific Islanders.* Honolulu: University of Hawai'i Press, 2014.
Throughout Oceania, there has historically been a rich tradition of language and practice for people who iden-tify outside of the Western gender binary and outside of heteronormative practices: *mahú, fa'afafine, fakaleiti.* This anthology includes essays that look at ancient tra-ditions in the Pacific Islands and the ways that imperi-alism and colonialism affect our understanding of these cultures.

Bloom, Amy. *Normal: Transsexual CEOs, Crossdressing Cops, and Hermaphrodites with Attitude.* London: Bloomsbury, 2003.
Bloom questions what we mean by "normal" in our soci-ety. Once she begins writing about people on the trans spectrum as well as people with differences in sex devel-opment (DSD/intersex), it becomes clear that we should be questioning ideas of "normal." This is a very accessible and often humorous book.

Bockting, Walter, and Eric Avery, eds. *Transgender Health and HIV Prevention: Needs Assessment Studies from Transgender Communities across the United States.* New York: Haworth Medical Press, 2005.

In this work, various authors discuss the impact that AIDS and HIV have had on trans communities—specifically trans women of color. Each essay focuses on a specific location with "needs-based" assessments: Boston, Houston, and Philadelphia, for example. This will be of interest to anyone who is focused on social justice.

Bockting, Walter, and Sheila Kirk, eds. *Transgender and HIV: Risks, Prevention, and Care.* New York: Haworth Press, 2001.

Chapters in this book include ones focusing on social service needs, substance abuse and prevention, and discussions about gender affirmation surgical procedures and being HIV+. This is a more medically focused book, but it is an excellent resource for the medical field where there are still not nearly enough resources about trans people outside of the realm of gender affirmation surgical procedures.

Bond, Justin Vivian. *Tango: My Childhood, Backwards and in High Heels.* New York: Feminist Press, 2011.

Tango is a wonderful autobiography of growing up trans. Bond's story is completely accessible and brings a sense of humor to what were often heartbreaking and dangerous situations for young trans kids growing up in the 1970s. Many of these issues are still painfully relevant today.

Bono, Chaz, with Billie Fitzpatrick. *Transition: Becoming Who I Was Always Meant to Be.* New York: Plume, 2011.

As the child of stars Sonny Bono and Cher, Chaz Bono was always in the spotlight. Assigned female at birth, Chaz Bono came out as transgender in his thirties. This book is his autobiography and is written in a very engaging and accessible style.

Bornstein, Kate. *Hello Cruel World: 101 Alternatives to Suicide for Teens, Freaks, and Other Outlaws*. New York: Seven Stories Press, 2006.
> Trans teens are at a very high risk for attempted suicide. In this fun and engaging book, Bornstein takes on the very serious role of mentoring teens who feel like freaks—whether they are trans, queer, or have other reasons why they do not fit into societal categories of "normal." This small book is full of fun reassurances that being a teen is tough, and Bornstein includes lots of humorous cartoons and other visuals.

Bornstein, Kate, and S. Bear Bergman, eds. *Gender Outlaws: The Next Generation*. Berkeley: Seal Press, 2010.
> Bornstein and Bergman bring their sense of humor and wit to this intelligent and accessible group of essays that cover issues like the intersections of race, gender, and disability and the intersections of being trans and Jewish or Muslim. Topics like cisgender privilege and Transgender Day of Remembrance are also covered. The book begins with an entertaining interview between Bornstein and Bergman.

Bornstein, Kate. *A Queer and Pleasant Danger: A Memoir*. Boston: Beacon Press, 2012.
> Kate Bornstein's memoir is a beautiful example of the ways that autobiography can be life-changing for other people reading it. This is an engaging and accessible book about a trans activist pioneer.

Boyd, Helen. *She's Not the Man I Married: My Life with a Transgender Husband*. Emeryville: Seal Press, 2007.
> Helen Boyd's autobiography/biography of being a spouse to someone assigned male at birth who then transitions offers readers an excellent look at the ways transitioning genders can affect a relationship—specifically a marriage. The book is not sensationalist and the last chapters are

written by Boyd's spouse, Betty. This is a very personable account of gender affirmation within a heterosexual relationship that turns into a lesbian relationship.

Califia, Patrick. *Sex Changes: Transgender Politics*. San Francisco: Cleis Press, 2003.
Califia, who had been a prolific lesbian sex radical writer from San Francisco in the 1980s, has now become a major voice in trans culture. This book offers an engaging history of trans identity that includes early trans pioneers and contemporary trans rights activists.

Champagne, Roland A., Nina Ekstein, and Gary Kates. *The Maiden of Tonnerre: The Vicissitudes of the Chevalier and the Chevalière d'Eon*. Baltimore: Johns Hopkins University Press, 2001.
A contemporary book that looks at the memoirs of Chevalier/Chevalière d'Éon. Although these authors use male pronouns for d'Éon throughout this book, most contemporary historians now use a neutral pronoun out of respect for the fact that d'Éon appears to have been equally comfortable as a man and as a woman. This is one of the first English translations of the famous French statesperson and spy's life. Perhaps the most important component of this book is the final chapter, which is d'Éon's own writing about numerous Catholic saints who were assigned female at birth, but who became men in order to fully embrace religion. D'Éon writes, in the late eighteenth century, about a collective trans identity and trans community (although without using the term "trans").

Clarke, Julie. *Becoming Julie*. Edinburgh: Fledgling Press, 2014.
A beautiful autobiography and coming out story of Julie Clarke, who was assigned male at birth in the 1950s in rural Scotland. This is a completely accessible and compelling first-person account of a "regular" person who happens to be transgender. A very down-to-earth autobiography.

Cooney, Kara. *The Woman Who Would Be King*. New York: Crown, 2014.

This book offers students an interesting and accessible account of Pharaoh Hatshepsut from ancient Egypt. Rather than stay a queen, Hatshepsut insisted on using the masculine title of pharaoh, and she even wore a fake beard to show her masculinity and power. Cooney's book explores ideas of gender in ancient Egypt.

Cotten, Trystan T., ed. *Hung Jury: Testimonies of Genital Surgery by Transsexual Men*. Oakland: Transgress Press, 2012.

Cotten has compiled several essays that detail each man's experience with genital construction surgery. There is also an excellent section written by partners of trans men. For those wanting to know more about the specifics of phalloplasty, this is an accessible book that is not full of medical jargon.

Coyote, Ivan. *Tomboy Survival Guide*. Vancouver, BC: Arsenal Pulp Press, 2016.

Using carefully crafted short stories, Canadian Ivan Coyote takes readers on a moving tour of important moments and turning points in his life. This book is easy to read and hard to put down.

Cronn-Mills, Kirstin. *Beautiful Music for Ugly Children*. Woodbury: Flux, 2014.

Winner of the Stonewall Book Award, this young adult novel focuses on Gabe, a young trans teen, whom everyone wants to continue to call by his birth name. Gabe DJ's at a local radio station where he is out and proud about being Gabe.

Currah, Paisley, Richard M. Jung, and Shannon Price Minter, eds. *Transgender Rights*. Minneapolis: University of Minnesota Press, 2006.

Laws focusing on trans people are changing rapidly around the world; however, the essays in this book are still very relevant where laws, history, and politics are concerned. This book includes writing by numerous scholars and activists who have been, and continue to be, on the cutting edge of the fight for legal protections for trans people. People interested in legal issues like employment nondiscrimination and family rights will find this book useful.

De Erauso, Catalina. *Lieutenant Nun: Memoir of a Basque Transvestite in the New World.* Translated by Michele Stepto and Gabriel Stepto. Boston: Beacon Press, 1996.
This short and fast-paced memoir covers the life of Catalina/Don Antonio de Erauso who, as a teenager in 1599, escaped an abusive convent. After hiding in a nearby forest, de Erauso tears apart the nun's clothing and refashions the outfit into that of a young man. From there, de Erauso joins the Spanish army, travels to the Americas, and recounts numerous adventures including gambling and fighting in duels.

Devor, Aaron H. *Gender Blending: Confronting the Limits of Duality.* Bloomington: Indiana University Press, 1989.
Devor's book was one of the first to explore what today we might call non-binary gender expression. It is based on numerous interviews with people who were assigned female at birth and who identify as female, but whose gender expression blends masculinity and femininity to the point where they are sometimes taken to be men and sometimes women. This book looks at the constructions and constrictions of binary gender.

Devor, Aaron H. *FTM: Female-to-Male Transsexuals in Society.* Bloomington: Indiana University Press, 1999, 2016.
This groundbreaking book continues to be one of the most in-depth studies on trans men and their experiences in everyday life. Incorporating forty-five in-depth interviews, Devor's book covers issues about growing up trans,

sexuality and relationships, finding identity, deciding to transition, and life after transitioning.

Devor, Aaron H. *The Transgender Archives: Foundations for the Future*. Victoria: University of Victoria Libraries, 2014.
This book has beautiful examples of the various holdings in the world's largest transgender archive at the University of Victoria in Victoria, British Columbia. From underground trans zines to historic Japanese advertisements for Takarazuka (cross-gender performance), this book will give readers a sense of what is available in the archives.

Diamond, Morty, ed. *From the Inside Out: Radical Gender Transformation, FTM and Beyond*. San Francisco: Manic D Press, 2004.
Diamond's anthology of writings by people assigned female at birth who identify as trans men, genderqueer, or non-binary includes poems, essays, and short stories. This is an excellent book for anyone looking for short writings and the creative voices of trans people.

Docter, Richard F. *From Man to Woman: The Transgender Journey of Virginia Prince*. Northridge: DocterPress, 2004.
Richard Docter, a clinical psychologist focusing on gender research, has compiled an in-depth biography on Virginia Prince, a transgender pioneer. Prince was the founder and editor of one of the longest running trans magazines, *Transvestia*.

Dose, Ralf. *Magnus Hirschfeld: The Origins of the Gay Liberation Movement*. Translated by Edward H. Willis. New York: Monthly Review Press, 2014.
Magnus Hirschfeld was one of the first sexologists to recognize that sexual orientation and gender identity could inform each other, but are not the same. He was an early pioneer for trans rights when he worked with authorities in Berlin to make special identification cards for people

he referred to as transvestites—a word he coined. Some of the first gender-affirming surgeries were done at his research institute. This is an excellent biography of his life and work around LGBTQ+ issues in Weimar Berlin.

Driskill, Qwo-Li. *Asegi Stories: Cherokee Queer and Two-Spirit Memory.* Tucson: University of Arizona Press, 2016.
  Qwo-Li Driskill, who has written and edited numerous pieces on Two-Spirit people—including a book of poetry—now takes their focus to their Cherokee roots to explore Two-Spirit identity within the Cherokee Nation. Many indigenous cultures have long histories of Two-Spirit people in their tribes; however, in the Cherokee Nation, Two-Spirit history had almost been forgotten, until this book.

Driskill, Qwo-Li, Chris Finley, Brian Joseph Gilley, and Scott Lauria Morgensen, eds. *Queer Indigenous Studies: Critical Interventions in Theory, Politics, and Literature.* Tucson: University of Arizona Press, 2011.
  This book of academic essays written by a diverse group of writers is divided into three sections: "Performing Queer Indigenous Critiques," "Situating Two-Spirit and Queer Indigenous Movements," and "Reading Queer Indigenous Writing." This is a groundbreaking text that focuses beautifully on intersecting identities and intersecting oppressions.

Ekins, Richard, and Dave King, eds. *Blending Genders: Social Aspects of Cross-Dressing and Sex-Changing.* London: Routledge, 1996.
  This wide-ranging book of academic essays includes writings about heterosexual cross-dressers' clubs, the 1990s trans community in the Kings Cross station area of London, personal accounts of transitioning, and medical constructions of trans people. Some major writers and theorists in trans studies such as Stephen Whittle and

Mark Rees are included along with an excellent look at trans literary traditions over the past century.

Ekins, Richard, and Dave King, eds. *Virginia Prince: Pioneer of Transgendering.* New York: Haworth Medical Press, 2005.
This book of essays includes several written by Virginia Prince, who was a pioneer in the field of transgender studies. It was also simultaneously published as *International Journal of Transgenderism* 8, no. 4 (2005). Prince and her often controversial ideas about the nature of trans people are the focus of this text.

Ellis, Havelock. *Studies in the Psychology of Sex Volume VII: Eonism and Other Supplementary Studies.* Philadelphia: F. A. Davis, 1928.
Havelock Ellis was a sexologist famous for taking a sympathetic approach to gay, lesbian, and bisexual people. In this volume, he focuses specifically on what today we would call trans identities. The subtitle of the volume, "Eonism," refers to the famous French trans figure Chevalier/Chevalière d'Éon.

Enke, Anne, ed. *Transfeminist Perspectives: In and Beyond Transgender and Gender Studies.* Philadelphia: Temple University Press, 2012.
Often, feminism and transgender studies are at odds, although they need not be. This is an excellent set of essays from feminist theorists who discuss why feminist studies and trans studies must go together. From essays about trans and intersex student athletes to the ramifications of trans rights and immigration laws, this is a cornerstone text.

Erickson-Schroth, Laura, ed. *Trans Bodies, Trans Selves: A Resource for the Transgender Community.* Oxford: Oxford University Press, 2014.
This book, which is modeled on the famous feminist text *Our Bodies, Our Selves,* is an outstanding resource book

for trans people and their allies. The book is a virtual "how to" on all things relating to trans health and well-being and includes interviews and stories from a diverse group of trans people around the world.

Ewert, Marcus. *10,000 Dresses*. Illustrations by Rex Ray. New York: Seven Stories Press, 2008.

Bailey was assigned male at birth, but every night Bailey dreams of wearing beautiful dresses. This is an outstanding children's book because the author uses "she" pronouns for Bailey, who identifies as a girl, despite all of the adults in the book insisting Bailey is a boy who cannot wear dresses. It is a powerful look at pronouns and the strength of friendship.

Feder, Ellen K. *Making Sense of Intersex: Changing Ethical Perspectives in Biomedicine*. Bloomington: Indiana University Press, 2014.

This outstanding book investigates the ethical dilemmas in Western medicine concerning people who have differences in sex development (DSD). Feder looks at the ways that Western medicine has categorized babies with DSD as needing "emergency" surgery because they embody non-binary biological sex. Interviews with doctors and people with DSD shed light on the ethical concerns of pushing all bodies into a sex binary.

Feinberg, Leslie. *Stone Butch Blues*. New York: Firebrand Books, 1993.

This is Feinberg's iconic semi-autobiographical novel about a gender-diverse person growing up in a culture that depends on the rigidity of the gender binary. This book won numerous awards and remains in the top 10 of LGBT "must reads."

Feinberg, Leslie. *Transgender Warriors: Making History from Joan of Arc to RuPaul*. Boston: Beacon Press, 1996.

Leslie Feinberg's classic book that looks at trans history through the ages and interweaves hir own story into the fabric of the narrative. The depth of research combined with the accessibility of the writing makes this an absolute "must read" for anyone interested in trans culture and trans people. This book makes a terrific jumping-off point for further research on various historic figures.

Feinberg, Leslie. *TransLiberation: Beyond Pink or Blue.* Boston: Beacon Press, 1998.

In this very accessible book, Leslie Feinberg mixes together hir own story of becoming a trans activist along with profiles of other trans activists. Of particular note, Feinberg includes an extensive interview with Sylvia Rivera, one of the trans women of color who led parts of the early LGBT liberation movement in the United States.

Gaillardet, Frédéric. *The Memoirs of Chevalier d'Eon.* Translated by Antonia White. London: Anthony Blond, 1970.

This is an interesting book. On the one hand, it was written by someone who, today, we would refer to as transphobic and patronizing toward d'Éon. On the other hand, it is one of the few sets of translations into English of the infamous Chevalier/Chevalière d'Éon's own writings, so in that regard, this is an excellent source.

Garber, Marjorie. *Vested Interests: Cross-Dressing and Cultural Anxiety.* New York: Routledge, 1992.

Garber's classic academic and accessible text on cross-dressing examines some of the ways that cultures have historically looked at clothing as signs of gender identity and social status. From medieval sumptuary laws that made cross-dressing illegal because there was worry that peasants would pass as aristocracy, to the ways that various pieces of religious clothing for men are gendered as female, Garber supplies readers with some excellent questions about clothing and culture through the ages.

Girshick, Lori B. *Transgender Voices: Beyond Women and Men.* Hanover: University Press of New England, 2008.
This book uses interviews and social theory to explore various ways of being trans in the world. From social constructions that are tied to biological sex to coming out, gender policing, and gender liberation, Girshick covers a lot of trans issues with a focus on trans men in particular.

Gonzalez-Polledo, E. J. *Transitioning: Matter, Gender, Thought.* London: Rowman and Littlefield International, 2017.
This highly theoretical book is an ethnographic exploration of trans men's experiences outside of a strict gender binary. This is an interdisciplinary piece that uses anthropology, trans studies, and feminist studies to examine bodies and lives in transition, both literally and metaphorically.

Green, Jamison. *Becoming a Visible Man.* Nashville: Vanderbilt University Press, 2004.
This iconic and groundbreaking book explores what it means to be a trans man in our culture. The writing is accessible and engaging as Green not only explores his own life and struggles as a trans man, but he also looks to larger cultural issues where gender identity, stereotypes, and labels are concerned.

Haefele-Thomas, Ardel. *Introduction to Transgender Studies.* New York: Harrington Park Press, 2018.
This is the first introductory textbook in the field of transgender studies. The twelve chapters are global in their focus and explore trans history, culture, and people from ancient times to the present day. Also included within each chapter are "Writings from the Community" so that

voices of trans people around the world are also present in the text.

Halberstam, Jack (Judith). *In a Queer Time and Place: Transgender Bodies, Subcultural Lives*. New York: New York University Press, 2005.

Jack Halberstam (this older publication still uses his name assigned at birth) is a queer and trans theorist and historian. In this important book of essays looking at the ways trans men's bodies and lives are seen, Halberstam focuses on transgender biography, theories of queer and trans positionalities, and trans contexts within U.S. cultural studies.

Hoffman, Sarah, and Ian Hoffman. *Jacob's New Dress*. Illustrations by Chris Chase. Chicago: Albert Whitman, 2014.

Jacob is a boy who likes to wear dresses. He identifies as a boy. This true story, which is written by the parents of a child whose gender expression does not fall strictly on the gender binary, is empowering in its show of parental support for a child being bullied by classmates at school. It is also clear that, culturally, we put way too much emphasis on what being either a boy or a girl is supposed to look like.

Holmes, Rachel. *Scanty Particulars: The Life of Dr James Barry*. London: Viking, 2002.

This is one of the few respectful and well-written biographies on Dr. James Miranda Barry who, more often than not in history, is written about as the first *woman* surgeon in Britain. Dr. Barry, though, lived his entire life as a man, and Holmes looks at the ways that we can claim Barry as a historic trans figure. Also of note, Dr. Barry spent most of his career in the British colonies giving care to people with leprosy and people indigenous to the places Britain colonized.

Hoyer, Niels, ed. *Man into Woman: The First Sex Change—A Portrait of Lili Elbe.* London: Blue Boat Books, 2004.
Lili Elbe is known as the first person in Europe to undergo a Western medical gender affirmation surgery in 1931. Sadly, she died a year later from medical complications and infections from the surgery. Elbe's writings, which were translated into English by Niels Hoyer, were first published in 1933.

Hurst, Mitchell, and Robert Swope, eds. *Casa Susanna.* New York: Powerhouse Books, 2005.
In upstate New York in the 1960s, there was a special house for weekend retreats called Casa Susanna. The people who went to Casa Susanna had been assigned male at birth and lived as men, but while they were at this special house, they would dress like, and feel themselves to be, women in a time when cross-dressing was illegal and could land a person in jail and end many careers. This book is a compilation of the beautiful photographs taken on those weekends of people who today would likely identify as trans women. This is an outstanding pictorial history.

Irving, Dan, and Rupert Raj, eds. *Trans Activism in Canada: A Reader.* Toronto: Canadian Scholars' Press, 2014.
This anthology of essays focuses on trans activism in Canada. Sections of this book include an exploration of historical and contemporary perspectives, individual and community approaches to trans activism, and a look at transforming various bureaucracies and health care. This is an outstanding and diverse compilation of essays.

Jacobs, Sue-Ellen, Wesley Thomas, and Sabine Lang, eds. *Two Spirit People: Native American Gender Identity, Sexuality, and Spirituality.* Chicago: University of Chicago Press, 1997.
This book of theoretical essays written by Indigenous Two-Spirit people offers an array of topics that concern

Two-Spirit identities within a contemporary context. Of particular note, many of the essays discuss Two-Spirit identities as encompassing the LGBTQ2+ spectrum within the context of postcolonial recovery.

Jenkins, Andrea. *The T Is Not Silent: New and Selected Poems.* Minneapolis: Purple Lioness Productions, 2015.
Andrea Jenkins, award-winning poet, historian, and first African American openly trans woman elected to the city council of a major city in the United States, delivers a beautiful selection of poems in this book. From her own autobiographical "Black Pearl" to poems calling for social justice for trans women of color, this is an empowering book of poetry.

Johnson, E. Patrick, ed. *No Tea, No Shade: New Writings in Black Queer Studies.* Durham: Duke University Press, 2016.
Although this book is not solely focused on black trans people, there are numerous essays focused on black trans people and black trans experience. From black drag to explorations of gender fluidity within African American queer communities, this theoretical book looks at the intersections of race, sexual orientation, gender identity, and gender expression.

Jones, Rhian E. *Petticoat Heroes: Gender, Culture and Popular Protest in the Rebecca Riots.* Cardiff: University of Wales Press, 2015.
This accessible and outstanding book looks at the nineteenth-century Rebecca Riots in Wales (these riots were caused by poor people being taxed exorbitant amounts of money by the wealthy). One of the major components of these riots were men cross-dressed as women. This is the first historical account that takes various gender issues into consideration—particularly looking at gender outside of a strict binary.

Kane-DeMaios, J. Ari, and Vern L. Bullough, eds. *Crossing Sexual Boundaries: Transgender Journeys, Uncharted Paths.* Amherst: Prometheus Books, 2006.

    The editors of this anthology have compiled numerous stories, essays, and poems from trans people discussing their lives as trans. The autobiographies in this book discuss gender transition, family, and community. An excellent selection of personal stories by trans people.

Keig, Zander, and Mitch Kellaway, eds. *Manning Up: Transsexual Men on Finding Brotherhood, Family, and Themselves.* Oakland: Transgress Press, 2014.

    This anthology of nonfiction essays from twenty-seven trans men explores their experiences in their families and in their communities. This incredibly diverse collection includes voices of queer and straight trans men from diverse ethnic, cultural, and socioeconomic backgrounds.

Kilodavis, Cheryl. *My Princess Boy: A Mom's Story about a Young Boy Who Loves to Dress Up.* Illustrations by Suzanne DeSimone. New York: Aladdin, 2009.

    This beautifully illustrated children's book is written by a mother whose child is gender nonconforming. The book is for young children, but it is a fantastic example of early education, school acceptance, and anti-bullying.

King, Nia (interviewer), and Jessica Glennon-Zukoff and Terra Mikalson, eds. *Queer and Trans Artists of Color: Stories of Some of Our Lives.* San Bernardino: CreateSpace Independent Publishing Platform, 2015.

    Nia King has interviewed numerous queer and trans people of color for this biography. Unlike many biographies that tend to be more social science based, the people interviewed here are all artists. This is an outstanding look at artists who discuss the intersections of being queer and/or trans and who deal with issues of race and class in their art and in their lives.

Krieger, Irwin. *Counseling Transgender and Non-Binary Youth: The Essential Guide*. London: Jessica Kingsley, 2017.
Irwin Krieger is a clinical social worker who has, for the past decade, focused his work with trans teens, adults, and their families. This book is an accessible "how to" guide for people who serve as counselors for trans teens and their families. The book focuses on the impacts of stigma on trans teens, medical transition, family therapy, and issues around school and beyond.

Kuklin, Susan. *Beyond Magenta: Transgender Teens Speak Out*. Somerville, MA: Candlewick Press, 2014.
The stories of the six teens interviewed in *Beyond Magenta* illustrate beautifully the diverse spectrum of trans experience and intersecting identities. Their stories range from crossing the gender binary completely, to refusing to be labeled within a binary, to looking at differences of sex development (intersex) as part of a non-binary and multifaceted sex and gender schema. In their own images and stories, these teens invite readers to hear about their varied experiences.

Kulik, Don. *Travesti: Sex, Gender and Culture among Brazilian Transgendered Prostitutes*. Chicago: University of Chicago Press, 1998.
For many trans women in Brazil, often the only kind of work is sex work. Trans women are also among the most frequent homicide victims in Brazil. This is an excellent sociological and cultural exploration of the lives of trans women in Brazil who also do sex work. The author uses interviews to delve into the lives of these women.

Lester, CN. *Trans Like Me: A Journey for All of Us*. Great Britain: Virago Press, 2017.
CN Lester is an academic and activist who has written an engaging book that looks at numerous issues in trans

studies. Lester's experience as trans informs the writing about topics like trans children, pronouns, and the denial of trans history.

Maroon, Everett. *The Unintentional Time Traveler.* Maple Shade, NJ: Lethe Press, 2016.
> Written by a trans author, this is a terrific young adult book that explores fluidity within the gender binary. When sixteen-year-old Jack agrees to try a new experimental treatment for his seizures, he finds himself transported back into the 1920s and into the body of Jacqueline. Over time, the main character navigates within both poles of the gender binary, and also asks the reader to call the gender binary into question.

Martin, Fran, Peter A. Jackson, Mark McLelland, and Audrey Yue, eds. *AsiapacifiQUEER: Rethinking Genders and Sexualities.* Urbana: University of Illinois Press, 2008.
> This diverse compilation of essays focusing on gender and sexual orientation in Asian, Pacific, and Oceania communities and cultures includes pieces about trans women in Malaysia, trans masculinity in Hong Kong, gender in Tom and Dee culture in Thailand, and the growing Fa'afafine community in New Zealand. This is an excellent book for anyone wanting to explore gender identities and expressions in various Asian cultures.

Mattilda a.k.a. Matt Bernstein Sycamore, ed. *Nobody Passes: Rejecting the Rules of Gender and Conformity.* Emeryville: Seal Press, 2006.
> This book is a collection of very accessible and engaging essays that focus on the intersections of race, class, trans identity, and trans embodiment. From short stories that focus on issues like parental violence against trans youth, to a short memoir about being a Syrian non-binary immigrant in the United States, Mattilda has compiled diverse perspectives on gender.

Maupin, Armistead. *The Days of Anna Madrigal.* New York: Harper Perennial, 2015.

Armistead Maupin has, over the course of four decades, created one of the most quintessential series of novels about San Francisco and a core group of characters who make up a chosen family. In this ninth and last book of the series, Maupin focuses on the matriarch of this family of "freaks" and "misfits": Anna Madrigal, who also happens to be a trans woman. For forty years, and throughout all of his books, Maupin has always given respect and dignity to Mrs. Madrigal, and now, finally, readers get her life story.

Merrill, Lisa. *When Romeo Was a Woman: Charlotte Cushman and Her Circle of Female Spectators.* Ann Arbor: University of Michigan Press, 2000.

Merrill's book offers an excellent look at women who played "breeches parts"—male roles on the stage in the nineteenth century. What set Charlotte Cushman apart, though, was that she was very out of the closet about her attraction to women, and she also became the first woman to be truly respected on the stage as a man. Most "gender-bending" roles on stage for women were in comedies; however, Cushman became famous playing Hamlet and Romeo. A beautiful study of gender fluidity on stage.

Ming, Lei, with Lura Frazey. *Life Beyond My Body: A Transgender Journey to Manhood in China.* Oakland: Transgress Press, 2016.

Surviving against all odds, including the use of underground and illegal testosterone, and a stint in prison for being transgender, Lei Ming is a trans man living in stealth in China. This book is his journey as a young trans man from a small village in a country where being transgender is still very difficult.

Mirandé, Alfredo. *Behind the Mask: Gender Hybridity in a Zapotec Community.* Tucson: University of Arizona Press, 2017.

Mirandé's book is an in-depth and outstanding study of gender diversity in the Juchitán region of Mexico where a large number of citizens are Muxes—trans and gender-fluid people. The book includes narratives of Muxes as well as an excellent chapter on Two-Spirit Muxe Zapotec identity.

Morgan, Ruth, Charl Marais, and Joy Rosemary Wellbeloved, eds. *Trans: Transgender Life Stories from South Africa*. Auckland Park, South Africa: Jacana, 2009.
This beautiful book of life stories includes personal narratives and art that explore trans people in South Africa, a country long torn by violent apartheid rule. What makes this book unique is that South Africans of *all* races and ethnicities are included.

Murdock, Knave. *TransCat*. Six issues. Seattle: Northwest Press, 2014.
TransCat is billed as "America's first trans superhero!" This series of comics focuses on a diverse group of friends fighting for social justice with a specific focus on gender equality. These are engaging and accessible comics for young teens.

Najmabadi, Afsaneh. *Professing Selves: Transsexuality and Same-Sex Desire in Contemporary Iran*. Durham: Duke University Press, 2014.
In contemporary Iran, gender affirmation surgery is legal if the trans person receiving the hormones and surgery professes that they will be heterosexual after the procedure. Najmabadi's research explores the current Iranian laws that allow for gender affirmation, yet criminalize homosexuality. This book explores the intersections of the law, medicine, and religion.

Namaste, Viviane. *Sex Change, Social Change: Reflections on Identity, Institutions, and Imperialism* (2nd ed.). Toronto: Women's Press, 2005.

Namaste's outstanding study that focuses on culture in the Canadian province of Quebec tackles difficult topics such as trans people in sex work, trans people in prison, and trans people with HIV/AIDS. For both academics and activists, Namaste has written beautifully about the intersections of feminist and trans theory as well as the ways that decisions by people in power affect the day-to-day lives of trans people. The personal essays included are very compelling.

Nanda, Serena. *Neither Man nor Woman: The Hijras of India.* Belmont, CA: Wadsworth, Cengage Learning, 1999.
This is an outstanding ethnography on the *hijras* in India—a group of third-gender people who have existed in India for over 2,000 years. Nanda interviews various *hijras* and records their life stories within the larger context of Indian postcolonial culture.

Nestle, Joan, and Clare Howell, and Ricki Wilchins, eds. *Genderqueer: Voices from Beyond the Sexual Binary.* Los Angeles: Alyson Books, 2002.
This was one of the first books to use the term "genderqueer" and to include essays written by, for, and about trans and genderqueer people. Before the term "nonbinary" was coined, this book was working with the same ideas. Of particular note, Joan Nestle, who has always been a lesbian feminist activist, writes about the need for cisgender lesbians to support trans people. The anthology is full of stories, poems, and essays that are fully accessible.

Noble, Jean Bobby. *Sons of the Movement: FtMs Risking Incoherence on a Post-Queer Cultural Landscape.* Toronto: Women's Press, 2006.
Calling into question a white supremacist sex and gender binary system, the theoretical essays in this book interrogate white masculinity and the expectations of what being a man means. Noble looks to various trans and queer

embodiments and the intersections of being antiracist, trans, queer, and feminist.

Pessin-Whedbee, Brook. *Who Are You? The Kid's Guide to Gender Identity.* Illustrated by Naomi Bardoff. London: Jessica Kingsley, 2017.

As a kindergarten teacher and a mother of a gender-nonconforming child, Pessin-Whedbee wanted to create a book that she could use in her own classrooms to explain the complexities of gender identity. This is an outstanding children's book that focuses on racial and gender diversity and gives children a chance to discuss how they identify their gender.

Ponsonby, Miranda. *The Making of Miranda: From Gentleman to Gentlewoman in One Lifetime.* Gretton, Northamptonshire: Noble Books, 2009.

Miranda Ponsonby, assigned male at birth, was born into a wealthy family in England. Before her transition, she was a Household Cavalry officer connected to the royal family; after her transition, at the age of sixty, she became a nurse. In her mid-seventies, she created this first-person account of her life.

Power, Terri. *Shakespeare and Gender in Practice.* Houndmills, Basingstoke: Palgrave, 2016.

There has been a lot of research and work done on cross-dressing in Shakespeare's plays, which were written during the Elizabethan era when women were not allowed on the stage. In this book, the focus is on contemporary cross-dressing and gender transgressions in productions of the Bard's plays. This is an excellent source on the ways that Shakespeare's plays can be seen as trans performance.

Robertson, Jennifer. *Takarazuka: Sexual Politics and Popular Culture in Modern Japan.* Berkeley: University of California Press, 1998.

The world-famous Takarazuka Revue, which was founded in 1913, is a Japanese singing and performance group comprised entirely of women. However, there are prized positions in the revue for women who embody masculinity both on stage and in day-to-day life. Robertson's book is an outstanding historic and sociological study of the Japanese phenomenon.

Rudacille, Deborah. *The Riddle of Gender: Science, Activism, and Transgender Rights*. New York: Anchor Books, 2006.
Prompted by the coming out of a close friend, Rudacille decided to research trans identities through history and science. Although some of her language is now a bit dated, each of her chapters includes a conversation she has with various trans people in the fields of history, medicine, and activism. For those conversations, this book still makes an excellent contribution to the field.

Savage, Sarah, and Fox Fisher. *Are You a Boy or Are You a Girl?* PRC: Print Ninja, 2015.
Tiny and their family have moved to a new town, and now Tiny has to navigate a new school situation in which everyone keeps asking them if they are a boy or a girl. Tiny refuses to fall into being pushed on one side of the gender binary or the other. Although classmates bully Tiny, the teacher winds up being a great ally. This is an excellent book that looks at the experience of a non-binary trans child.

Schultz, Jackson Wright. *Trans/Portraits: Voices from Transgender Communities*. Hanover, NH: Dartmouth College Press, 2015.
Schultz's book explores the stories of more than thirty trans people in the United States. The trans voices included are from diverse ethnic, religious, racial, and socioeconomic backgrounds and include people all across the gender and sexual orientation spectrum.

Sears, Clare. *Arresting Dress: Cross-Dressing, Law, and Fascination in Nineteenth-Century San Francisco.* Durham: Duke University Press, 2015.

Sears has created an accessible and fascinating history of people who cross-dressed in order to embody their true gender identity in San Francisco in the nineteenth century. The historic accounts are supported by outstanding research and archival material, which bring the people discussed to life. Sears takes intersecting identities into account—in particular in the chapter focusing on the ways that Chinese immigrants in San Francisco were discriminated against.

Seliger, Mark. *On Christopher Street: Transgender Stories.* New York: Rizzoli, 2016.

This book includes stunning photographs of trans people who live in the neighborhood around Christopher Street, which is famous for being the place where the Stonewall Riots happened at the start of the modern-day LGBTQ rights movement. Seliger's book also includes moving stories from the people pictured.

Skidmore, Emily. *True Sex: The Lives of Trans Men at the Turn of the 20th Century.* New York: New York University Press, 2017.

From the starting point of examining "female husbands" in the nineteenth century, Skidmore explores the lives of various trans men in the United States in both rural and urban settings. This is an outstanding and accessible history.

Smith, Brice D. *Lou Sullivan: Daring to Be a Man among Men.* Oakland: Transgress Press, 2017.

Lou Sullivan was an openly gay trans man who lived in a time when many gender affirmation clinics would not assist trans people unless they planned to be heterosexual after their affirmation surgery. Lou Sullivan paved the way for queer trans people, specifically queer trans men. This is the first biography that focuses on Lou Sullivan's life and his political activism and work.

Spoon, Rae. *First Spring Grass Fire.* Vancouver: Arsenal Pulp Press, 2012.

Canadian non-binary trans writer and musician Rae Spoon has created a story about a non-binary trans teen in Alberta, Canada. The narrator of the book grows up in an evangelical household and often finds themselves being dragged to religious revivals. They are also struggling with a father with mental health issues and an abusive home environment. This is a poignant coming-of-age story.

Spoon, Rae, and Ivan E. Coyote. *Gender Failure.* Vancouver: Arsenal Pulp Press, 2014.

Coyote and Spoon have taken material from their live shows that have toured Europe and North America and compiled their experiences into stories and essays about the ways that they both fail at fitting into the gender binary. In a broader sense, the authors look at the ways the gender binary holds everyone hostage.

Stanley, Eric A., and Nat Smith, eds. *Captive Genders: Trans Embodiment and the Prison Industrial Complex*—Expanded Second Edition. Oakland: AK Press, 2015.

From bathhouse raids in Toronto in 1981 to violence against trans people of color, this activist and political book of essays examines trans people who have been victimized by, fought against, and continue to try and change the prison-industrial complex. Included in the book are excellent essays on pioneering activists like Miss Major Griffin-Gracy and younger activists who continue to work against violence against trans people.

Street Transvestite Action Revolutionaries: Survival, Revolt and Queer Antagonist Struggle. Untorelli Press, online zine. https://untorellipress.noblogs.org/files/2011/12/STAR.pdf.

Sylvia Rivera and Marsha P. Johnson, two trans women of color who were among the trans protesters who were present at the Stonewall Inn in New York City in 1969 when the modern LGBTQ rights movement was first ushered in, were soon ignored by mainstream white gay and lesbian people who did not want the new movement to be too radical. Thus, Street Transvestite Action Revolutionaries (STAR) was born. This is their manifesto from the early 1970s, which reads as both a historic piece as well as a contemporary call for direct action.

Stryker, Susan. *Transgender History: The Roots of Today's Revolution*, revised edition. New York: Seal Press, 2017.
    In her most recent edition of *Transgender History*, the trans historian Susan Stryker maps out the history of trans people with a predominant focus on the United States. The book is full of definitions, explanations of cross-dressing laws, and an outstanding list of resources for further research. This is an excellent history text for anyone who would like to begin to explore trans history.

Stryker, Susan, and Stephen Whittle, eds. *The Transgender Studies Reader*. New York: Routledge Press, 2006.
    Stryker and Whittle have compiled fifty original and reprinted essays ranging from nineteenth-century sexology pieces that helped set some of the dangerous stereotypes that still face trans people today to essays that focus on trans feminist theory. There is a wealth of diverse sources that cover numerous trans theories in this compilation.

Stryker, Susan, and Aren Z. Aizura, eds. *The Transgender Studies Reader 2*. New York: Routledge Press, 2013.
    This second compilation edited by Stryker and Aizura brings more diverse trans theoretical essays to the scholar interested in trans studies. In response to the first reader being too Western and Eurocentric in focus, this second

reader looks at gender variance in Japan, Latin America, and the Philippines. Both readers contain an outstanding array of essays in the field of study.

Styles, Rhyannon. *The New Girl: A Trans Girl Tells It Like It Is.* Great Britain: Headline, 2017.
Styles has written a fast-paced memoir of her life. From being assigned male at birth and struggling with her gender identity throughout childhood to beginning her transition at the age of thirty, this book takes readers on her journey.

Woolf, Virginia. *Orlando: A Biography.* London: Hogarth, 1928. New edition. London: Hogarth, 1933.
What happens when someone lives for 300 years as a man, falls asleep for ten days, and then wakes up as a woman who continues on with her life for another 300 years? This is modernist British author Virginia Woolf's fantastical story about gender fluidity and the course of British history over a 600-year period.

Journals

Currah, Paisley, and Susan Stryker, eds. *TSQ: Transgender Studies Quarterly.* Durham: Duke University Press, ongoing.
TSQ is an outstanding academic journal that is published four times a year. Each special edition focuses on a topic like trans archives, trans feminism, and trans pedagogy. The essays range from those by well-known scholars in the field to those by up-and-coming scholars.

Graham, Cynthia, ed. *The Journal of Sex Research.* Society for the Scientific Study of Sexuality. Ongoing.
A high-quality scholarly scientific interdisciplinary sex research journal that frequently has articles about trans, non-binary, and Two-Spirit people.

Haefele-Thomas, Ardel, ed. *Victorian Review: An Interdisciplinary Journal of Victorian Studies.* Special edition: Trans Victorians. Baltimore: Johns Hopkins University Press, forthcoming 2019.

In this special edition of *Victorian Review*, the essays range from an investigation of a nineteenth-century cross-dressing trial in London that is now being explored in terms of trans identity, trans literature, and trans interpretations of the Welsh Rebecca Riots. Trans is explored within a historic context, and these academic essays break new ground in exploring a trans past.

International Journal of Transgenderism. Various special editors. New York: Haworth Medical Press, ongoing.

With a focus on various medical, social, and cultural issues surrounding trans people and their access to health care, this academic journal provides numerous issues with focused themes like HIV and AIDS in the trans community, poverty and health care in the trans community, substance abuse and recovery in the trans community, and methods of outreach for care providers to the trans community.

Pfeffer, Carla A. Guest ed. *Journal of Homosexuality* 61, no. 5 (2014). Special edition: Trans sexualities.

The eleven authors from Canada, the Netherlands, the United Kingdom, and the United States write about trans sexuality from the perspectives of anthropology, communications, English, film studies, gender studies, linguistics, philosophy, photography, psychology, public health, and sociology.

Zucker, Kenneth, ed. *Archives of Sexual Behavior.* International Academy of Sex Research. Ongoing.

A high-quality scholarly scientific interdisciplinary sex research journal that frequently has articles about trans, non-binary, and Two-Spirit people.

Art, Film, Media, and Television

Abma, Daniel. *Transit Havana*. Kloos & Co. Medien GmbH, 2016.

Alex Bakker, trans author from the Netherlands, wrote the screenplay to create this outstanding documentary that looks at the complexities of the Cuban government's attempts to welcome Western doctors who will perform gender affirmation surgeries for trans women waiting for the procedures. The relationships between socialism, trans rights, poverty, and sex work are all explored in depth.

Alencastre, Dante. *Raising Zoey*. Alencastre Productions, 2016.

Zoey Luna is a trans youth who is able to transition smoothly with the support of a loving family. This documentary film is an excellent example of the positive impact family support and love can have for trans kids.

Anbe, Brent, and Kathryn Xian. *Ke Kulana He Mahu: Remembering a Sense of Place*. Zang Productions, 2001.

This award-winning and groundbreaking documentary film took the festival circuit by storm in 2001 because it was the first film to explore the devastation of Western imperialism in Hawai'i in terms of the ways that *mahu* (third-gender) people were silenced. Anbe and Xian's film includes interviews with local people who are *mahu* alongside historic accounts of the history of Hawai'i.

Arnold, Chris. *Trans*. Rose Works/Sex Smart Films, 2012.

At times, this documentary film can be sensationalist; however, it is an important film in that it shows one family that is completely supportive of their trans child who is under the age of ten. Another important focus in this film is on Dr. Christine McGinn, a trans surgeon who, along with her wife, runs the Papillon Gender Wellness Clinic in Pennsylvania.

Bartlett, Neil. *Stella*. London: Oberon Books, 2016.
Bartlett's twenty-first-century play explores the life of a nineteenth-century figure, Ernest Boulton, better known as Stella, who was arrested numerous times in London on masquerading charges. Until recently, Boulton has been regarded as a gay man who went out in public in drag; however, given archival evidence and a more in-depth historic look, there is an excellent argument to be made that Boulton was Stella, a trans woman. This play beautifully explores the intersections of gender identity and sexual orientation and the ways that past laws and culture would conflate the two.

Beauchamin, Michael, Lory Levy, and Gretchen Vogel. *Two-Spirit People*. Frameline Release, 1992.
This groundbreaking short documentary was the first of its kind to look at the lives and experiences of Two-Spirit people. Several Two-Spirit people are interviewed in the film.

Ben-Moshe, Billy. *Melting Away*. Doron Eran. 2011.
This is a sensitive and well-acted film about parents who reject their teenaged son when they discover that he performs drag, and later lives as a woman. When the father is dying of cancer, the mother reconnects with their child, now a woman. The daughter dresses as a nurse and cares for her father, who doesn't recognize her at first. In the end, the family heals before the father dies.

Berliner, Alain. *Ma Vie En Rose*. Centre Nationale de la Cinématographie, 1997.
This Belgian classic—"My Life in Pink" in English—may be old now, but it is still a beautifully done film that looks at a trans child whose family does not understand that

they have a little trans daughter rather than a little cisgender son. The cruelty of neighbors, bullies at school, and
even within the nuclear family, is heartbreaking.

Bohigian, Amy. *Rural Transcapes*. Watershed, 2014.
Christopher Moore, the founder of the TransConnect
Program, asked the director to make an educational film
about trans health and medical care in his rural area of the
Kootenays in British Columbia, Canada. This is a thirty-
minute film focusing on trans people in the area as well as
two doctors who work with the community to make safe
spaces in health care.

Davis, Kate. *Southern Comfort*. Docurama, 2000.
When trans man Robert Eads found out he had less than
a year to live because he was dying from ovarian cancer,
he invited filmmaker Kate Davis into his life and his
extended trans community in rural Georgia. The outcome is one of the fullest, simplest, and most beautifully
humane documentaries about trans people.

DeGuerre, Marc. *Transforming Gender*. Gender Project in
association with the Canadian Broadcasting Corporation, 2015.
https://www.cbc.ca/doczone/episodes/transforming-gender
This documentary is an excellent introduction to what life
is like for eleven trans and non-binary people living in
Canada and the United States. The people interviewed
range from young children to an elder in their nineties.

Dugan, Jess T., and Vanessa Fabbre. *To Survive on This Shore:
Photographs and Interviews with Transgender and Gender Non-
Conforming Older Adults*. https://www.tosurviveonthisshore.com/
Jess T. Dugan and partner Vanessa Fabbre have collabo-
rated to create this stunning photo exhibit that includes
interviews with trans elders who are often forgotten
in mainstream society and in trans communities. These
images and stories resonate with beauty and strength.

Ernst, Rhys. *Lou Sullivan*. Part of Ernst's *We've Been Around*. Webseries by Focus Features, 2016. http://rhysernst.com /portfolio/weve-been-around/ Accessed on March 29, 2018.

The docuseries focuses on trans people in the past whose stories have almost been forgotten. Lou Sullivan was a gay trans man and the founder of FTM International. He was a pioneer who forged the way for gay, lesbian, and bisexual trans people to be out as queer and trans. Sullivan died from AIDS in 1991.

Ernst, Rhys. *S.T.A.R.* Part of Rhys Ernst's *We've Been Around*. Webseries by Focus Features, 2016. http://rhysernst.com/port folio/weve-been-around/ Accessed on March 29, 2018.

Street Transvestite Action Revolutionaries was founded by Stonewall Inn rebellion veterans Marsha P. Johnson and Sylvia Rivera when the LGBTQ+ movement they helped start decided that it was more interested in the rights of cisgender gay men and cisgender lesbians.

Ernst, Rhys. *Wilmer and Willie Broadnax: "Little Axe" & "Big Axe."* Part of Ernst's *We've Been Around*. Webseries by Focus Features, 2016. http://rhysernst.com/portfolio/weve-been-around/ Accessed on December 12, 2017.

Wilmer "Little Axe" Broadnax looks at the relationship between trans gospel singer Wilmer Broadnax and his brother, Willie, who always protected him in the various bands they played in.

Feder, Sam. *Kate Bornstein Is a Queer & Pleasant Danger*. A Sam Feder Film, 2014.

Kate Bornstein is a trans pioneer, artist, and activist. Feder's documentary film explores her decades of work as a true gender outlaw who always resists categorical boxes.

France, David. *The Death and Life of Marsha P. Johnson*. Public Square Films, 2017.

This incredibly slick and controversial documentary focuses on the probable murder of Marsha P. Johnson. The film is controversial because the filmmaker, who had a large budget, did not acknowledge help from members of the trans community—including use of some archival footage. That being said, the film does an excellent job of exploring the fact that this pioneer was murdered and that the NYPD did not seem to care.

Freeman, Mark, and Nathaniel Walters. *Transgender Tuesdays*. Healing Tales Productions, 2012.
The Tom Waddell Clinic in San Francisco's Tenderloin neighborhood is a free clinic. On Tuesday nights, it becomes solely a trans clinic. This film chronicles the first primary care trans clinic in the United States. The film is an outstanding educational piece that includes interviews with over twelve patients, doctors, and nurses who started the program.

Goldson, Annie, and Peter Wells. *Georgie Girl*. Women Make Movies, 2001.
Goldson's award-winning documentary focuses on the life of Georgina Beyer, the first out trans person in the world to serve as a member of parliament. Beyer is Maori and from New Zealand, and this film follows her career as she moves from being elected governor of a conservative rural and white province in New Zealand to her success in parliament.

Grahn, Neil. *Queen of the Oil Patch*. Great Pacific Media, 2018.
This reality TV series broadcast on the Aboriginal Peoples' Television Network follows Mikisew Cree First Nation and Fort McKay resident Massey Whiteknife, a successful CEO and philanthropist with an occupational health and safety firm in northern Alberta, as Massey increasingly moves into living as a woman named Iceis Rain.

Guzmán, Mary. *Mind If I Call You Sir?: A Discussion Between Latina Butches and Female-to-Male Transgendered Latinos.* StickyGirl Productions, 2004.

Although this film is now a bit dated, it still remains one of the few films focusing on Latinx trans people. The conversation between two different sets of "gender outlaws"— butch lesbians and trans men—is unique and interesting.

Hart, Phoebe. *Orchids: My Intersex Adventure.* A Women Make Movies Release, 2010.

In this Australian documentary, the filmmaker, who has differences of sex development (DSD), travels across Australia to interview other people who also have DSD. She focuses on the myths that there are only two options when it comes to biological sex.

Heidenreich, Erin. *Girl Unbound: The War to Be Her.* Blackacre Entertainment, 2016.

Maria Toorpakai lives in Waziristan, one of the most conservative places controlled by the Taliban. But Maria is an athlete, and in order to play sports, disguises herself as a boy. This documentary follows Maria's success and the ways that presenting publicly as a young man becomes very complex.

Hooper, Tom. *The Danish Girl.* Focus Features, 2015.

This 2015 feature-length biopic focuses on Lili Elbe, possibly the first person to undergo gender affirmation surgery with Western medical practices in the early twentieth century. Of particular note, when the actual surgery took place, Magnus Hirschfeld, the famous sexologist, was present to advise.

Hyde, Sophie. *52 Tuesdays.* Closer Productions, 2014.

In this Australian drama, a sixteen-year-old girl learns that her mother is going to transition to male. They are only able to see one another one day a week—on Tuesdays. To make the film more realistic, it was only filmed on Tuesdays over the course of one year.

Kasino, Michael. *Pay It No Mind: Marsha P. Johnson*. Redux Pictures, 2012.

Along with her soulmate, Sylvia Rivera, Marsha P. Johnson was one of the founders of Street Transvestite Action Revolutionaries. She was an African American trans woman who was well known throughout the LGBTQ+ community in New York, and an elder treasured by her community. Her death, which community members knew was suspicious, was written off by the New York City Police Department as a suicide. This documentary uses outstanding archival footage to look at her life and her work.

Kohan, Jenji. *Orange Is the New Black*. Netflix, 2013–.

Netflix's iconic prison drama features trans actor and activist Laverne Cox in a groundbreaking role for an African American trans woman.

Lahood, Grant. *Intersexion*. Ponsonby Productions, 2012.

This multiple-award-winning documentary from New Zealand considers numerous people who have differences of sex development (DSD). Their personal stories underscore the ordinariness of biological sex that is nonbinary. The people interviewed are from all walks of life.

Lebow, Alisa. *Outlaw*. A Women Make Movies Release, 1994.

This is an outstanding short documentary featuring Leslie Feinberg, the trans icon who wrote *Transgender Warriors* and *Stone Butch Blues*. This is Feinberg's video manifesto in which ze asks people to reconsider their stereotypes about "natural" gender.

Livingston, Jennie. *Paris Is Burning*. Art Matters, 1990.

The focus of this groundbreaking documentary film is the New York City drag ball scene. It follows the lives of African American and Puerto Rican drag queens and trans people living at or below the poverty level who compete in underground drag balls. This iconic film, though, is much more about gender, race, and class in America.

Loven, Hillevi. *Deep Run*. A Women Make Movies Release, 2015. This documentary focuses on Cole, a young trans man who lives in an evangelical Christian community in rural North Carolina. Cole and his girlfriend, Ashley, who also identifies as queer, both have to navigate being kicked out of the church and family, and bullied in the community. An excellent look at the difficulties trans people face in religiously conservative rural settings.

Ophelian, Annalise. *Major!* Floating Ophelia Productions, 2015. Miss Major Griffin-Gracy is an elder African American trans activist who founded TGI Justice, a nonprofit organization that works with trans and people with differences of sex development (DSD) who are incarcerated. From being a Stonewall veteran to working for social justice her entire life, this multi-award-winning documentary pays tribute to Miss Major's continuing legacy.

A Place in the Middle: A Strength-Based Approach to Gender Diversity and Inclusion. PBS 2015. This short film follows Kumu Hina, a trans Hawaiian cultural icon and teacher, as she works with middle and high school students, some of whom are *mahū*, an Indigenous Hawaiian and Pacific Island trans identity.

Reed, J. Mitchel, and Lucah Rosenberg-Lee. *Passing: Profiling the Lives of Young Transmen of Color*. Frameline, 2015. With this outstanding exploration of the intersecting identities of race and masculinity, this film focuses on trans men of color who completely live as cisgender. What does it mean to be trans and to present your gender so that people do not see the trans part of your identity?

Shattuck, Sharon. *From This Day Forward.* PBS, 2015.
Most films that focus on trans people in families concentrate on trans youth coming out to parents or guardians and hoping to gain their acceptance. In this film, documentary filmmaker Sharon Shattuck focuses on her own family as one of her parents comes out as transgender.

Shavelson, Lonny. *Three to Infinity: Beyond Two Genders.* Photowords Films, 2015.
This documentary film considers people who do not identify within the gender binary. The diverse group of people interviewed identify as agender, genderqueer, non-binary trans, or other terms that convey their sense of rejecting a rigid gender binary.

Silverman, Gabriel, and Fiona Dawson. *TransMilitary.* SideXSide Studios, 2018.
Trans people comprise around 15,000 members of the U.S. military; however, as this film chronicles, their position in the military is unstable. Through interviews with entry-level and high-ranking military people who are trans, this outstanding documentary looks at the ways that President Obama's lifting the military ban made major changes, and yet President Trump's pronouncements about reinstatement of the ban has made life more difficult.

Storyhive. *Safety in Numbers.* 2018. https://www.youtube.com/watch?v=dQwS7LqfJys
This documentary eloquently traces some of the history of what it was like for trans people in the early parts of the twentieth century and how we got from there to where we are today. The stories are brought to life through interviews with elders who lived it then and young trans people who are experiencing being trans and non-binary today.

Stryker, Susan. *Screaming Queens: The Riot at Compton's Cafeteria.* Frameline, 2005.

Trans historian Susan Stryker's film takes a look at a trans riot in the Tenderloin neighborhood in San Francisco in 1966. The film is important not only as a history of the local trans community in San Francisco in the 1960s, but also in making the argument that trans people—and trans women of color in particular—were fighting for their rights and resisting police harassment *before* the 1969 Stonewall Riots.

Surat-Shaan Knan. *Twilight People: Stories of Faith and Gender Beyond the Binary.* https://www.twilightpeople.com/the-project/

This series of photographs and interviews offers a look into the lives of trans people of faith within the Abrahamic religions. The show first opened in London, England, in 2016 to huge acclaim and is currently on tour; however, many of the images and interviews are available on the website.

The Wachowskis and J. Michael Straczynski, *Sense8.* Netflix Original Series, 2015–2018.

The Wachowski siblings, who are both trans women, and cisgender man Michael Straczynski have created one of the most unique and trans-positive shows ever made. The series follows eight people (sensates) who can all occupy one another's bodies. One of the eight is Nomi, a trans woman who is also a lesbian, played by trans actress Jamie Clayton.

Zolten, Sam. *Just Call Me Kade.* Frameline, 2002.

Zolten's short documentary follows a fourteen-year-old trans boy through his transition. This is an incredibly positive film that depicts Kade's supportive family in Tucson, Arizona.

Websites

The Bilerico Project: http://bilerico.lgbtqnation.com/2008/02/transgender_history_trans_expression_in.php
Historic website that focuses on trans history from ancient times to the present.

Digital Transgender Archive, Trans History, Linked: https://www.digitaltransgenderarchive.net/
This archive is all and only digital. It provides links to digitized items in hard-copy archival collections around the world.

Gay History and Literature: Essays by Rictor Norton: http://rictornorton.co.uk/
Although this online set of historic essays sounds as if it is focused only on gay history and literature, Rictor Norton has several entries that are trans focused. This website is well worth a look, particularly for those doing historical research that is pre-twentieth century.

A Gender Variance Who's Who: https://zagria.blogspot.com/
An excellent resource for historical and contemporary figures in trans life.

The Transgender Oral History Project at the University of Minnesota's Jean-Nickolaus Tretter Collection: https://www.lib.umn.edu/tretter/transgender-oral-history-project
Transgender oral histories are recorded and accessible to students here. Includes filmed interviews as well as transcripts in pdf format. An outstanding source for any contemporary history, biography, or autobiography research project.

Organizations and Outreach

The Chair in Transgender Studies: https://uvic.ca/transchair/
The world's only chair in Transgender Studies is a research leadership and community outreach office dedicated to

building and sharing scholarship by and about trans, non-binary, and Two-Spirit people; educating the public; and sponsoring community-building events. It is located at the University of Victoria in Victoria, British Columbia, Canada.

El/La Para Trans Latinas: http://ellaparatranslatinas.yolasite.com/about-us.php
Works to promote survival and quality of life for trans Latinas in the San Francisco Bay Area.

GATE: https://transactivists.org/
International trans and bodily diversity outreach organization.

Moving Trans History Forward conferences: https:/uvic.ca/mthf/
A series of biennial international conferences sponsored by the Chair in Transgender Studies that draw together trans, non-binary, and Two-Spirit community activists, researchers, educators, artists, service providers, and allies. Conferences consider both the history of trans activism and research, and the crucial issues that impact trans, non-binary, and Two-Spirit people today and in the future.

National Center for Transgender Equality: https://transequality.org/
Works throughout the United States on various issues of equality facing trans people.

The Sylvia Rivera Law Project: https://srlp.org/
Accessible legal and advocacy help for all trans people, based in New York City.

TGI Justice Project: http://www.tgijp.org/
TGI Justice works on changing the prison-industrial complex and the transphobic ways this system works with trans people.

The Transgender Archives: https://uvic.ca/transgenderarchives/
This is the world's largest trans archive. Free and open to
the public at the University of Victoria, British Columbia,
Canada. It contains records from twenty-three countries
on all continents except Antarctica, in fifteen languages,
that go back well over a century.

Transgender Europe (TGEU): https://tgeu.org/
Working for the equality of all trans people in Europe.

Transgender Law Center: https://transgenderlawcenter.org/
An advocacy and referral group for trans people, located
in Oakland, California.

Introduction

This chronology gives a timeline of numerous people, places, and important events relating to trans, non-binary, Two-Spirit, and gender-diverse people in history, art, culture, and society. It provides a simplified history of the rich complexities of gender among people, events, and cultures dating back to the ancient world.

1478–1458 BCE   Pharaoh Hatshepsut becomes the fifth pharaoh of the Eighteenth Dynasty of Egypt and rules for twenty years of prosperity; assigned female at birth, Pharaoh Hatshepsut refused to be called "Queen" and ruled as a man, including wearing traditional king's clothing and the ceremonial fake beard that all pharaohs wore.

190 CE   Rabbi Yehudah HaNasi completes the compilation of the Jewish books of the Mishnah, which describe six sexes.

204 CE   The Roman emperor Elagabalus is born; Elagabalus will rule for a short time between 218 and 222 and is often

A Pakistani student exits the first transgender school in Lahore on April 21, 2018, after the first day of class. The school, The Gender Guardian, was inaugurated on April 16 by the NGO Exploring Future Foundation (EFF). This is the EFF's first project. (ARIF ALI/AFP/Getty Images)

remembered as a terrible ruler in part because Elagabalus, who was assigned male at birth, clearly wanted to be a woman.

400 CE Four *māhū*, who are third-gender people, sailed from Tahiti to Hawai'i; they were healers and set up a long-standing tradition in the Hawai'ian Islands regarding the spiritual and sacred identity of the *māhū*.

1412 Jeanne d'Arc is born on the feast of Epiphany (in older Christian traditions this is on January 6) in Domrémy, a hamlet on the border of France, to parents who are humble farmers who work on common village pastures.

1431 Jeanne d'Arc's trials begin in Rouen, where at first she is accused of witchcraft, but is eventually put to death, in part for refusing to wear women's clothing. She is burned at the stake on May 30.

1455 Pope Calixtus orders that the trial of Jeanne d'Arc (Joan of Arc) be reconsidered by a court of lawyers and clergy; they find that d'Arc's condemnation and execution twenty-four years earlier was unjust.

1626 Pope Urban VIII gives Catalina/Don Antonio de Erauso an unusual choice: decide to live as a woman and a nun or as a man and an adventurer. De Erauso chooses to return to living as a man, as she had been doing for years.

1777 The Chevalier/Chevalière d'Éon is told by the French king, Louis XVI, to permanently wear women's clothing; d'Éon complies since they had already been read as a woman for decades. However, d'Éon's one bit of rebellion was that in their women's frocks, they always wore the Medal of Honor given to them after their work as a captain in the Dragoons— the medal itself would have gendered d'Éon as a man.

1778 Captain James Cook of the Royal British Navy first steps onto the shores of Hawai'i, where he and his crew misunderstand the third-gender people who are *māhū* as sinful and homosexual; this is the beginning of European religion, laws, and culture being used in carrying out a violent colonization of the Hawaiian Islands.

1809   A boy who was assigned female at birth, James Miranda Barry, enrolls at the University of Edinburgh's Medical School where he becomes one of the youngest medical students accepted to the institution, as well as one of the youngest students to receive special permission to take courses in gynecology, which was seen as inappropriate for younger male students. In his post in South Africa, Barry would use this knowledge to carry out one of the first successful caesarian sections in which both infant and birth parent survived.

1810   The Chevalier/Chevalière d'Éon dies in poverty in London, England; prior to burial, doctors strip d'Éon's body and announce that d'Éon is a man, although d'Éon had lived as both a man and a woman.

1828–1829   The French Egyptologist, Jean-François Champollion, goes to the temple at Deir el-Bahri where he discovers hieroglyphics that used female gender endings to describe a king; his discovery leads to the resurrection of the history of Pharaoh Hatshepsut.

1840   Richard von Krafft-Ebing, commonly known as the "grandfather of sexology," is born in Austria; his foundational research in sexology describes many cases of gender variance but fails to make a distinction between sexual orientation, gender identity, and gender expression.

1865   Dr. James Miranda Barry dies of dehydration and complications from dysentery in London during a heat wave on July 25; the charwoman, Sophia Bishop, does not heed his request not to be stripped and washed in preparation for burial. Five days later, after Dr. Barry is buried in Kensal Green Cemetery, Sophia Bishop appears at the Horse Guards to let the army know that one of their most highly decorated surgeons was most surely assigned female at birth.

1866   Frances Thompson, a trans woman and freed slave, along with other African American women who were brutalized during the Memphis Massacre (when white police and white Confederate Army officers raped, murdered, and brutalized the South Memphis African American community for over a week), speaks to a congressional committee comprised of white men from Washington D.C.; it is the first time in U.S. history that a group of African American women are legally permitted to testify.

1868   On May 14, the sexologist Magnus Hirschfeld is born in Kolberg, Prussia (Kolobrzeg, Poland).

1876   Frances Thompson is arrested on masquerading charges in Memphis, Tennessee, and then is put on display at the men's prison where she becomes ill; she dies in November after her prison experience.

1885   Harry Benjamin, who in 1966 will publish the groundbreaking book *The Transsexual Phenomenon*, is born on January 12 in Berlin, Germany.

1886   We'wha, a Zuni Two-Spirit person, is received by President Grover Cleveland in Washington, D.C. as a "Zuni Princess."

1886   The English translation of Richard von Krafft-Ebing's *Psychopathia Sexualis* is published so that English-speaking people who have not been schooled in the typical medical and scientific language of German have access to all of his case studies on gender diversity and the broad spectrum of sexual orientation.

1912   Virginia Prince, an early trans woman activist in the twentieth century, is born into a middle-class white family in Los Angeles; she will become one of the most influential American trans people of the twentieth century.

1915   Michael Dillon is born on May 1 and will become the first known trans man to undergo gender affirmation procedures, starting with hormone treatments in 1939. He fell in love with trans woman Roberta Cowell, who did not return his affection.

1917   Reed Erickson is born. He will go on to found the highly influential Erickson Educational Foundation in 1964, which supported gay and trans equality.

1919   Magnus Hirschfeld establishes the Institut für Sexual-wissenschaft (often translated into English as Institute for Sex Research or Institute for Sexology) in Berlin, the first institution of its kind in the world.

1928   The English sexologist Havelock Ellis publishes *Eonism and Other Supplementary Studies* in which he uses the example of the late Chevalier/Chevalière d'Éon's life and experience as a historic trans person to coin the phrase "Eonism" for people who live in a gender different from their sex assigned at birth.

1930   Lili Elbe, who was assigned male at birth, undergoes the first known gender affirmation surgery in Berlin; Magnus Hirschfeld is present during the procedure to help advise the surgeon on the proper construction of a vagina and labia.

1931   Lili Elbe dies from infections and complications from her various gender affirmation procedures.

1933   On May 10, the Nazis burn the library of Magnus Hirschfeld's Institut für Sexualwissenschaft.

1935   On May 14, his sixty-seventh birthday, Magnus Hirschfeld dies in exile in Nice, France, where he is cremated and his ashes interred at the Caucade Cemetery.

1944   Michael Dillon, assigned female at birth, is officially registered as male in the United Kingdom.

1949   Sir Harold Gillies completes a phalloplasty on Michael Dillon, the first known on a trans man.

1951   Roberta Cowell, assigned male at birth, has her ID officially changed to female in the United Kingdom.

1951   On September 24, Christine Jorgensen begins her gender affirmation procedures at Gentofte Hospital in Copenhagen, Denmark, where doctors perform an orchiectomy in which her testicles were removed.

1952   On December 1, Christine Jorgensen's "sex change" becomes front-page news around the world.

1959   In May, police raid Cooper's Do-Nuts on Skid Row in Los Angeles because several of the customers are cross-dressed; however, the arrestees fight back in one of the first instances of trans resistance to police in the United States.

1960   Virginia Prince, an American trans woman and activist, founds one of the most important trans magazines: *Transvestia*.

1964   Reed Erickson, a trans man and philanthropist, creates the Erickson Educational Foundation; he donates millions of dollars to help promote gay and trans equality.

1966   In August, a trans riot breaks out at Gene Compton's Cafeteria located in the Tenderloin district of San Francisco when police raid the twenty-four-hour diner and begin strip-searching people who they think are violating the anti-masquerading laws.

1966   Dr. Harry Benjamin publishes a book that will forever change the face of gender affirmation procedures and access to them: *The Transsexual Phenomenon*.

1969   On Sunday, June 28, 1969, New York City police raid the Stonewall Inn, a bar in Greenwich Village that caters to LGBTQ2+ people. The clients, many of whom were trans people of color, including Miss Major Griffin-Gracy and Sylvia Rivera, fight back. The Stonewall Riots or the Stonewall Rebellion becomes a major historic moment for the beginnings of modern-day LGBTQ2+ liberation throughout the world.

1969   Dr. Stanley Biber, a surgeon in Trinidad, Colorado, performs his first gender affirmation surgery on a trans woman who has come to him and asked him to do so. Although he was not quite sure about performing the procedure, he studied diagrams from Johns Hopkins University Hospital and their gender affirmation clinic and was able to successfully operate on the woman.

1969   The First International Symposium on Gender Identity, jointly sponsored by the Erickson Educational Foundation and the Albany Trust, London, takes place July 25–27 at the Piccadilly Hotel, London, United Kingdom.

1972   With the help of the larger LGBTQ2+ community, Sylvia Rivera and Marsha P. Johnson are able to open STAR House for homeless and at-risk LGBTQ2+ youth in New York City.

1972   Sweden becomes the first country in the world to allow people to change their gender on their official government identification documents.

1977   The New York Supreme Court rules in favor of trans tennis player Renée Richards, who has sued the U.S. Tennis Association for the right to play the sport as a woman. She goes on to play in the U.S. Open in 1977 in the women's doubles, making it to the finals.

1979   In the United States, the Harry Benjamin International Gender Dysphoria Association (HBIGDA) is formed, named in honor of the work of sexologist Harry Benjamin. In 2007 it becomes known as the World Professional Association for Transgender Health (WPATH).

1979   The Harry Benjamin International Gender Dysphoria Association publishes the first version of the *Standards of Care*.

1980   Leslie Feinberg writes and publishes hir first work, *Journal of a Transsexual*, with World View Publisher in New York City.

1980   Dr. Preecha Tiewtranon begins offering gender affirmation procedures in Bangkok, Thailand.

1986   Dr. Harry Benjamin dies on August 24 in New York City at the age of 101. He has been a major voice and advocate for affirmative treatment for transsexual people.

1986   Lou Sullivan founds FTM International, which is an international outreach and advocacy organization focused on trans men.

1989   An American jazz musician from Oklahoma, Billy Tipton, falls ill at home; emergency medical technicians discover he has been assigned female at birth. From all accounts, the EMTs were very caring with Tipton and his family, although Tipton died.

1990 The term Two-Spirit is adopted in Winnipeg, Manitoba, at the Third Annual Inter-tribal Native American, First Nations, Gay and Lesbian American Conference. It is used as an umbrella term that includes lesbian, gay, bisexual, trans, non-binary, intersex, queer, and questioning people.

1992 Early in the morning of July 6, Marsha P. Johnson's body is found floating in the Hudson River; the New York Police Department rules it a suicide, but the LGBTQ2+ community argues that she has been the victim of a hate crime.

1993 The Tom Waddell Health Center in San Francisco, California, begins its "Transgender Tuesdays" health care outreach program to meet the basic health care needs of the trans community. People who identify anywhere on the trans spectrum are welcome, and no one is turned away for lack of money.

1993 In the U.S. state of Nebraska, Brandon Teena, a young trans man, is brutally raped and murdered by his peers when they find out he is trans. His story is told in a Hollywood film, *Boys Don't Cry*, which won an Oscar.

1993 Leslie Feinberg's book *Stone Butch Blues* is published.

1996 Leslie Feinberg publishes hir groundbreaking book on trans history: *Transgender Warriors: Making History from Joan of Arc to Dennis Rodman.*

1999 Robert Eads, a trans man from Toccoa, Georgia, dies in January from ovarian cancer that numerous doctors refused to treat. He is remembered as a robust member of the Southern Comfort transgender convention.

1999 Monica Helms, a trans woman and naval veteran, creates the internationally known and iconic pink, white, and blue transgender flag. It is first displayed at a Pride parade in Phoenix, Arizona, in 2000.

1999 Georgina Beyer, a Maori trans woman, becomes the first out trans person in the world elected to Parliament in New Zealand.

1999 Rita Hester, an African American trans woman, is murdered in Massachusetts by an offender fueled by rage against trans people. This tragic event marks the beginning of the "Remembering Our Dead" Web project as well as the First International Transgender Day of Remembrance, November 20, which is a day to honor and remember all of the trans lives lost through violence.

2000   California State Assembly Bill AB 537 passes, which changes the California Education Code to include a prohibition against discrimination and harassment of students based on sexual orientation and gender identity.

2000   Dr. Marci Bowers joins Dr. Stanley Biber's surgical team in Trinidad, Colorado. to train to become a gender affirmation surgeon.

2001   Gender Odyssey and Philadelphia Trans Health conferences start.

2002   Trans lawyer and activist Dean Spade founds the Sylvia Rivera Law Project based in New York City; the nonprofit organization focuses on the rights of all people regardless of age, gender identity, gender expression, race, ethnicity, ability, or socioeconomic status.

2002   The Transgender Law Center is founded in San Francisco as a nonprofit organization that works to change law, policy, and attitudes about gender identity and gender expression so that all people can live free from discrimination.

2002   On February 19, Sylvia Rivera dies of complications from liver cancer in a New York City hospital. In her own words, she was finally able to "cross the River Jordan" to be with her soulmate, Marsha P. Johnson, who had been murdered a decade before.

2002   Dr. Aaron Devor becomes the first out trans person to become an academic dean at a world-class research university.

2003   The National Center for Transgender Equality is established.

2004   Viktor Mukasa, a Ugandan trans man, founds Sexual Minorities Uganda (SMUG) in the face of the violent and legal oppression of LGBTQ+ people in Uganda.

2004   The Gender Recognition Act 2004 is passed by Parliament in the United Kingdom. It allows people to legally change their gender. It came into effect on April 4, 2005.

2005   Liesl Theron and Lex Kirsten found Gender DynamiX in South Africa, which becomes one of the major advocacy groups in the case of Caster Semenya's forced medical exams to prove that she is "enough" of a woman to compete in the Track and Field World Championships.

2005   Susan Stryker and Victor Silverman release their award-winning film *Screaming Queens: The Riot at Compton's*, a documentary that recovers the nearly lost history of a trans riot in 1966 in San Francisco.

2006   Voters in the state of Hawai'i elect Kim Coco Iwamoto to the state Board of Education, which makes her the highest elected trans official in the United States.

2007   The Supreme Court of Nepal issues a decision on third-gender identity that is, globally, the most comprehensive law enabling people to legally identify outside of the gender binary. Nepal was not the first country to legalize a third-gender identity, but this decision sets a legal precedent for the rest of the world.

2007   The Harry Benjamin International Gender Dysphoria Association changes its name to the World Professional Association for Transgender Health.

2009   Chaz Bono, the child of celebrities Sonny Bono and Cher, comes out publicly as a trans man.

2010   Michelle Suárez Bértora becomes the first known trans person to complete a university degree in Uruguay. Four years later, in 2014, she becomes the first trans person elected to the Uruguayan legislature.

2010   Marilyn Roxie creates the genderqueer flag that is now used as an international symbol.

2010   Transgender Intersex Africa (TIA) is formed to work on outreach to trans, non-binary, and intersex people in some of the most disadvantaged communities, including rural areas and areas with predominantly Black populations with socioeconomic barriers still left over from the British apartheid regime.

2010   Lana Lawless, a trans woman, sues the LPGA over their requirement that women golfers needed to be assigned female at birth. She won and they removed the requirement.

2011   The Catherine White Holman Wellness Centre, which offers respectful primary care services for trans, non-binary, and Two-Spirit people, opens in Vancouver, British Columbia, Canada.

2011   CeCe McDonald, a trans woman, is sentenced to forty-one months in prison in Minnesota after she stabbed a man who brutally attacked her. The LGBTQ2+ community rallies around the injustice of her arrest.

2011   Kye Allums becomes the first openly out trans man to play any Division 1 NCAA sport in the United States. He plays basketball for George Washington University in Washington, D.C.

2011   Janet Mock, an African American author and editor of People.com, comes out as she shares her teenage transitions story. Her writings have been inspiring for many young trans people.

2011   The Transgender Archives are launched at the University of Victoria. They are the world's largest collection of trans history in the world.

2012   Rock musician Laura Jane Grace comes out as transgender in a *Rolling Stone* article; two years later, her band, Against Me!, releases their album *Transgender Dysphoria Blues*.

2012   On May 24, 2012, Argentina's president, Cristina Fernandez de Kirchner, signs the Gender Identity Bill into law, making Argentina the first nation in the world where people can change their gender identity without a judge's or doctor's signature. It also obligates their health care plans to cover gender affirmation and obligates clinics to prescribe hormones and provide gender affirmation procedures on demand.

2013   Dancer and choreographer Jin Xing becomes the first transsexual celebrity in the People's Republic of China when she serves as a judge on China's *So You Think You Can Dance?* television show.

2014   Li Yinhe, a famous scientist, sexologist, and LGBT rights advocate in the People's Republic of China, publicly announces that her partner of fifteen years, Zhang Hongxia, is a trans man. In China, Li Yinhe is seen as a radical feminist and sexuality rights advocate. Her announcement bolsters a still predominantly underground LGBTQ+ rights movement.

2014   The art of Zackary Drucker and Rhys Ernst is displayed as part of the Whitney Biennial. Their lives together as a couple who are both in transition toward gender affirmation are on public display in a major venue.

2014   The first Moving Trans History Forward conference takes place at the University of Victoria, Canada.

2015   The magazine *Vanity Fair* releases a special issue with Caitlyn Jenner on the cover and an exclusive interview with the former Olympian and celebrity. Annie Leibovitz's photographs of Jenner accompany the article.

2015   On July 25, Ireland passes the Gender Recognition Act.

2015   A portrait of Sylvia Rivera is added to the National Portrait Gallery in Washington, D.C., becoming the first portrait displayed there of a trans person.

2015   In November, Tangerine Community Health Center, Southeast Asia's first transgender-focused general health care clinic, opens in Bangkok, Thailand.

2016   In January, the Chair in Transgender Studies is established at the University of Victoria in British Columbia. Founded by Dr. Aaron Devor, who serves as the inaugural chair, it is the only such chair in the world.

2016   The National Center for Transgender Equality releases the statistics for the 2015 national survey of trans people, the largest ever to be conducted in the United States. Topics include school environment, employment, and health care.

2016   Kael McKenzie is sworn in as the first transgender judge in Canada. He is Métis and honors both Western and Two-Spirit traditions in his speech.

2016   Canada adopts nationwide legal protections against discrimination on the basis of gender identity and gender expression.

2017   A newborn, Searyl Atli Doty, in British Columbia, Canada, becomes the first known baby in the world to be issued a "U" gender-neutral sex marker on a health card. The baby's parent, Kori Doty, who is non-binary trans, fought a legal battle to make sure that a binary gender marker was not placed on the government document.

2017   In the United States, the state of Oregon becomes the first to add a third gender option on driver's licenses; California, Maine, Massachusetts, and Washington, D.C. follow suit within a year of the Oregon ruling.

2017   Joyita Mondal, India's first transgender judge, is sworn in; she has risen through the political ranks after having been homeless and a sex worker.

2017   Andrea Jenkins becomes the first African American trans woman elected to a public office in a major U.S. city—Minneapolis.

2018   On May 17, Sexual Minorities Uganda's (SMUG) International Day Against Homophobia, Biphobia and Transphobia is shut down by police and the minister of Ethics and Integrity.

2018   Sean Dorsey becomes the first out trans person from the United States to perform at the prestigious Joyce Theater in New York City with their AIDS show, *The Missing Generation*.

2018   On June 19, the World Health Organization (WHO) announces that gender identity disorder and related categories are proposed to be removed from the classifications of mental and behavioral disorders.

2018   The LGBT International Powerlifting Congress includes an open gender category in the July powerlifting competition. Powerlifting becomes the first known sporting event in the world to include an open gender category for persons who identify as non-binary, genderqueer, gender-expansive, or any other gender category outside of the male/female binary.

Introduction

The language of gender diversity is rapidly changing and used in different ways in various cultural communities. We have done our best to provide basic definitions of some often-encountered terms. It is likely that other people would define many of these terms differently. Indeed, a few years from now, we probably would too!

It is also important to remember that social change is uneven. What is a cherished identity to one person may be interpreted as derogatory and offensive to others. The core lessons to remember when choosing what words to use are that there is strength in diversity, that words can heal or hurt, and that every person deserves to be treated with kindness and respect.

AFAB   Assigned female at birth (also FAAB).

Agender   When a person does not identify with any gender.

Ally   A person who is cisgender and fully supportive of trans, non-binary, and Two-Spirit people.

AMAB   Assigned male at birth (also MAAB).

Asegi udanto   In Cherokee culture, this term denotes a person who does not adhere to the gender binary—someone who is third gender.

Autogynephilic   A controversial term used to describe people who were assigned male at birth, who live their everyday lives as men, and who find it sexually arousing to periodically dress as women. Many people find this term highly offensive while some people identify with it.

Cisgender   A person whose assigned sex at birth and subsequent gender socialization and gender identity line up with one another.

Colonialism   The practice of taking control of another country or region by occupying the region with settlers, exploiting it economically, and rewriting laws and customs.

Cross-dressing   A once widely used term, not used as much today. The wearing of the clothing of the other binary gender. Generally considered a more benign term than transvestite.

Drag   Theatrically exaggerated parody performance of one of the binary genders.

DSD   People whose sex characteristics are not entirely male or entirely female are said to have differences of sex development, or disorders of sex development, or may be known as intersex.

DSM   *Diagnostic and Statistical Manual of Mental Disorders,* published by the American Psychiatric Association. Widely used in North America to diagnose gender-diverse people who wish to transition.

Enby   Comes from the initials N.B. for nonbinary. Enby is now shorthand for someone who identifies outside of the gender binary.

Eunuch   A male who has had his testicle removed (castrated).

First Contact   Refers to when European explorers first came into contact with a particular Indigenous people.

FTM   Female-to-male. Once a widely used term to describe transmasculine people; rarely used today outside of scientific literature.

Gender   A social category assigned at birth on the basis of the sex assigned at birth.

Gender affirmation procedures   Social and medical procedures used to assist people to live comfortably in accordance with their gender identities when they are not the same as those assigned at birth.

Gender binary A system of social organization that treats gender as consisting of only men/boys and women/girls, and does not allow any other genders.

Gender-diverse When used as an adjective, this refers to people whose gender falls outside of the gender binary.

Gender dysphoria, Gender incongruence Technical diagnostic terms used by medical personnel to describe gender-diverse people who request medical assistance to change their gender expression or sex.

Gender identity The felt gender of a person, which may not be the same as the gender assigned at birth.

Gender variance A broad term to describe the full spectrum of gender identities and gender expressions.

Genderqueer An older term for non-binary. Coined by Rikki Anne Wilchens. Like non-binary people, genderqueer people reject strict binary gendered categories.

Hermaphrodite A term that comes from the ancient Greek and is a combination of the names of the Greek gods Hermes and Aphrodite. It denotes a person who is understood to be biologically male and female. This is an old term for someone who has differences of sex development (DSD)—also known as intersex. It is generally not used today and is considered derogatory by many people.

Heteronormativity The idea that everyone should be cisgender, heterosexual, and have a stereotypical gender expression.

Hijra A third-gender category of people in India who are usually assigned male at birth, but who go through a special spiritual ceremony in which they undergo castration and sometimes also a penectomy in a ritual dedicated to the deity Bahuchara Mata.

Homosexual An older term for people who experience same-sex desire.

ICD *The International Classification of Diseases and Related Health Problems,* published by the World Health Organization of the United Nations, is widely used in most of the world to diagnose gender-diverse people who wish to transition, and many other medical conditions.

Imperialism One country exerting its power and control over another country or region, usually through military force.

Intersex See DSD.

Māhū A third-gender category possibly originating from Tahiti before 400 CE and now generally associated with third-gender people indigenous to the Hawai'ian Islands.

Misogyny People who have a prejudice against, and even hatred of, people who express femininity. Misogyny often is defined as "woman hating."

MTF Male-to-female. Once a widely used term to describe transfeminine people; rarely used today outside of scientific literature.

Nadleeh A gender category outside of the Western male/female binary in traditional Navajo culture. Navajo culture recognizes five genders.

Non-binary People whose gender identity is not strictly within the gender binary. They may not identify with binary categories at all, or may be fluid or creative about how they combine or express aspects of the binary categories. Non-binary people usually prefer the singular "they/them/their" pronouns.

Passing An unpopular term for when a person who has transitioned is recognized as the gender they are expressing. It has a negative connotation that implies falsification.

Queer Historically, this term was very homophobic; however, starting in 1990, gay, lesbian, bisexual, and trans people have reclaimed it as an empowering umbrella term for the LGBT2+ people who are not heteronormative.

Sex A social category assigned at birth on the basis of physical characteristics such as genitals and/or sex chromosomes. Usually divided into male and female with the terms intersex or DSD used for all people whose sex status is not clearly male or female.

Standards of Care   *Standards of Care for the Health of Transsexual, Transgender, and Gender-Nonconforming People* are published under the auspices of the World Professional Association for Transgender Health. They are guidelines used around the world intended to ensure quality care for people undergoing medically supervised gender transitions.

TDOR   Transgender Day of Remembrance. A commemoration of all the people known to have been murdered each year due to transphobic violence. TDOR happens in places around the world on November 20 every year.

Trans man, Trans woman   A person on the transmasculine (trans man) or transfeminine (trans woman) spectrum who now lives as a gender other than the one they were assigned at birth.

Transgender, Trans, Trans*   Umbrella terms used to describe a wide range of gender-diverse people who do not feel that the gender assigned to them at birth was correct. Anyone who is not cisgender.

Transgenderist   An obscure term coined by Virginia Prince to mean a person assigned male at birth who lives full time as a woman without genital surgery. Widely considered to be one of the origins of the word transgender.

Transition   A word used to describe the process of changing one's gender away from the one assigned to them at birth.

Transmasculine   spectrum,   transfeminine   spectrum   Describes a range of identities of people who were assigned female (transmasculine) or male (transfeminine) at birth and no longer feel that was correct.

Transsexual   A once widely used term; falling out of use today. A person who desires and/or makes a binary sex and gender transition from male to female, or from female to male.

Transvestite   A once widely used term; rarely used today. A person who intermittently wears the clothing of the other binary gender, often for sexual purposes.

Two-Spirit   An umbrella term in English only used by people indigenous to the areas now known as the United States and Canada. Each Indigenous language has its own words, which have different nuances for each cultural group. Designates people who have spiritual qualities of both men and women. Can include people who also identify as lesbian, gay, bisexual, trans, queer, or intersex.

Wakatane and *Wakawahine*   Indigenous Maori terms for people who embody a third-gender identity.

Winkte   The Sioux word for people who are third gender in their culture.

WPATH   World Professional Association for Transgender Health. Largest professional group in the world devoted to the health needs of trans, non-binary, Two-Spirit, and other gender-diverse people.

X endings on words: Chicanx, Latinx, Mx   Since the terms Chicano/a and Latino/a reflect a gender binary, many scholars are now using an "x" or an @ sign at the end of these terms to include gender diversity outside of binary constructs. Several college and university programs in the United States have changed the name of their discipline accordingly. Likewise, Mx. is now an accepted gender-neutral title as opposed to the binary titles of Mr., Ms., Miss, and Mrs.

Ze/Hir pronouns   Trans activist, scholar, and author Leslie Feinberg, who felt that the binary categories of "she" and "he" pronouns was too constricting, invented these terms as a way to denote a non-binary status. These terms are attributed to Feinberg and are an earlier attempt to create gender-neutral pronouns. Today, "they" is often used as a gender-neutral pronoun in non-binary communities.

Note: page numbers followed by the letters "t" and "f" in italics indicate tables and figures, respectively.

About the Authors

Aaron Devor, PhD, initiated and holds the inaugural position as the world's only Chair in Transgender Studies. He is the Founder and Academic Director of the world's largest Transgender Archives, and Founder and host of the international, interdisciplinary Moving Trans History Forward conferences. He has been studying, writing, and teaching about transgender topics for more than thirty-five years. He is the author of numerous well-cited scholarly articles and three enduring books, *FTM: Female-to-Male Transsexuals in Society* (2016, 1997), *The Transgender Archives: Foundations for the Future* (2014) (a Lambda Literary Award Finalist), and *Gender Blending: Confronting the Limits of Duality* (1989). He has delivered more than thirty keynote addresses worldwide, advises policy makers, speaks frequently with the media, and has won many awards for his transgender work, including the Virginia Prince Pioneer Award, a national Equity Award, and awards from his university for Outstanding Community Outreach and for Advocacy and Activism in Equity and Diversity.

He was chosen as a Fellow of the Society for the Scientific Study of Sexuality, and elected as a senior member of the International Academy of Sex Research. He is Historian for the World Professional Association for Transgender Health (WPATH), has been involved in writing versions of the WPATH *Standards of Care for the Health of Transsexual, Transgender, and Gender Nonconforming People* since 1999, and is overseeing the translation of Version 7 into world languages.

Devor is an out trans man, a former Dean of Graduate Studies (2002–2012), a national-award-winning teacher, and a professor of Sociology at the University of Victoria in British Columbia, Canada.

Ardel Haefele-Thomas, PhD, is a non-binary trans activist, scholar, and teacher. During their doctoral work at Stanford University, they focused on nineteenth-century British cultural ideas about sex, gender, race, class, and nation through queer and postcolonial theories. For over a decade, Haefele-Thomas has served as Chair of LGBT Studies at City College of San Francisco, which is the first LGBT Studies department in the United States and the second in the world.

Their publications include *Introduction to Transgender Studies,* published by Harrington Park Press (Columbia University Press), which will be the first introductory textbook in this field of study in the world. They are also the author of *Queer Others in Victorian Gothic: Transgressing Monstrosity,* published by the University of Wales Press. Haefele-Thomas is also the guest editor for *Victorian Review's* special issue: *Trans Victorians,* which will mark the first time that trans topics have been considered in large scope within the field of Nineteenth-Century British Studies. Haefele-Thomas has published numerous essays in the field of Gothic Studies with a focus on intersecting identities in queer and trans gothic. Haefele-Thomas is a community activist for queer and trans rights and works at the college and city level in San Francisco to make sure that public spaces are safer for queer and trans people. They are also the international liaison for non-binary and intersex athletes for the LGBT International Powerlifting Congress and a delegate for the forthcoming Gay Games in Hong Kong.